GREAT SCENES *from the* OLD TESTAMENT

A Pictorial Archive of 160 Illustrations

JULIUS SCHNORR VON CAROLSFELD

DOVER PUBLICATIONS, INC.
Mineola, New York

Bibliographical Note

This Dover edition, first published in 2004, is a selection of all the Old Testament illustrations from *Die Bibel in Bildern,* originally published in German by Georg Wigand, Leipzig, in 1860. The English captions derive from a standard edition of the King James version of the *Holy Bible*.

Library of Congress Cataloging-in-Publication Data

Schnorr von Carolsfeld, Julius, 1794–1872.
[Bibel in Bildern. English]
Great scenes from the Old Testament : a pictorial archive of 160 illustrations / Julius Schnorr von Carolsfeld.
p. cm. — (Dover pictorial archive series)
ISBN 0-486-43949-6 (pbk.)
1. Bible—Illustrations. I. Title. II. Series.

N8026.S4613 2004
769.92—dc22

2004058272

Manufactured in the United States of America
Dover Publications, Inc., 31 East 2nd Street, Mineola, N.Y. 11501

Publisher's Note

ONE OF THE chief exponents of German Academic Romanticism, Julius Schnorr von Carolsfeld (1794–1872) was born in Leipzig, Germany. He began his career as a student of his father, Hans Veit Schnorr von Carolsfeld (1764–1841), also a painter, engraver, and draftsman. Inspired by early Renaissance art and the works of Albrecht Dürer, Julius Schnorr von Carolsfeld entered the Akademie in Vienna in 1811, studying art under German Neoclassical painter Friedrich Füger (1751–1818). In 1817, Schnorr von Carolsfeld went to Rome and became a member of the Nazarenes, a group of German and Austrian artists who sought to revive religious painting by returning to the spiritual values and purity of form of Renaissance models embodied in fresco painting and monumental art.

Associated with the Nazarenes until about 1827, Schnorr von Carolsfeld collaborated with Johann Overbeck, Peter von Cornelius, and Philipp Veit on a commission to decorate the entrance hall of the Villa Massimo in Rome with fresco murals. Soon after, he left Rome to accept a position at the Munich Academy. He eventually entered the service of King Ludwig I in Munich, bringing to Germany the art of wall painting that he had mastered in Italy years before. While in Munich, Schnorr von Carolsfeld received another important mural commission that required him to execute a series of frescoes depicting the *Nibelungenlied* in the Munich Residenz. In 1846 he settled in Dresden as a professor at the academy there and director of the Picture Gallery. He also created window designs for the Glasgow Cathedral and for St. Paul's Cathedral in London.

The major work of Schnorr von Carolsfeld's career, *Die Bibel in Bildern (The Bible in Pictures)* was a collection of 240 woodcut illustrations depicting scenes from the Old and New Testaments and the Apocrypha. It was published in Leipzig between 1852 and 1860, and expresses not only the artist's fascination with historic themes, but also exhibits some of the high points of his talent, namely, his meticulous attention to detail and linear clarity. The present edition reproduces all of the woodcuts from the Old Testament and the Apocrypha.

Contents

GREAT SCENES
from the
OLD TESTAMENT

A Pictorial Archive of 160 Illustrations

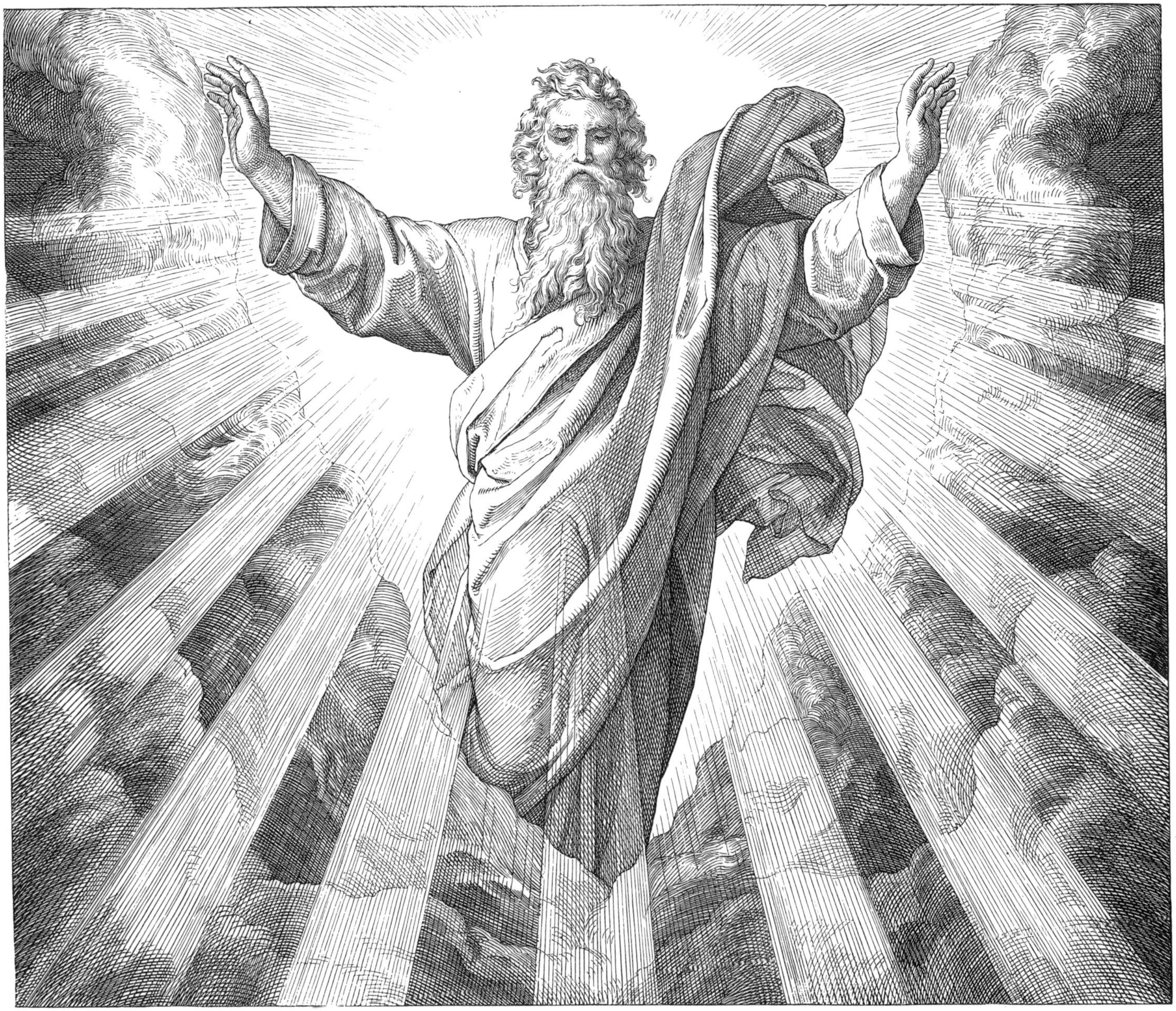

The First Day of Creation
Genesis. Chapter 1.

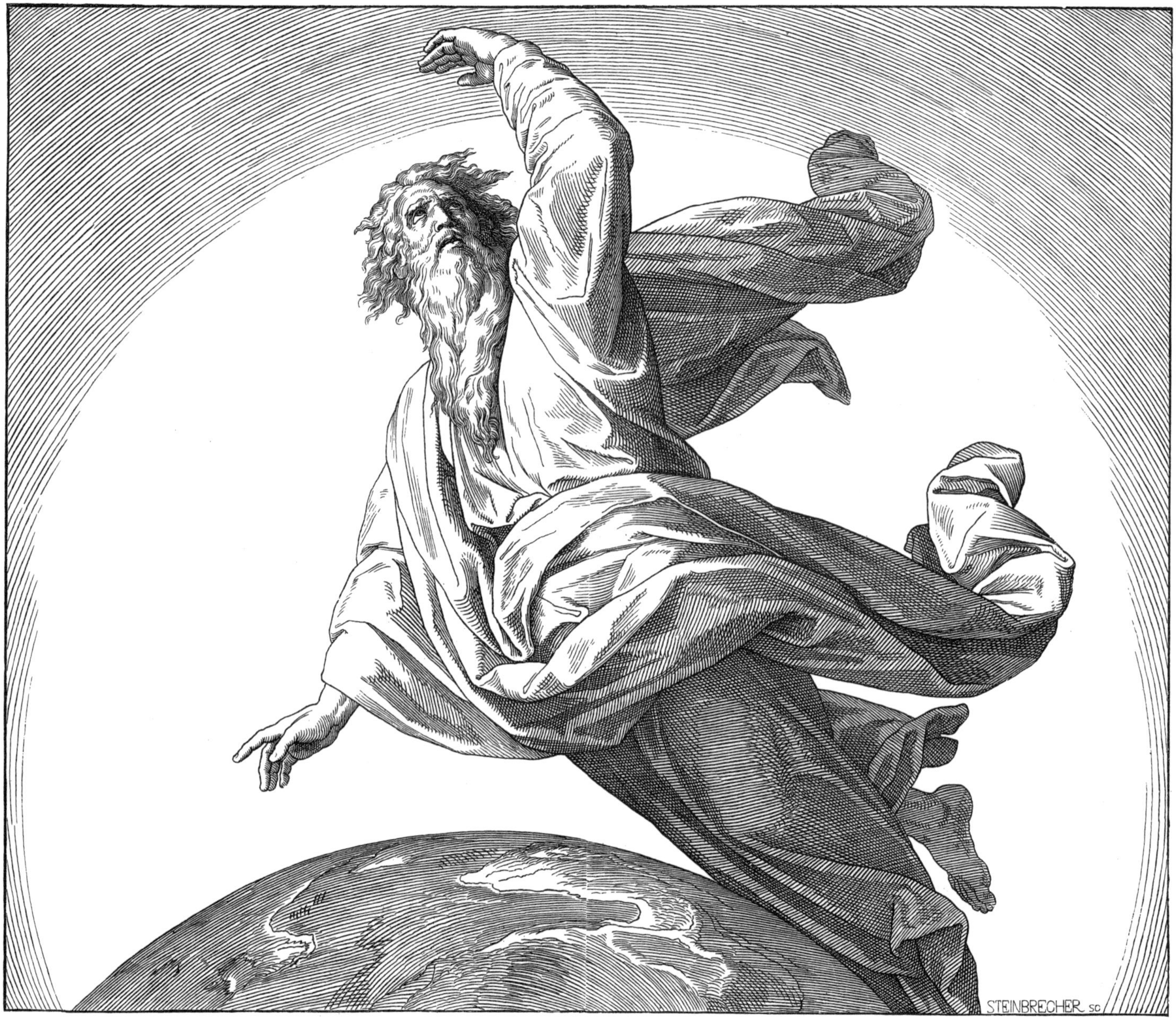

The Second Day of Creation
Genesis. Chapter 1.

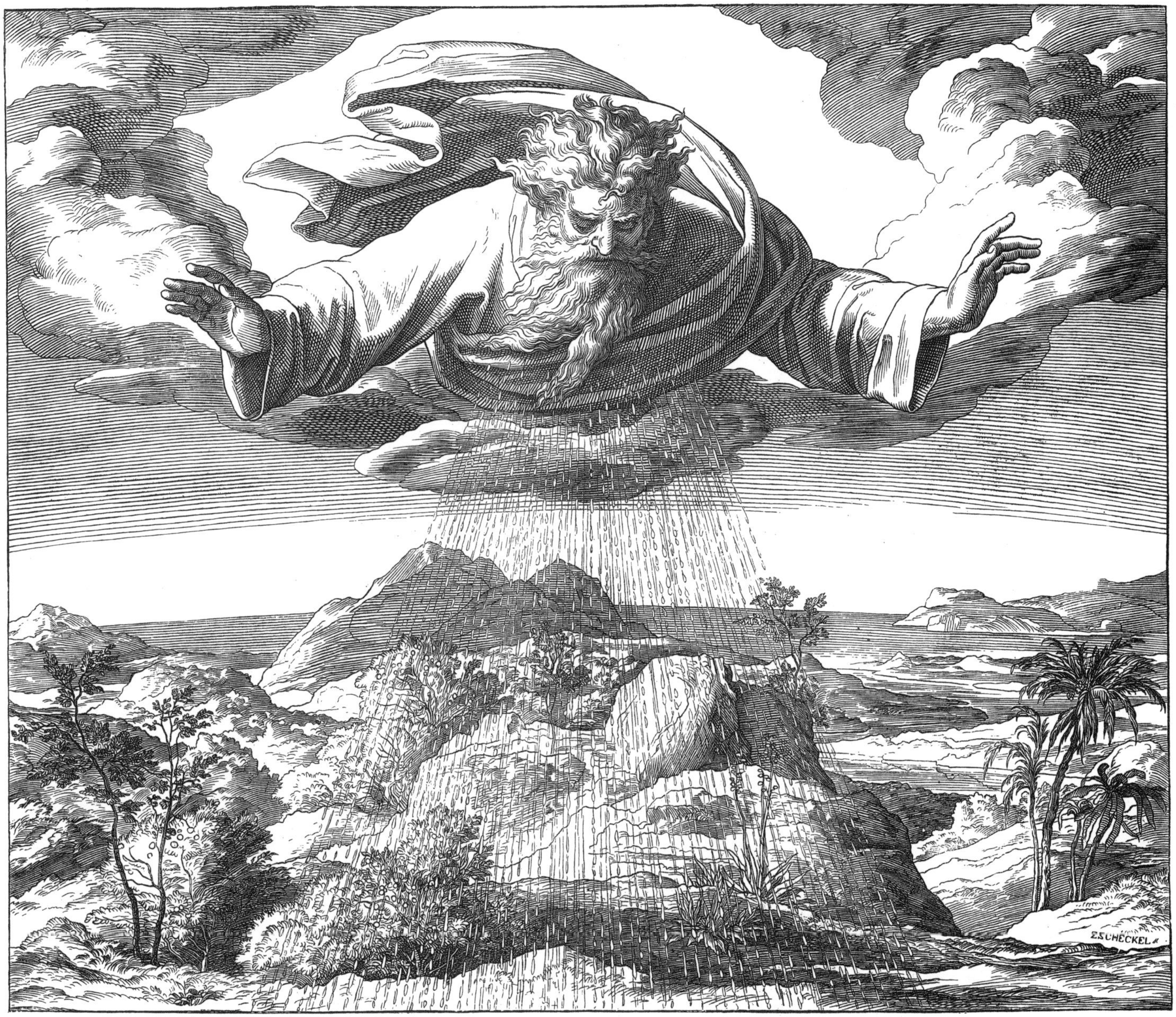

The Third Day of Creation

Genesis. Chapter 1.

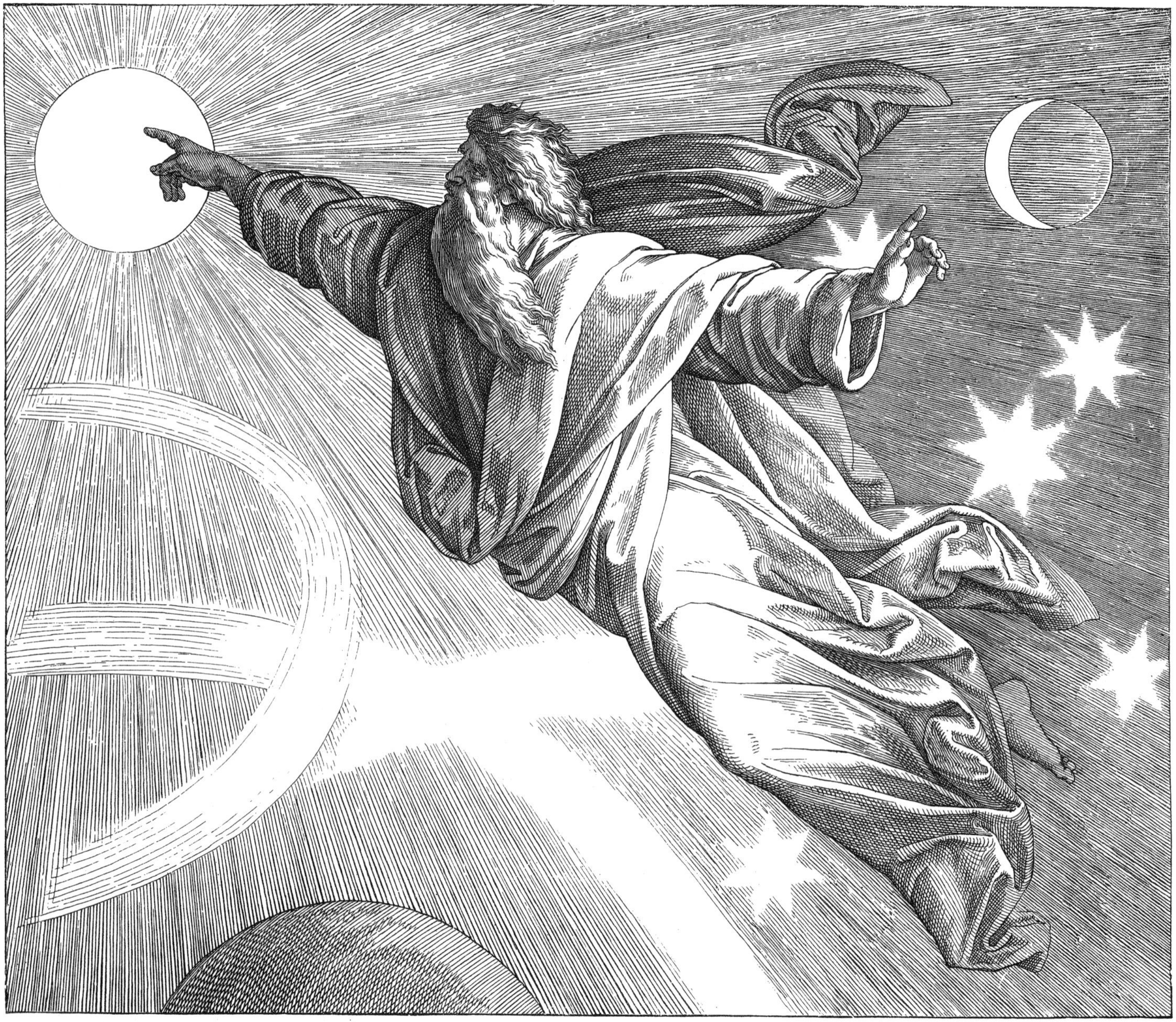

The Fourth Day of Creation

Genesis. Chapter 1.

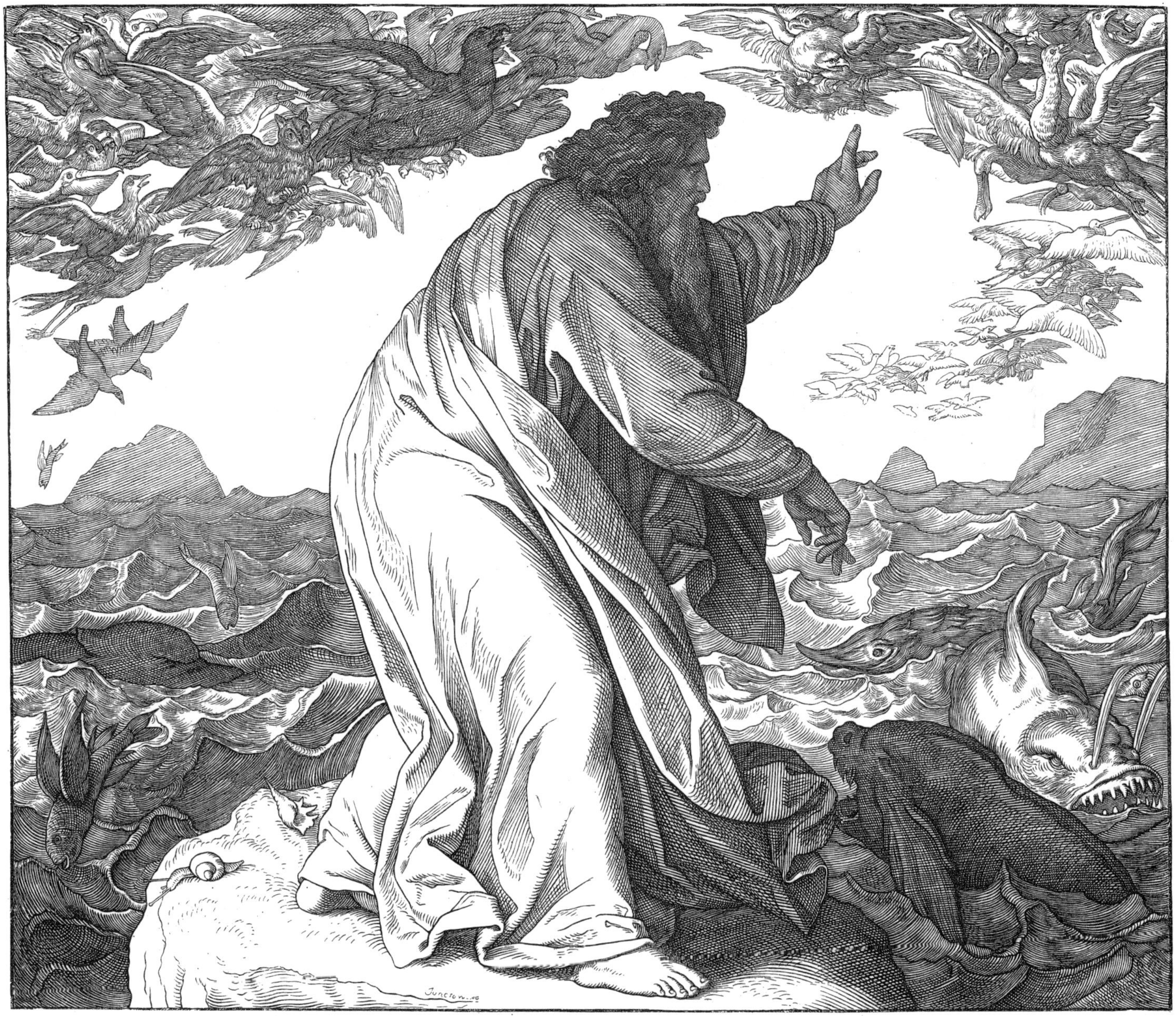

The Fifth Day of Creation

Genesis. Chapter 1.

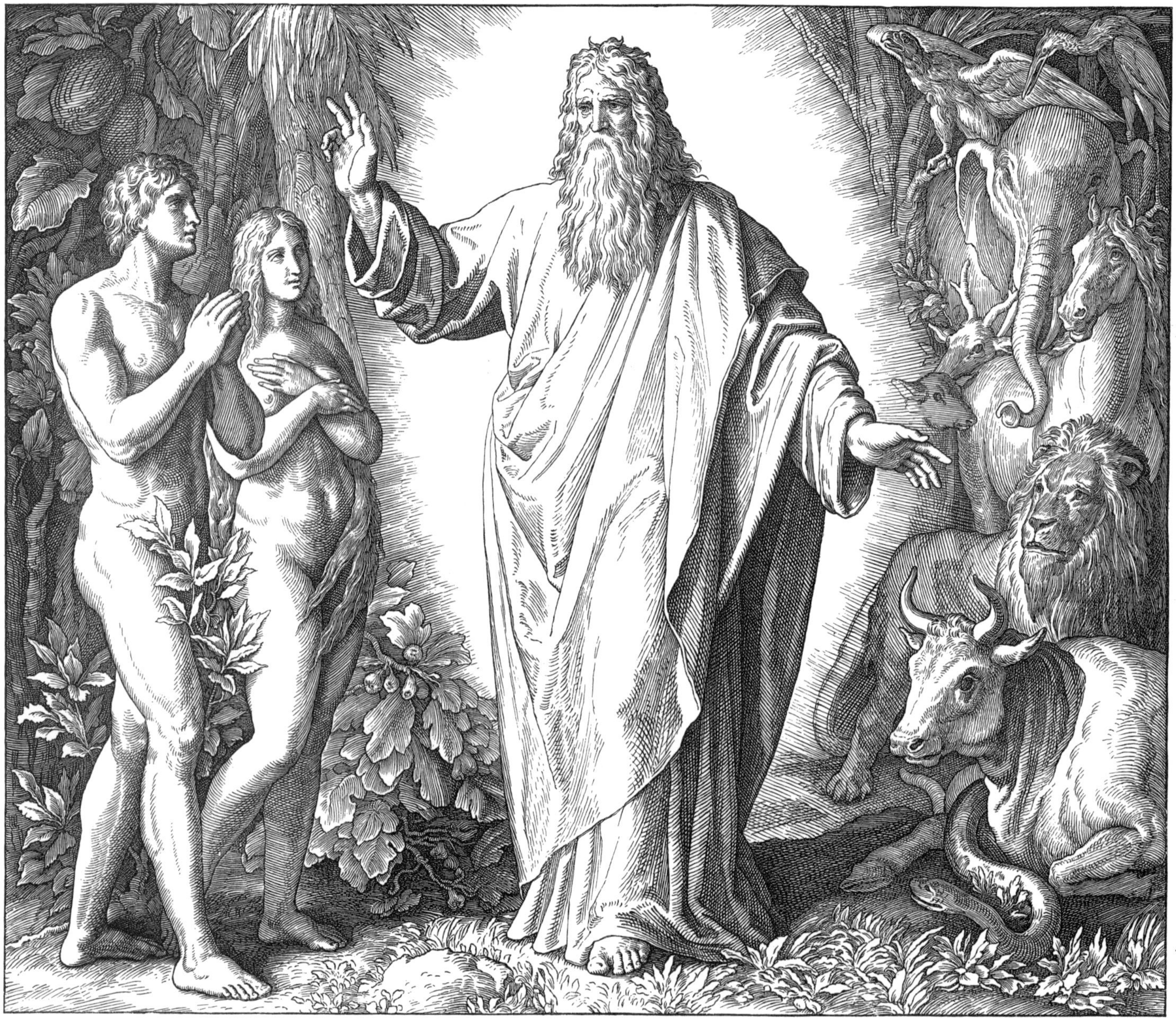

THE SIXTH DAY OF CREATION
Genesis. Chapter 1.

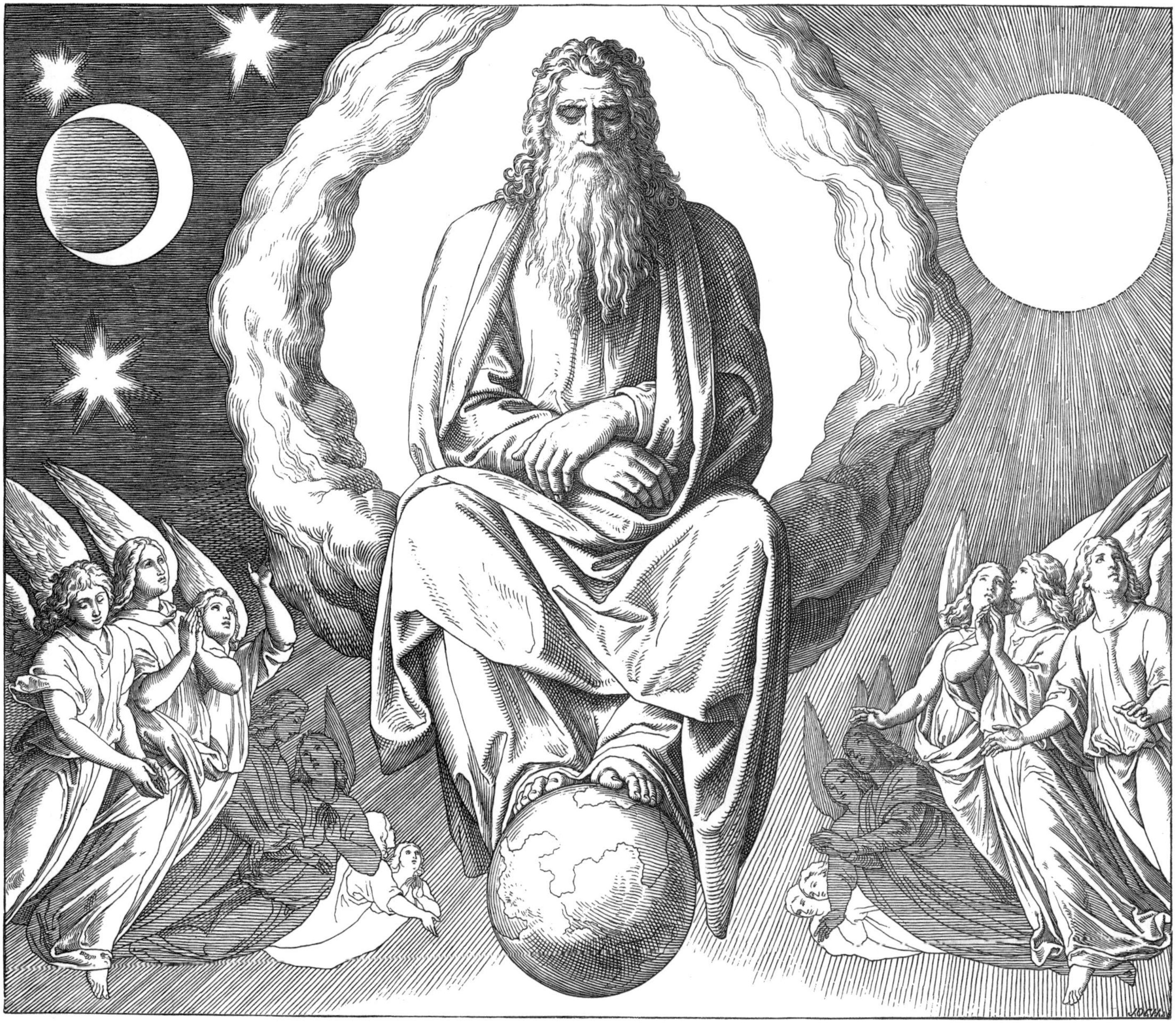

The Sabbath
Genesis. Chapter 2.

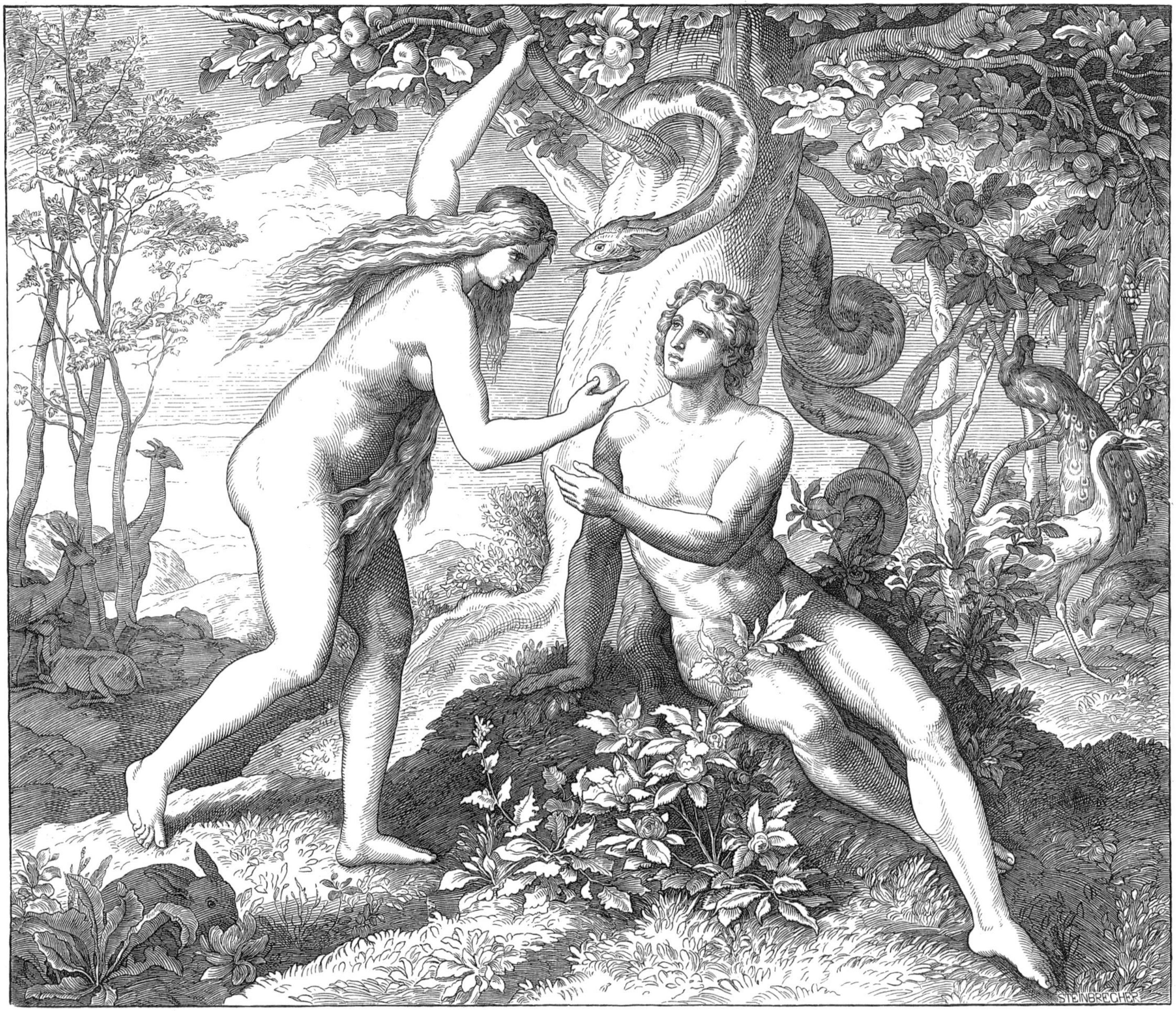

The Fall of Man

Genesis. Chapter 3.

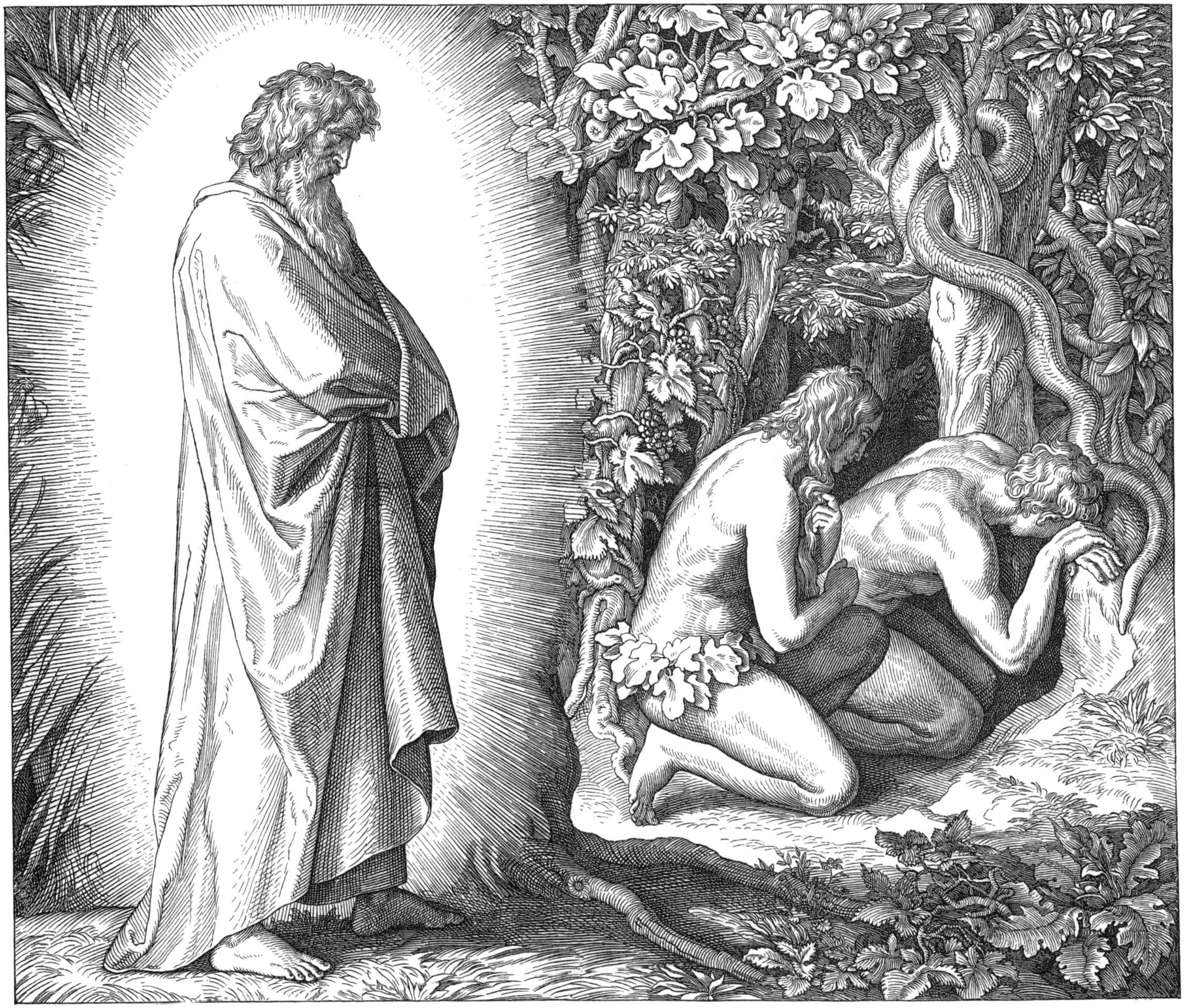

THE FIRST JUDGMENT OF GOD
Genesis. Chapter 3.

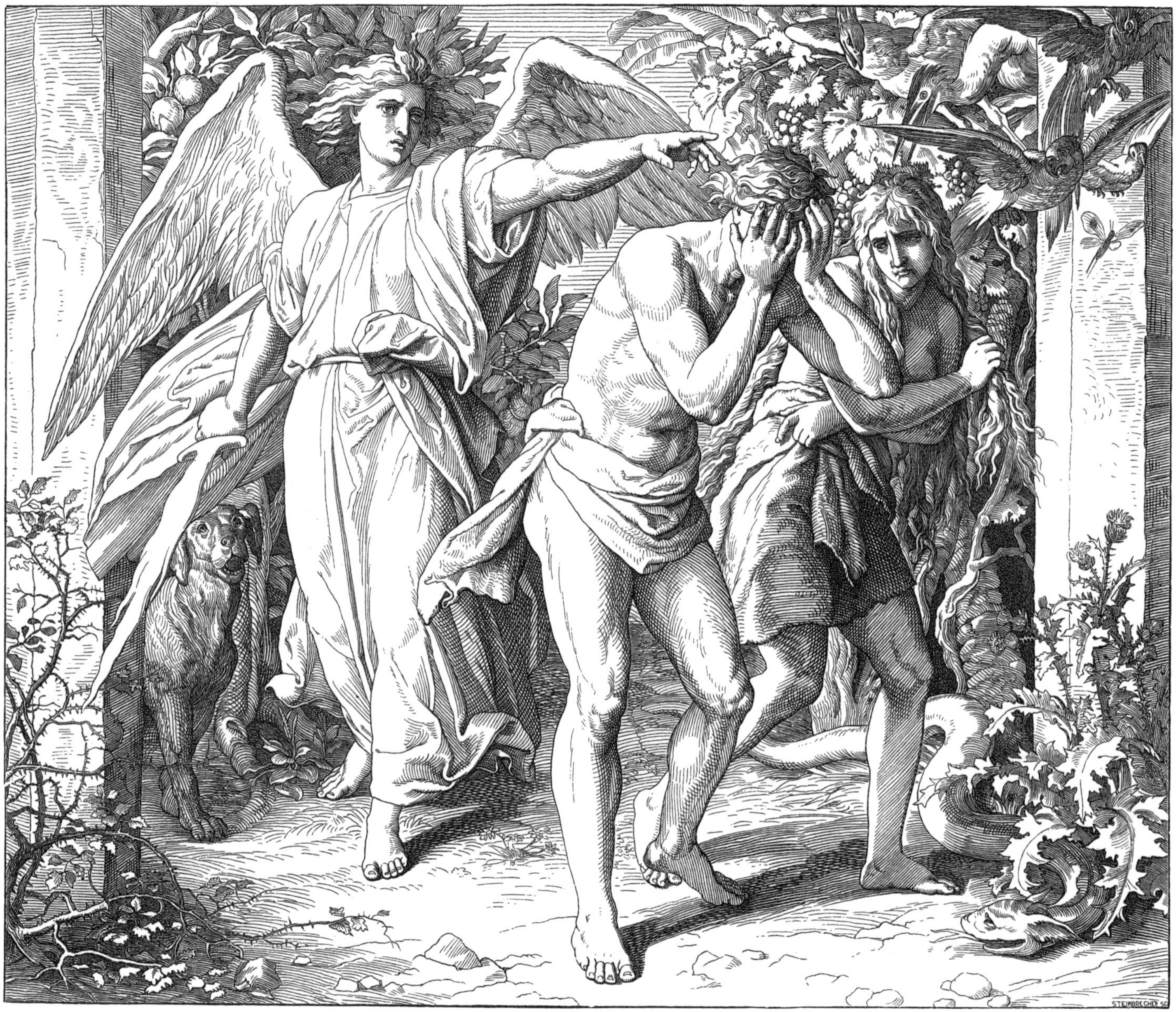

The Expulsion from Eden

Genesis. Chapter 3.

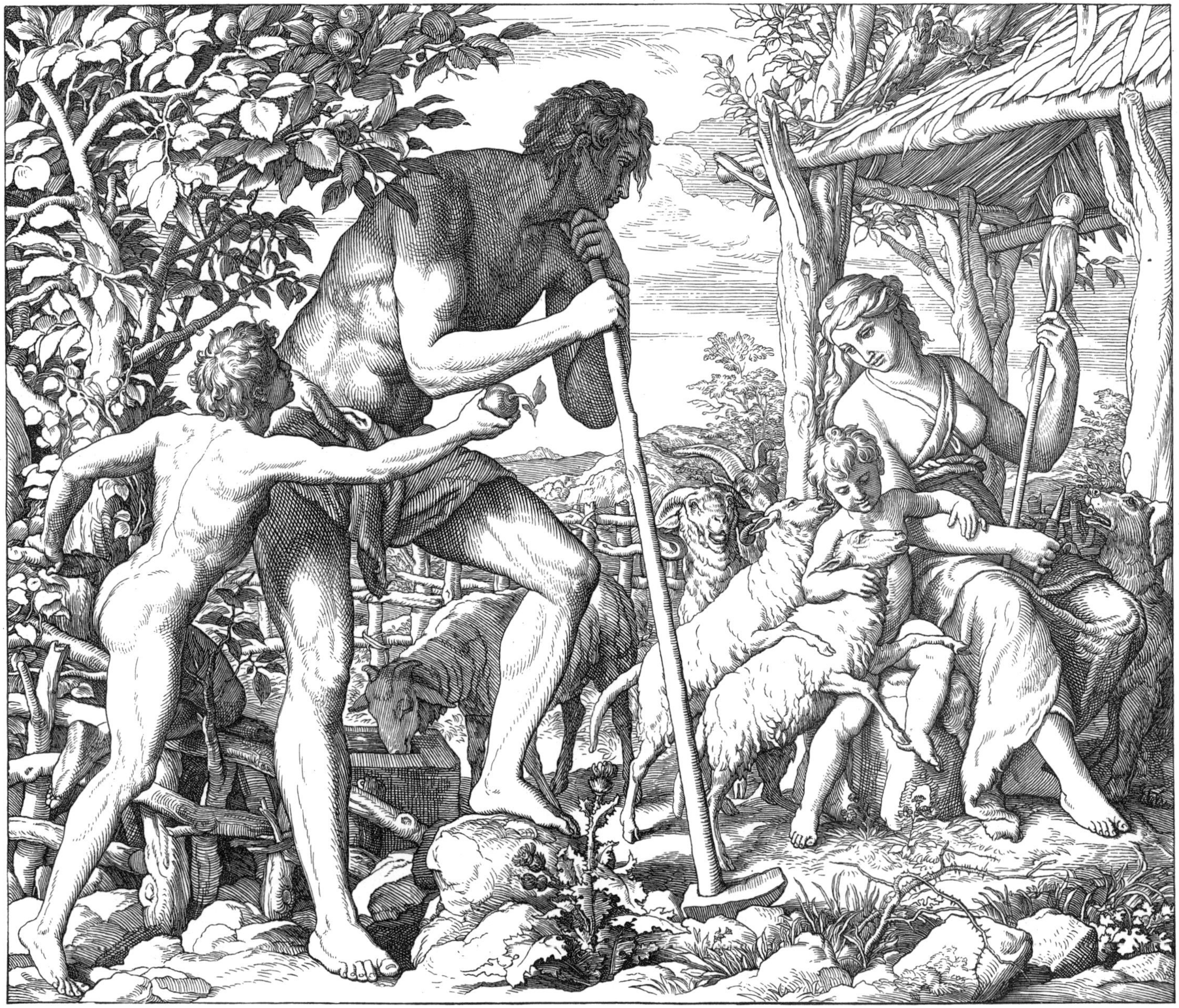

Adam and Eve After the Expulsion

Genesis. Chapter 3.

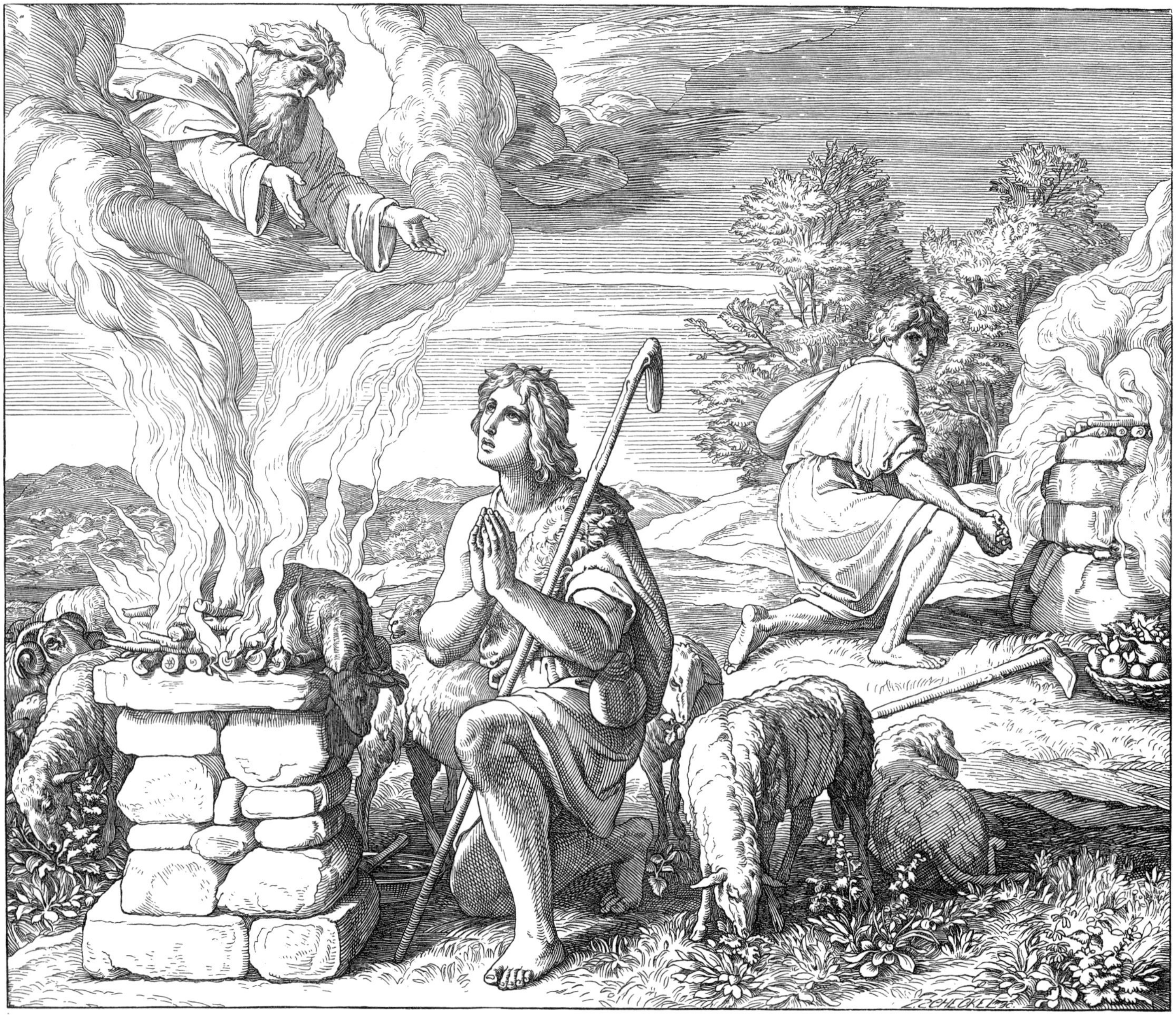

Cain and Abel's Offering

Genesis. Chapter 4.

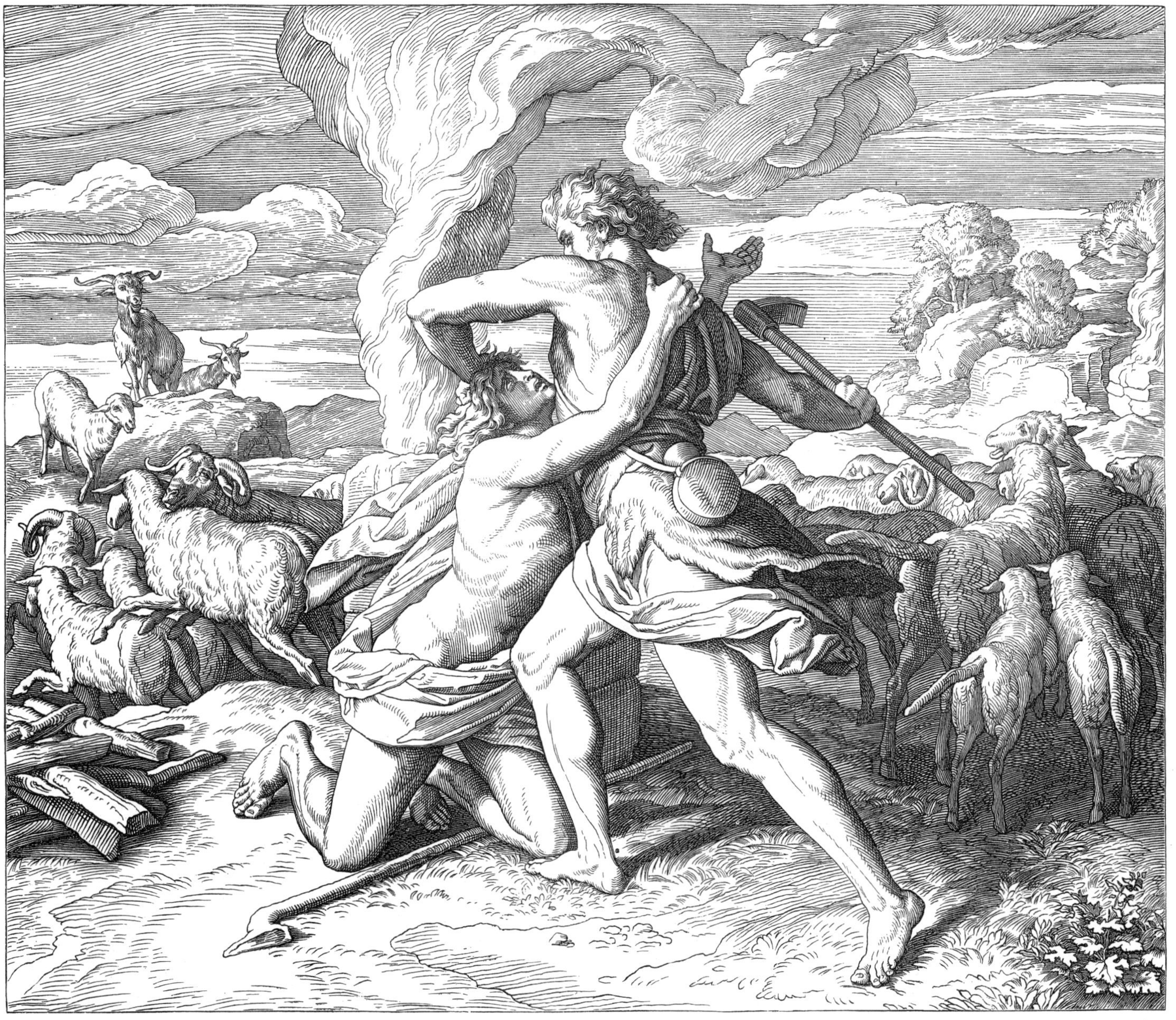

Cain Kills His Brother Abel

Genesis. Chapter 4.

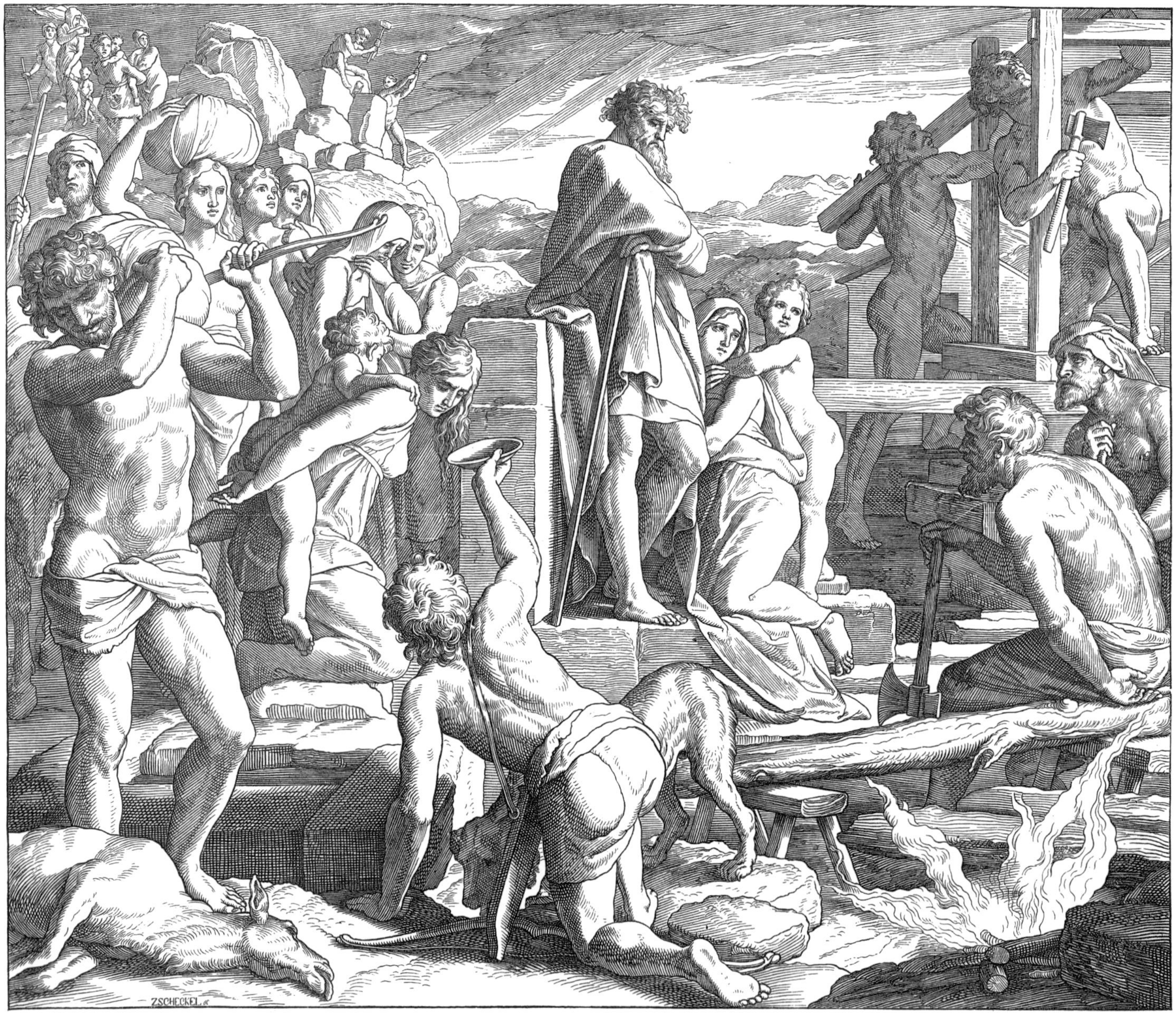

The Migration of the Canaanites

Genesis. Chapter 4.

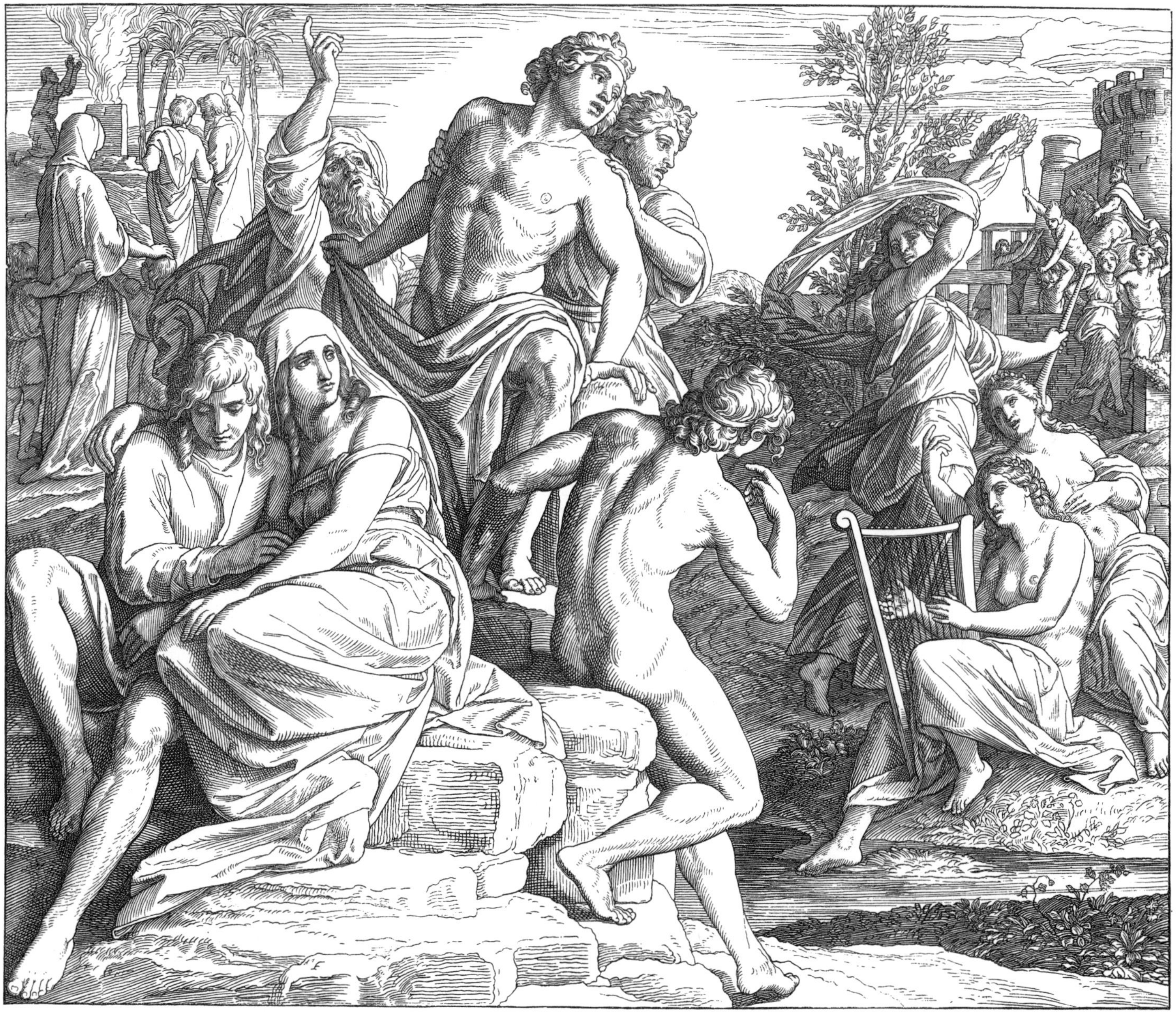

God's Children Mix with the Children of the World

Genesis. Chapter 6.

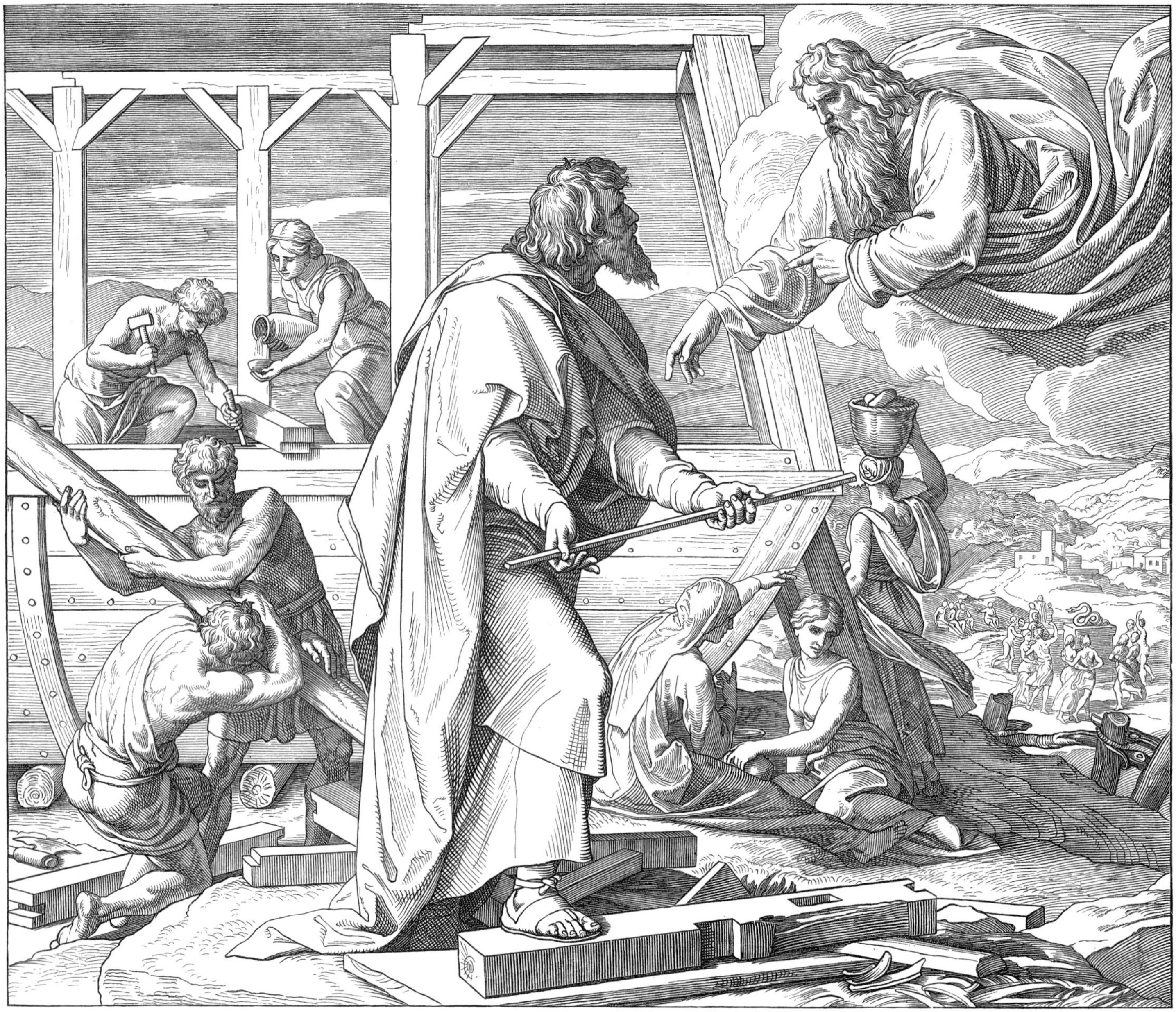

The Prophecy of the Flood
Genesis. Chapter 6.

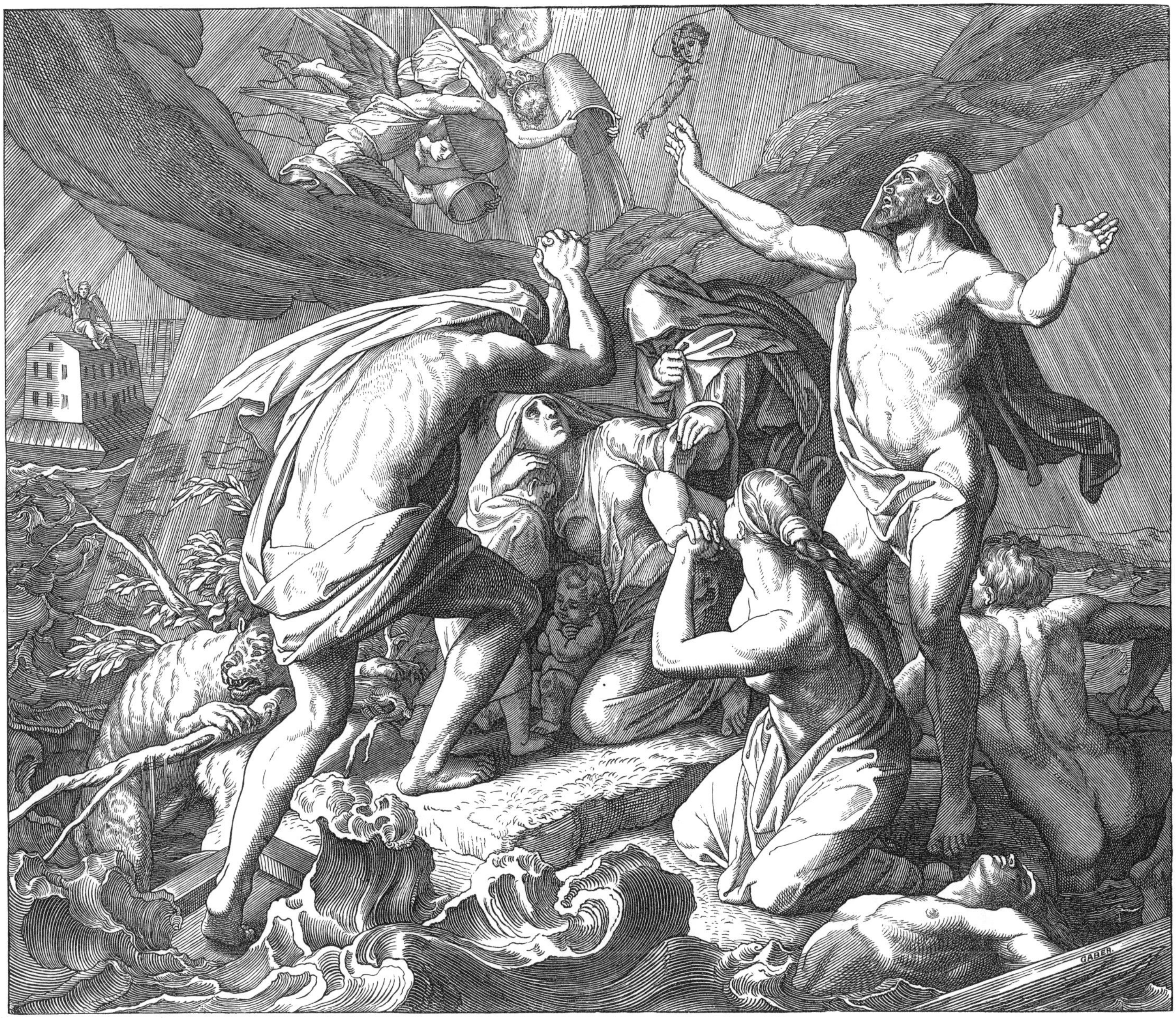

THE FLOOD
Genesis. Chapter 7.

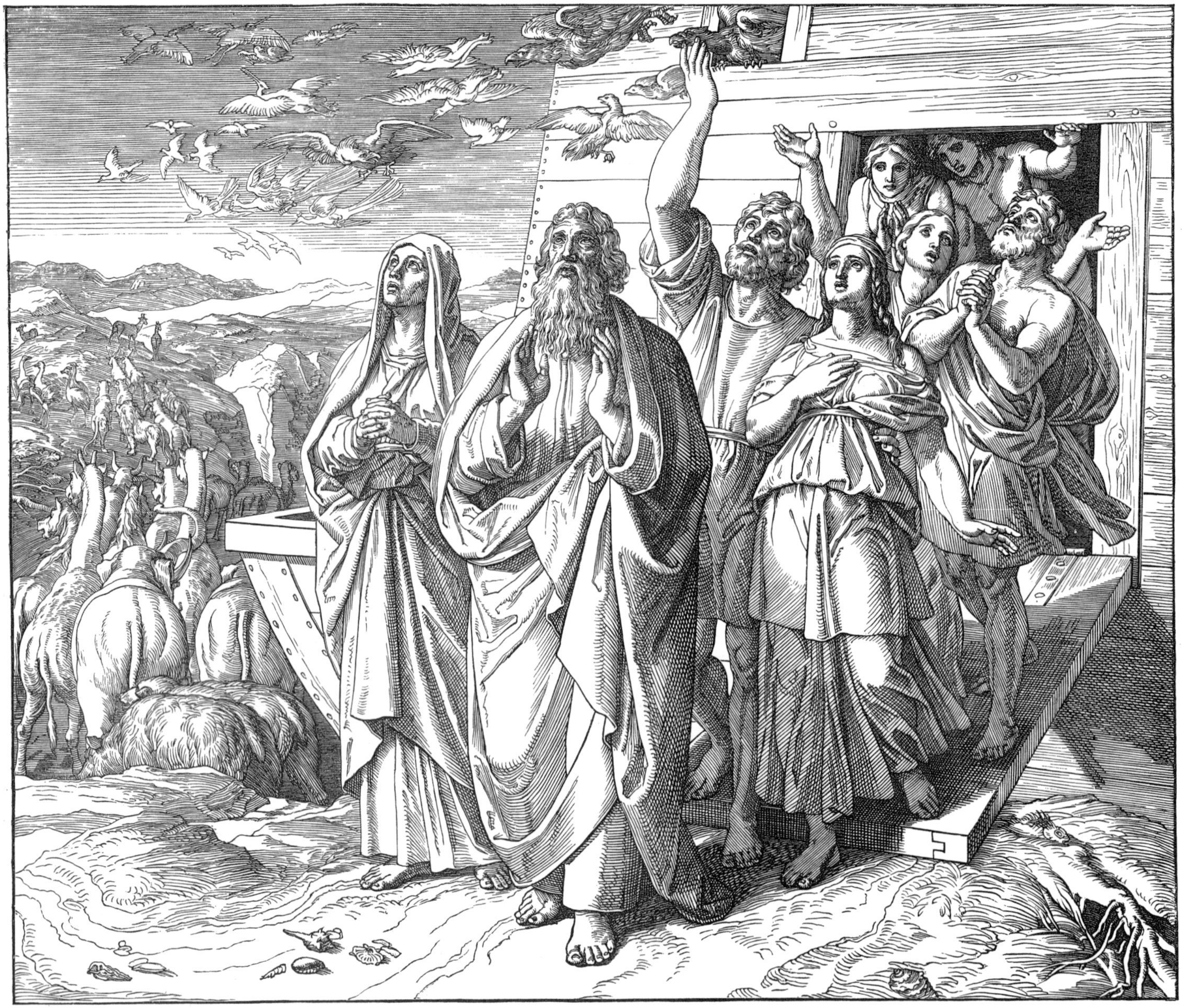

The Ark Rests Upon Ararat

Genesis. Chapter 8.

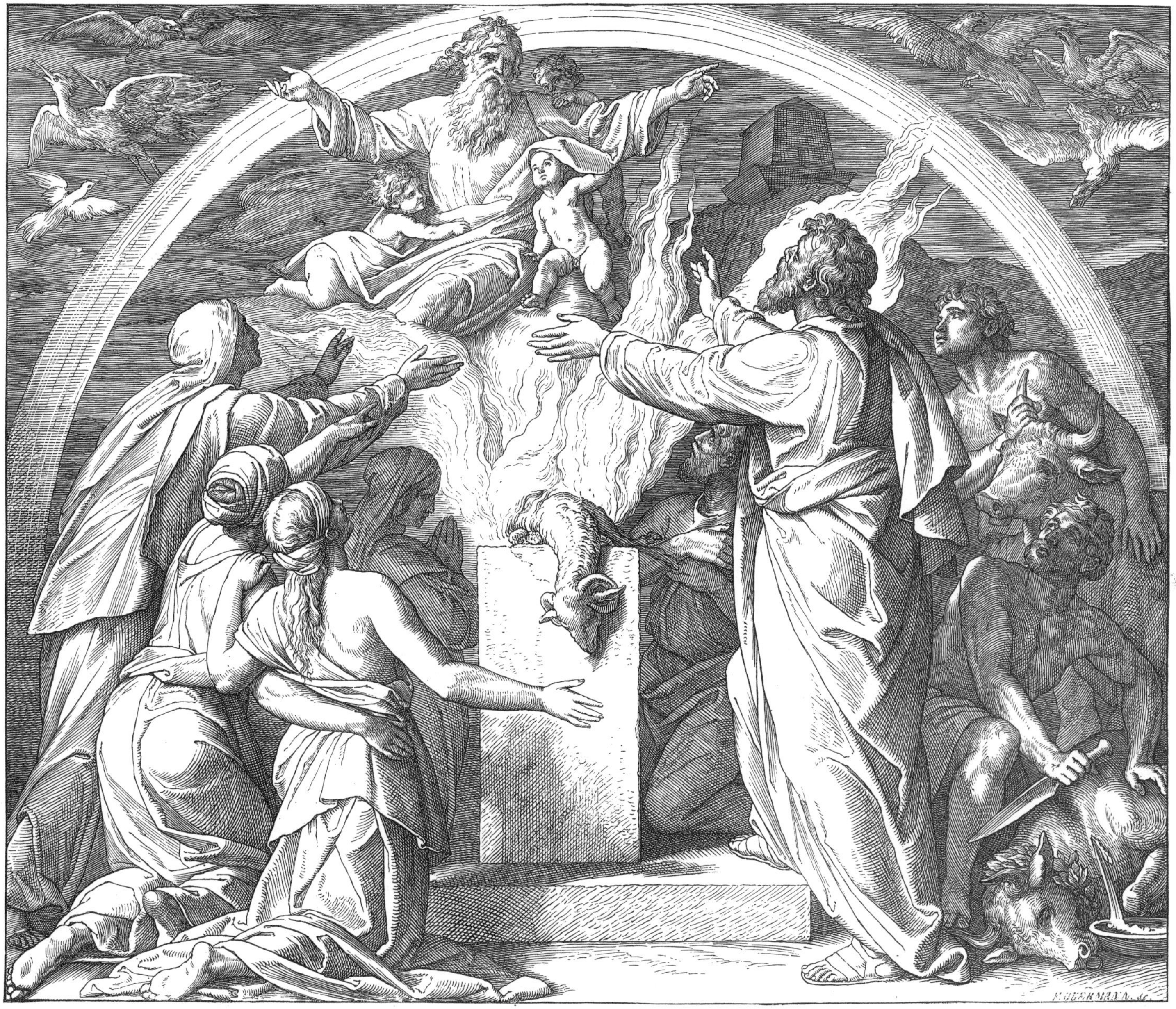

THE COVENANT OF THE RAINBOW
Genesis. Chapter 8.

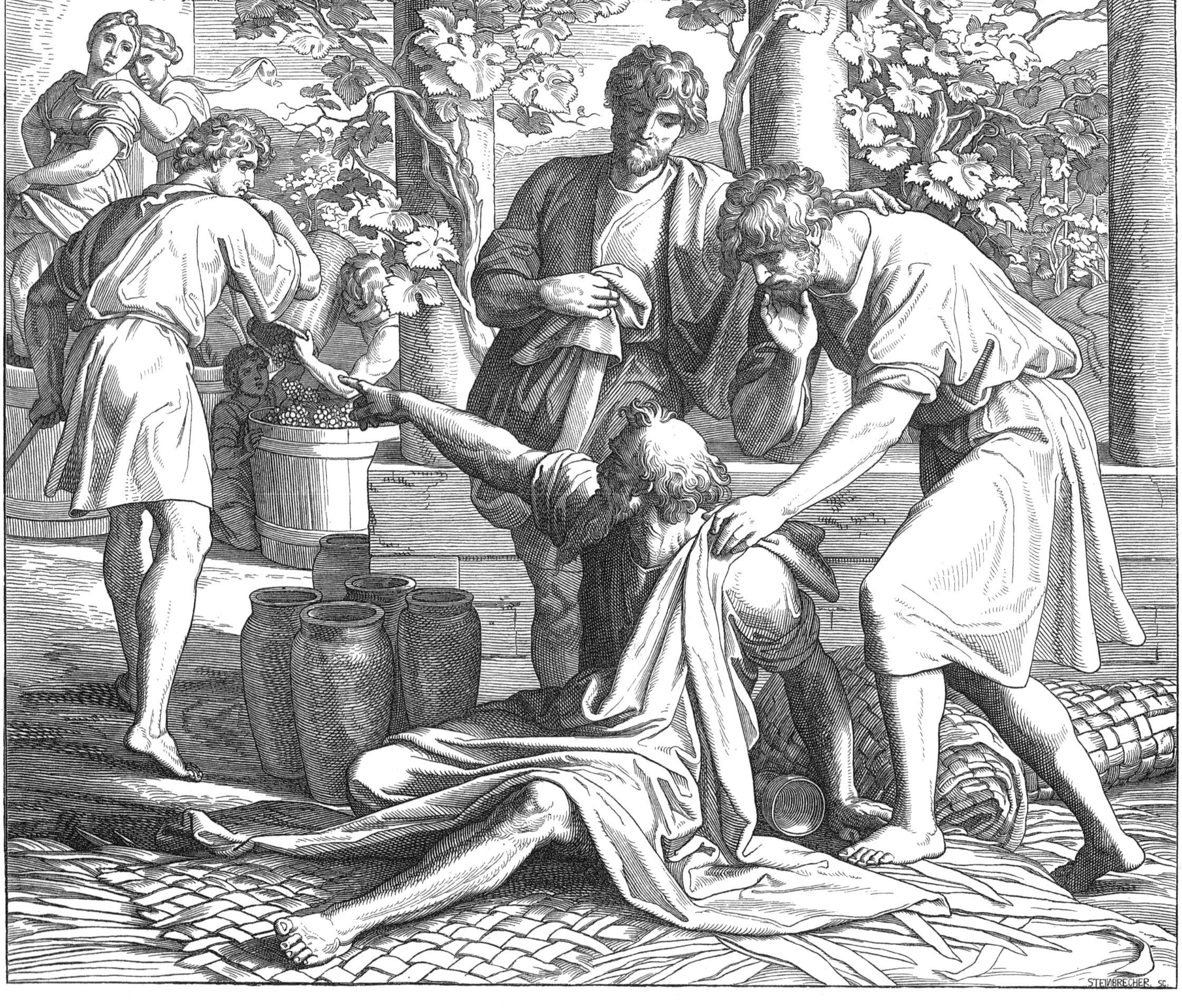

Ham Is Cursed by His Father

Genesis. Chapter 9.

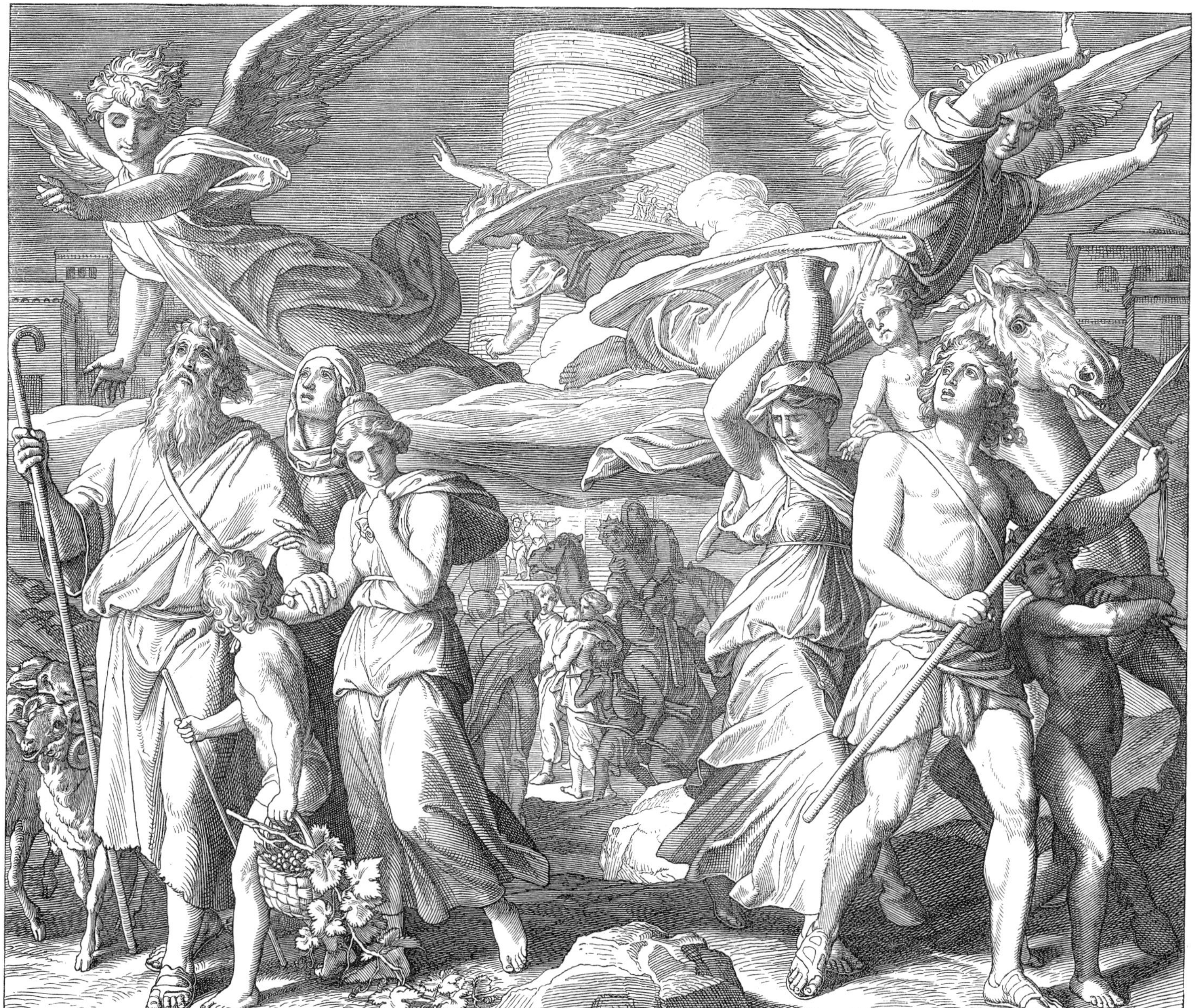

THE TOWER OF BABEL
Genesis. Chapter 11.

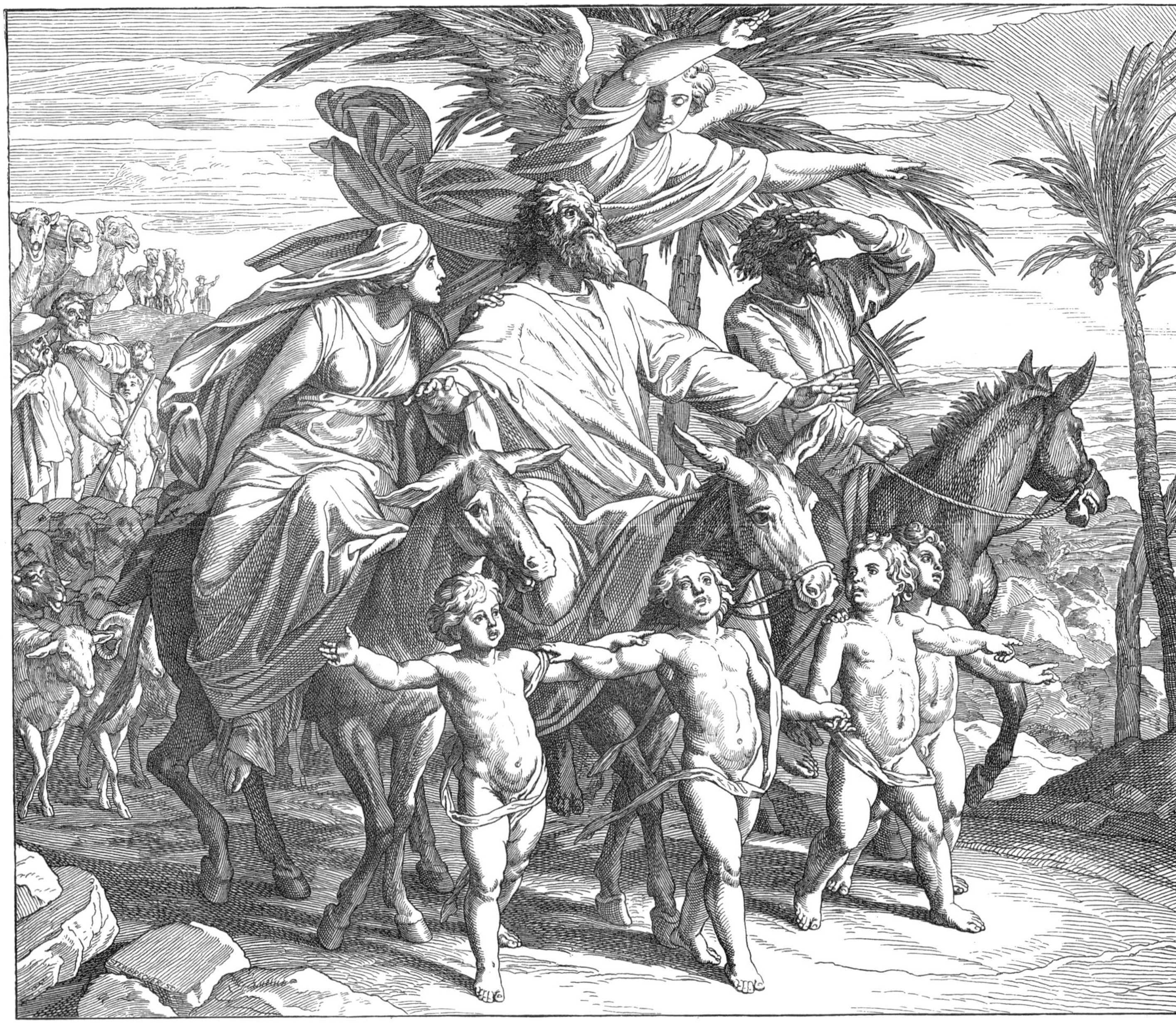

ABRAM SEES THE PROMISED LAND
Genesis. Chapter 12.

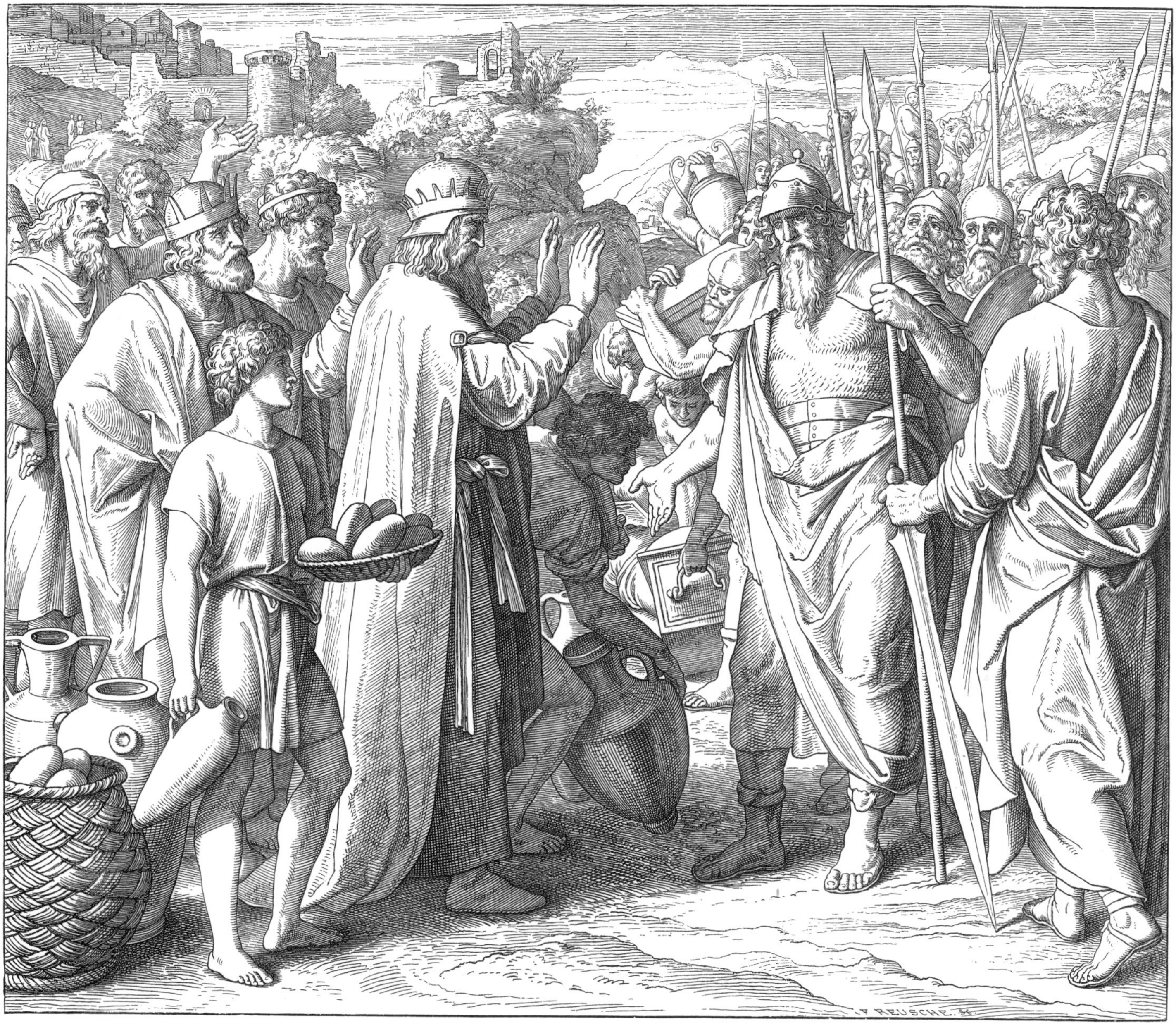

Abram Is Blessed by Melchizedek

Genesis. Chapter 14.

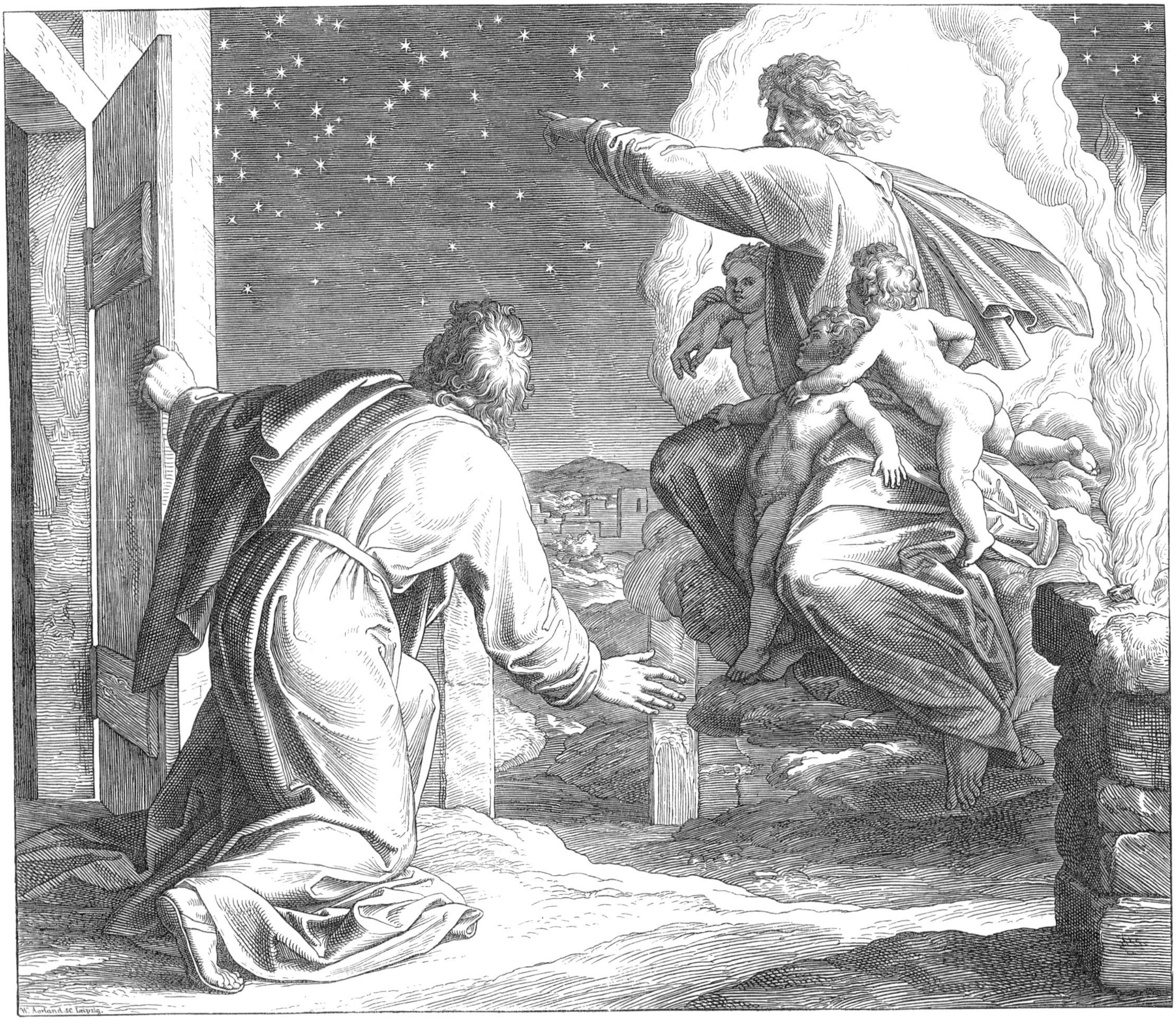

Abram Receives the First Promise

Genesis. Chapter 15.

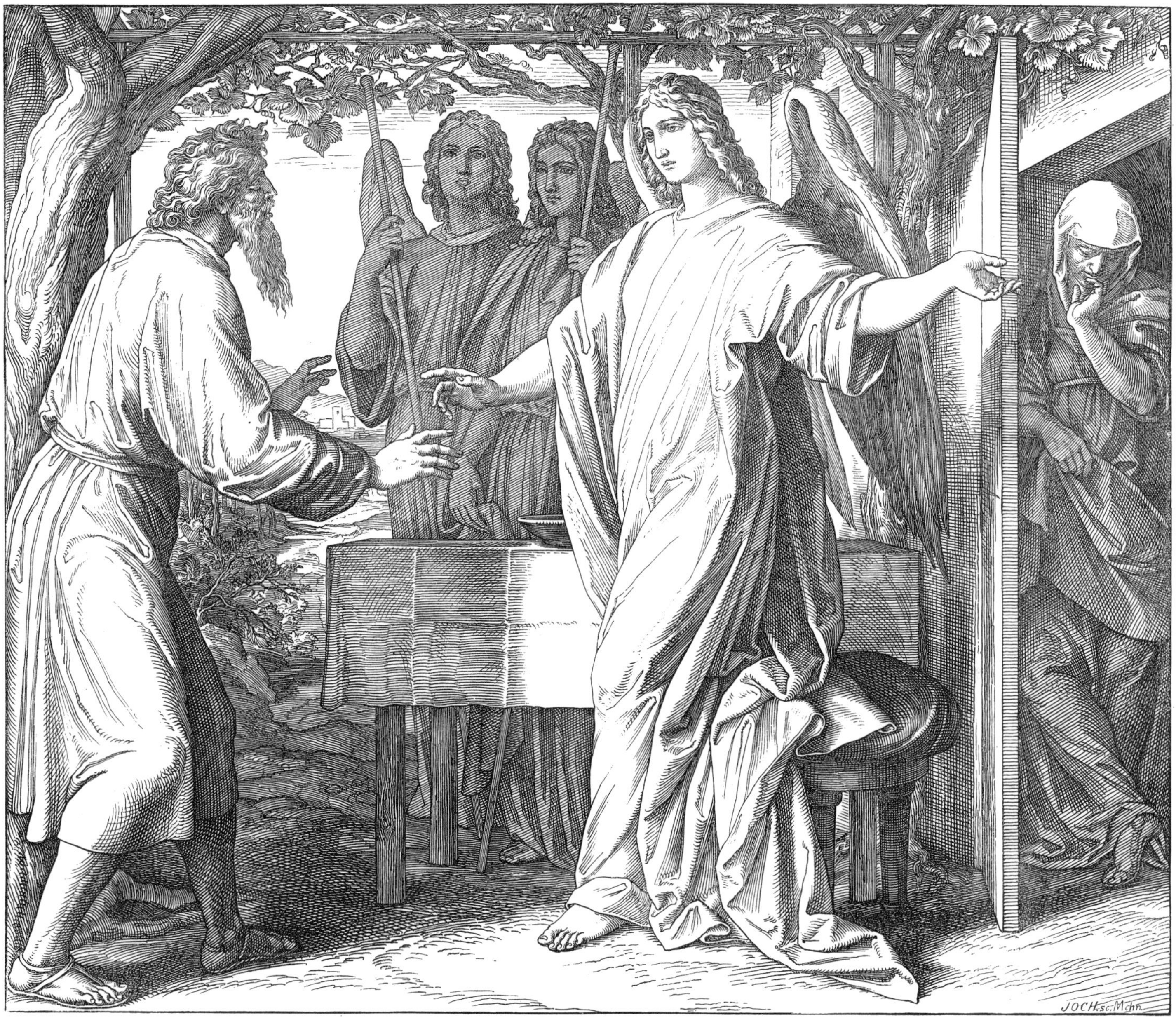

Abraham Receives God's Promise of a Son

Genesis. Chapter 18.

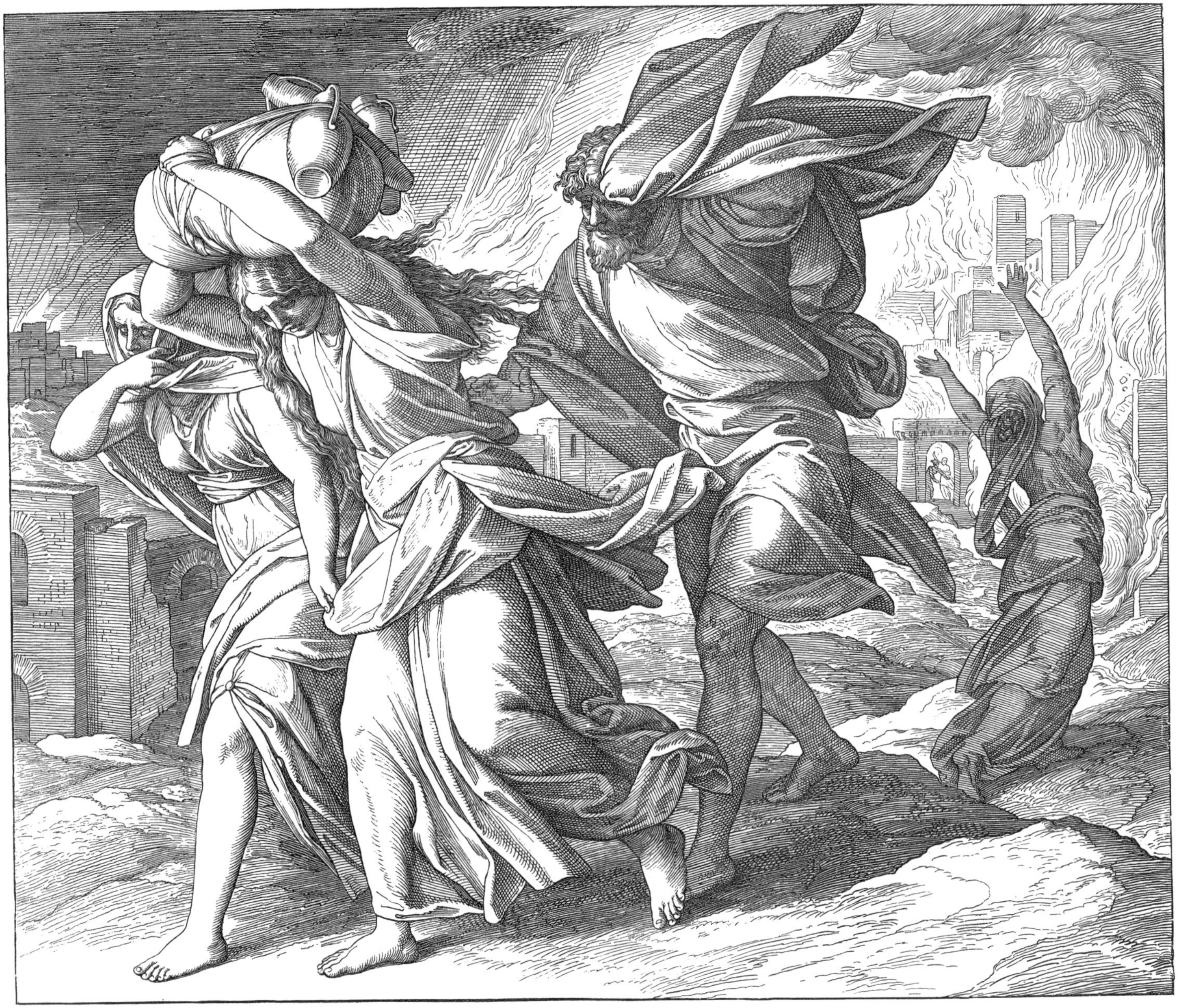

Lot Flees Sodom

Genesis. Chapter 19.

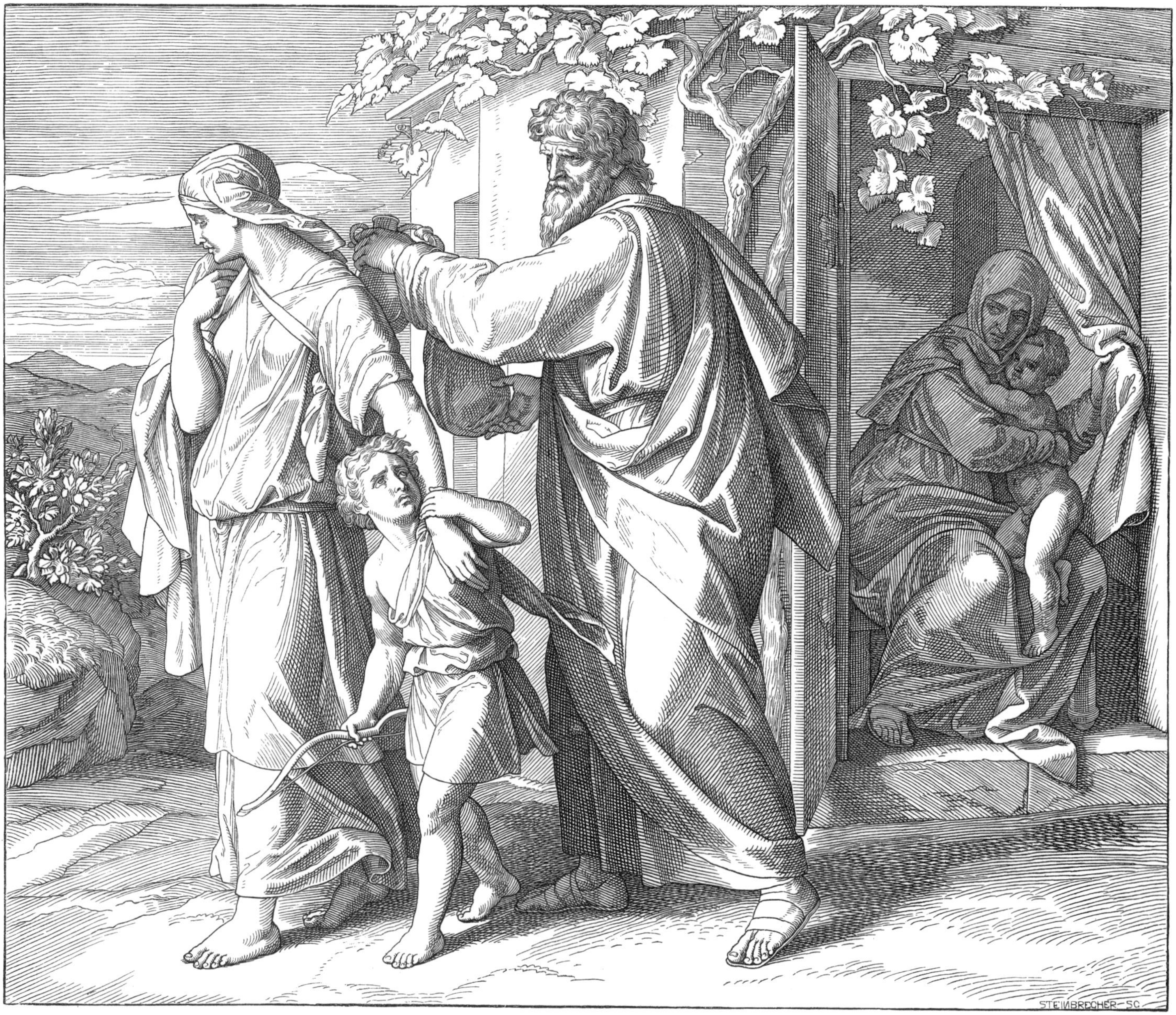

Ishmael and His Mother Are Driven Out
Genesis. Chapter 21.

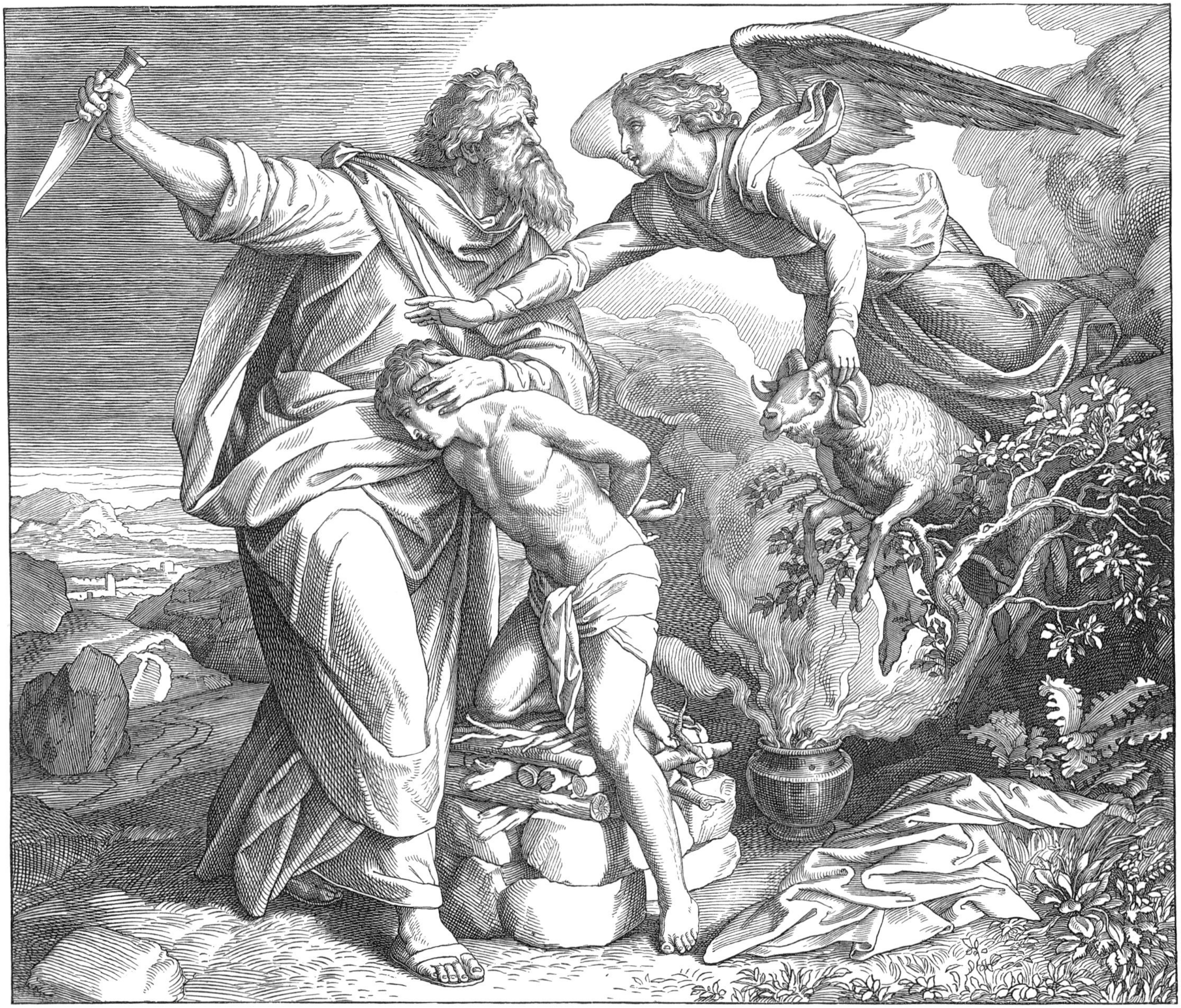

The Sacrifice of Isaac
Genesis. Chapter 22.

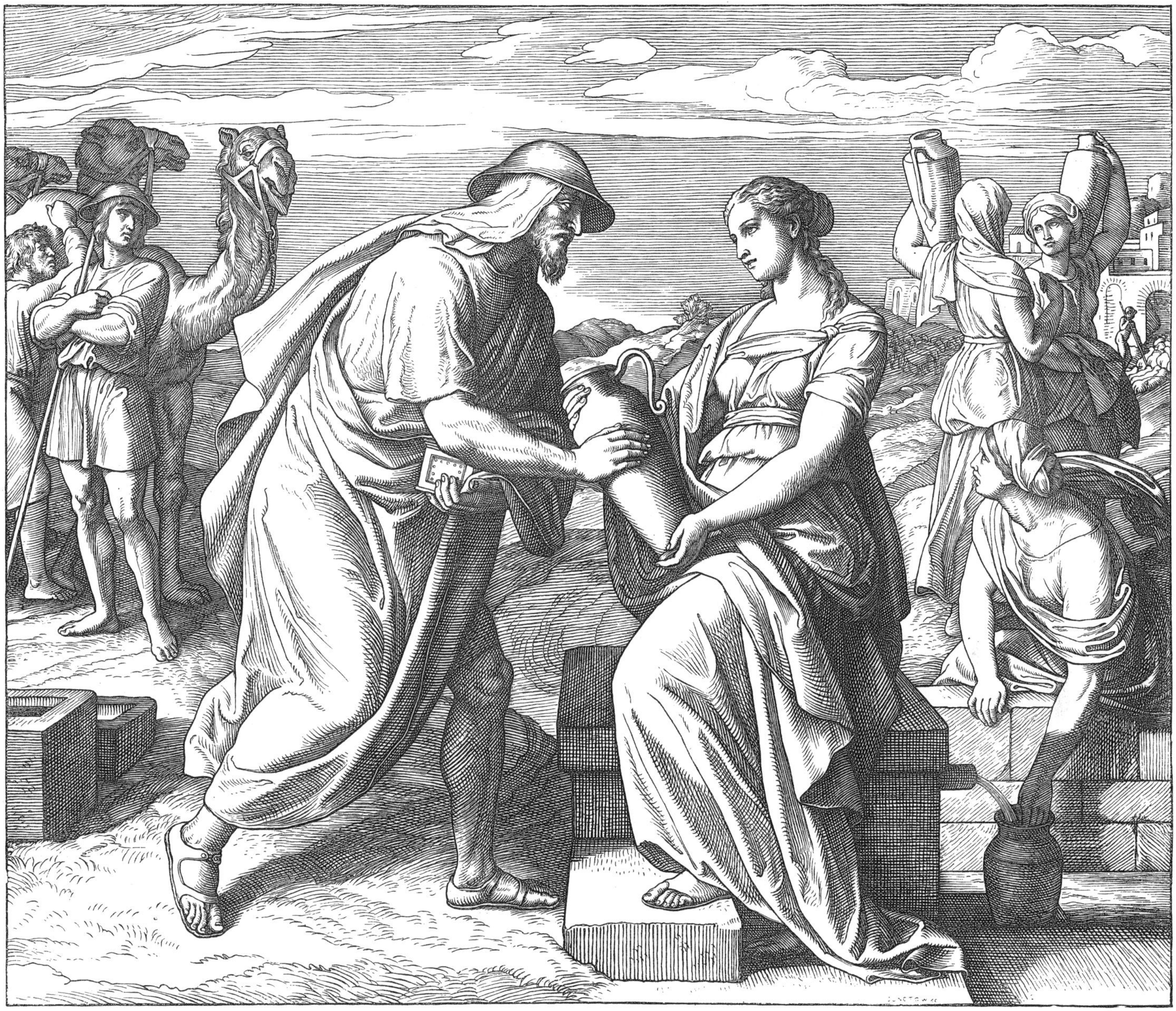

Rebekah Gives Abraham's Servant Water

Genesis. Chapter 24.

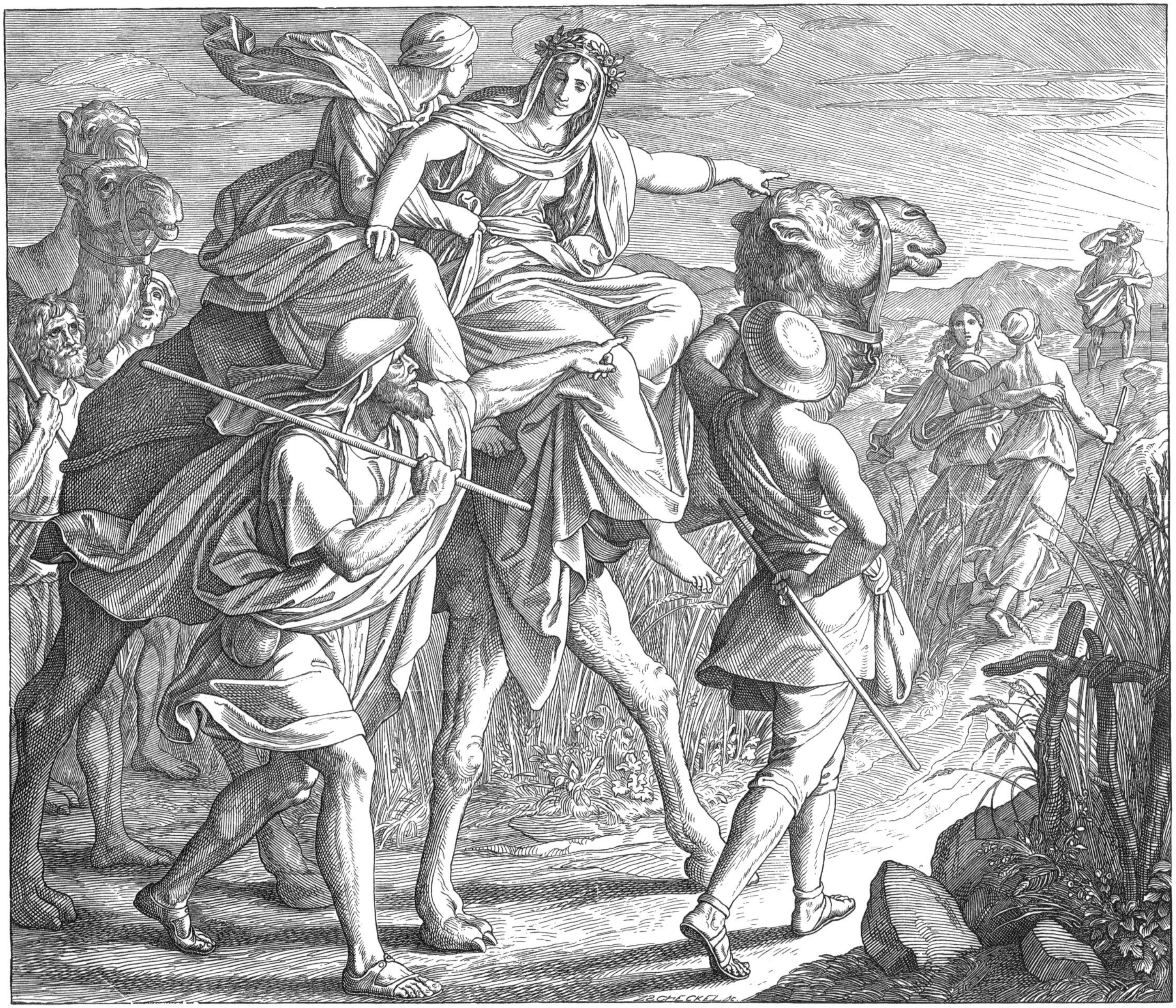

Rebekah Sees Isaac from Afar

Genesis. Chapter 24.

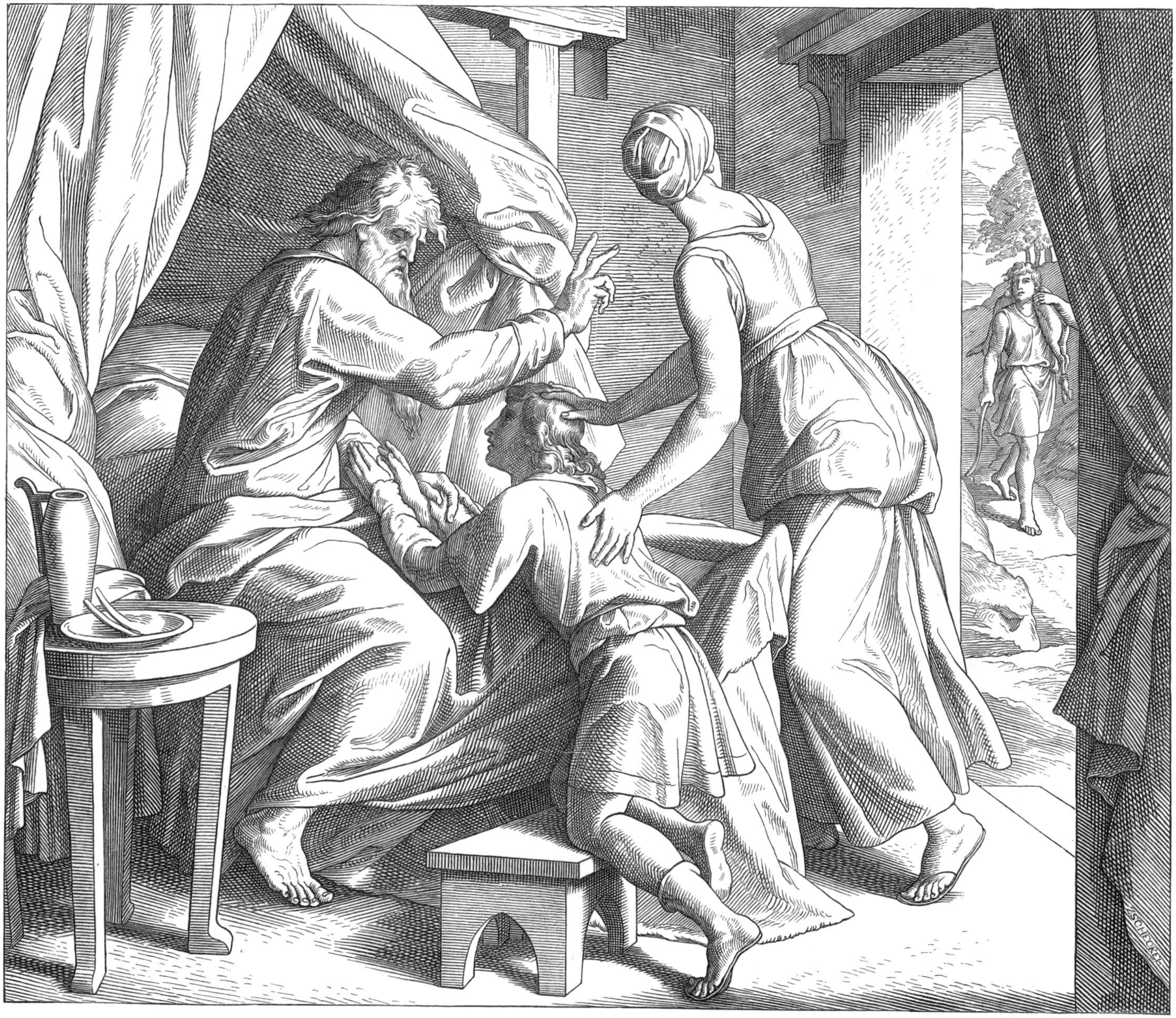

Isaac Is Deceived by Jacob

Genesis. Chapter 27.

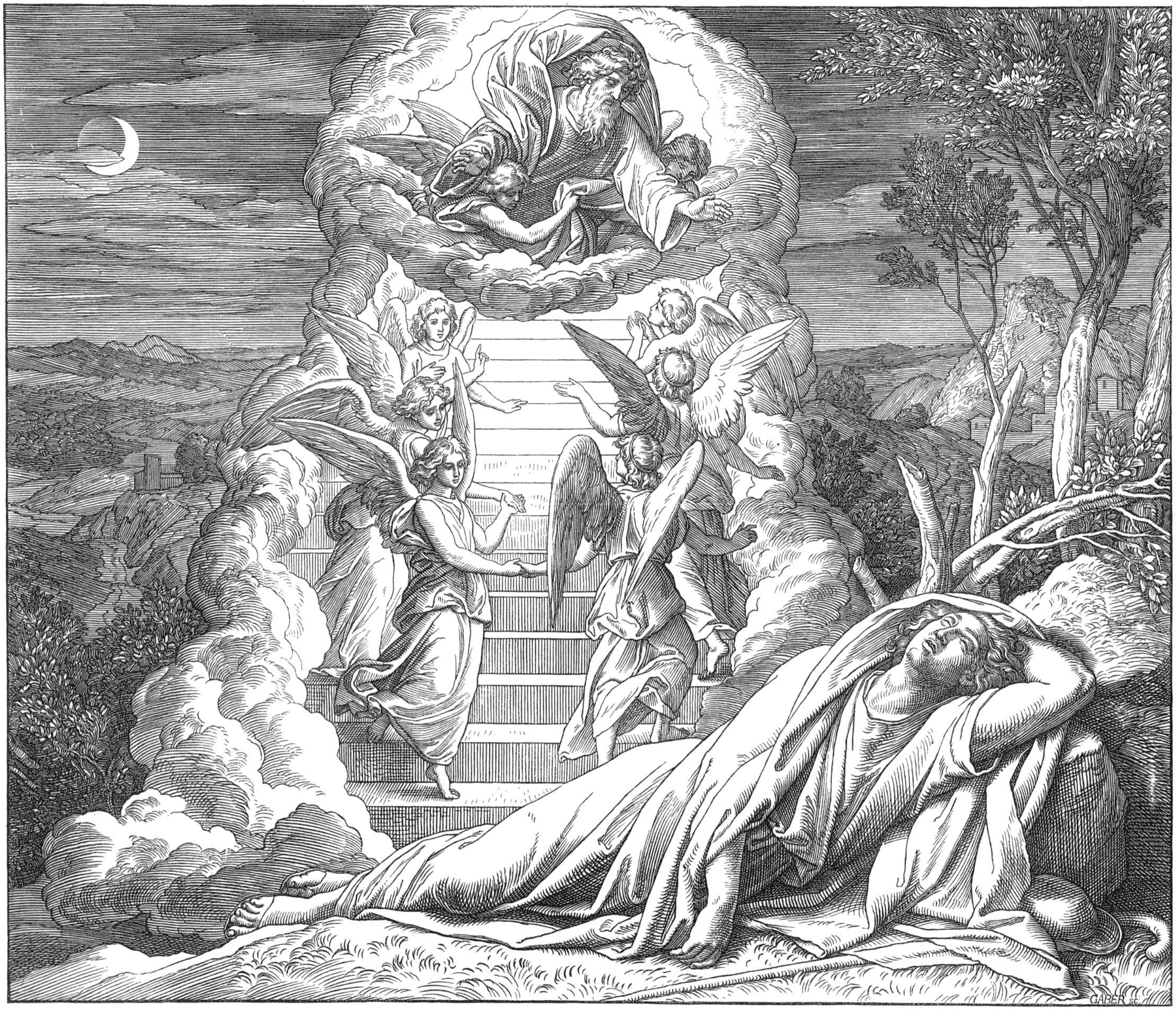

Jacob's Dream

Genesis. Chapter 28.

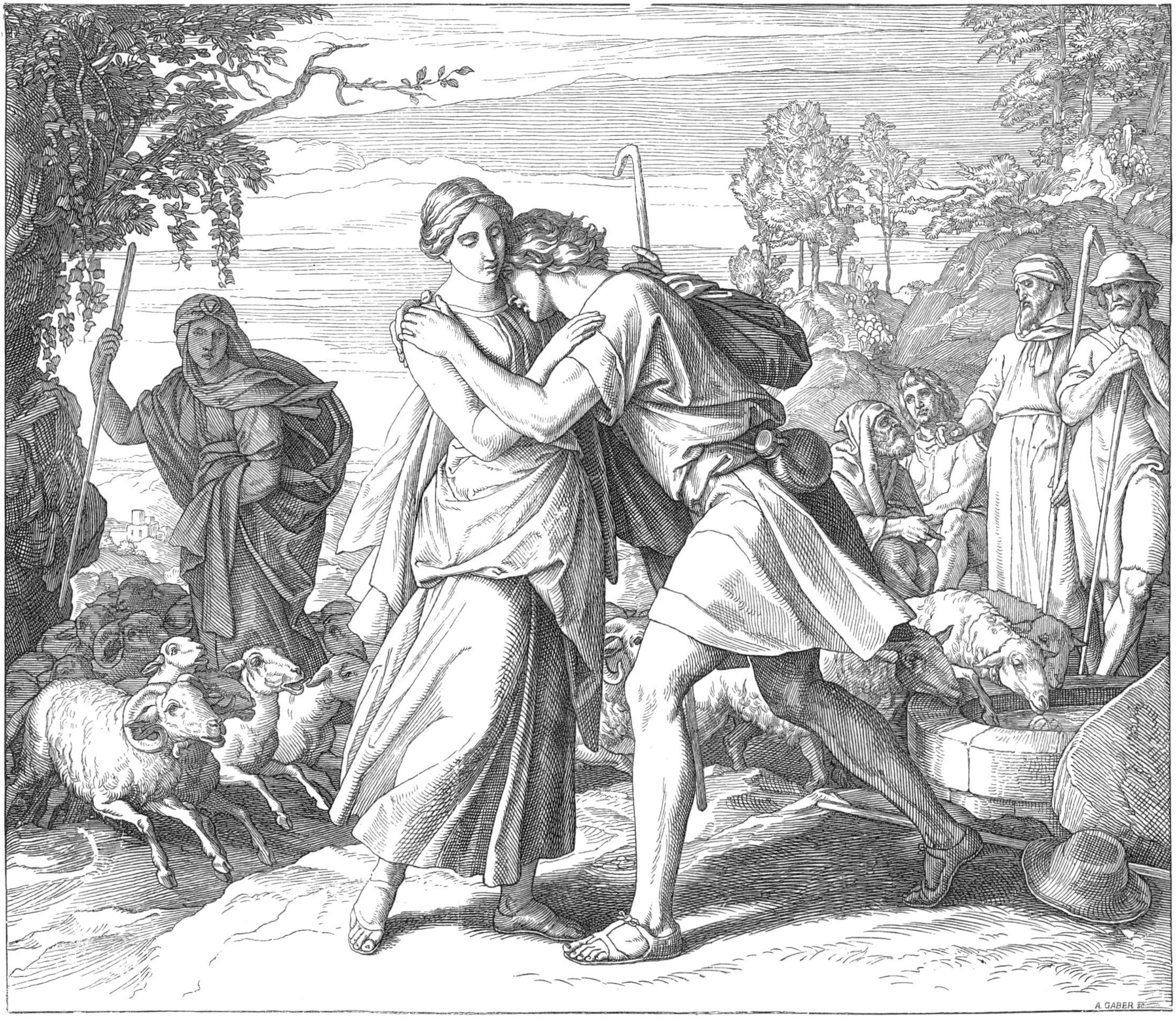

Jacob and Rachel at the Well

Genesis. Chapter 29.

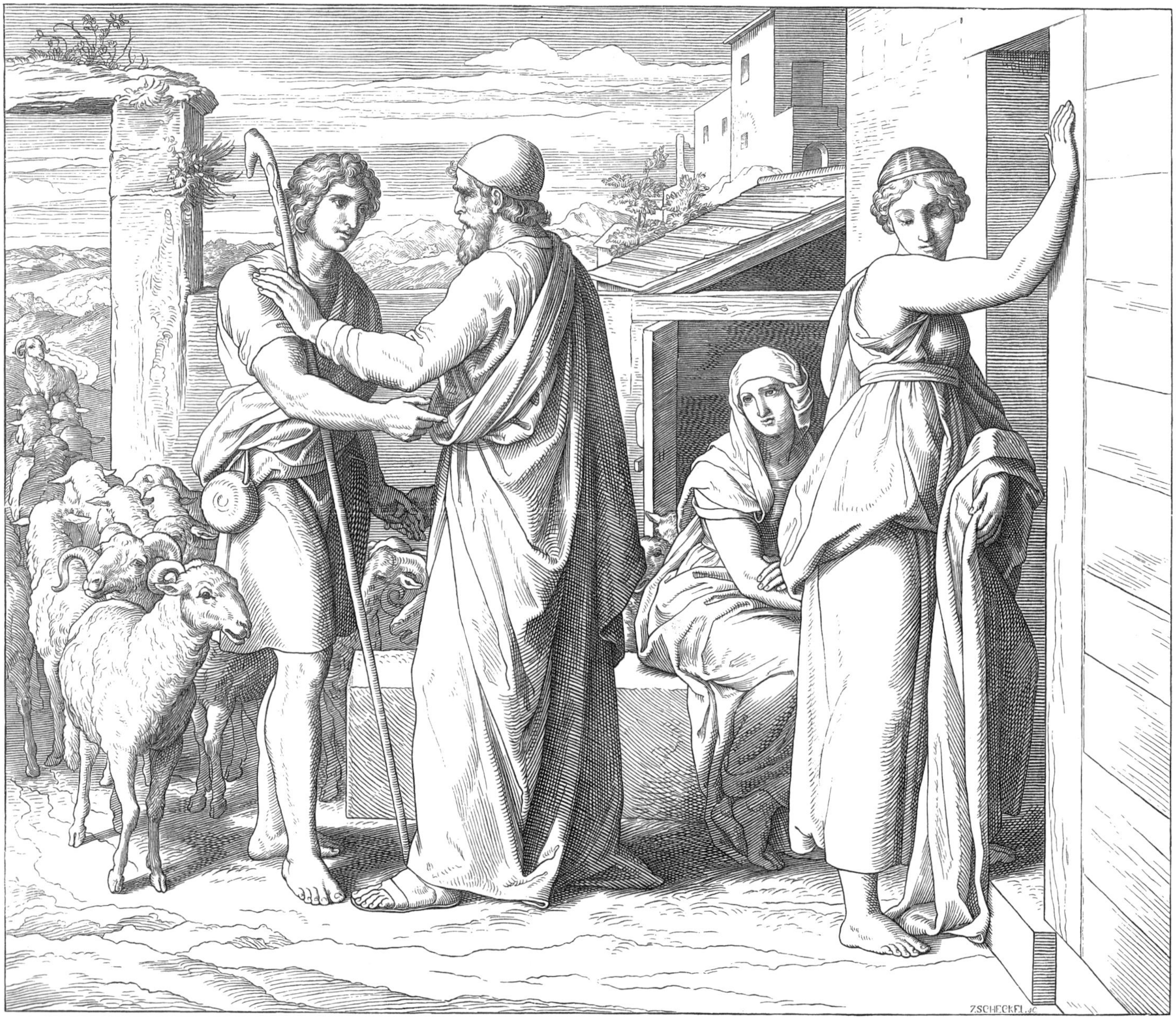

Jacob Seeks Rachel's Hand in Marriage

Genesis. Chapter 29.

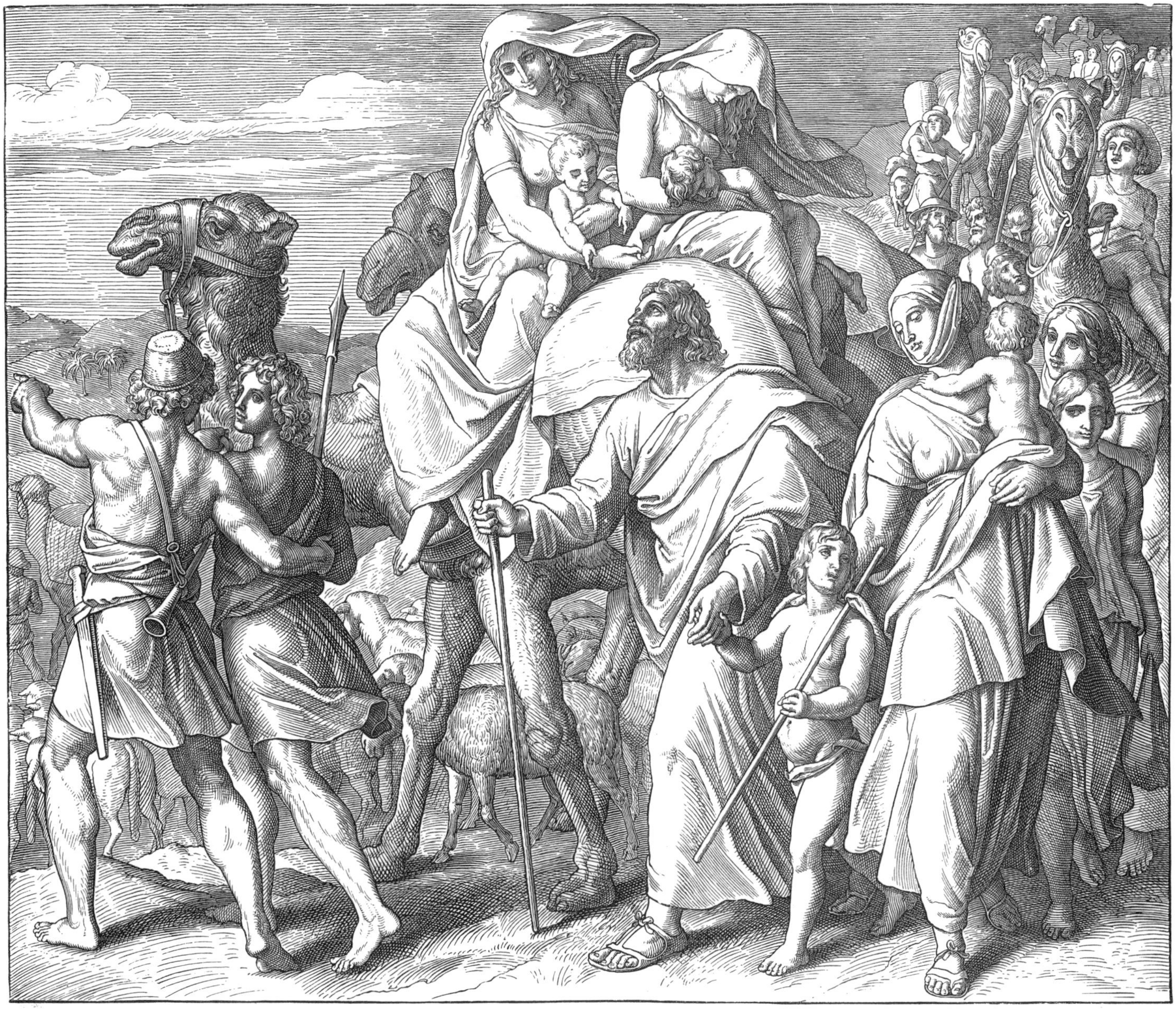

Jacob's Flight

Genesis. Chapter 31.

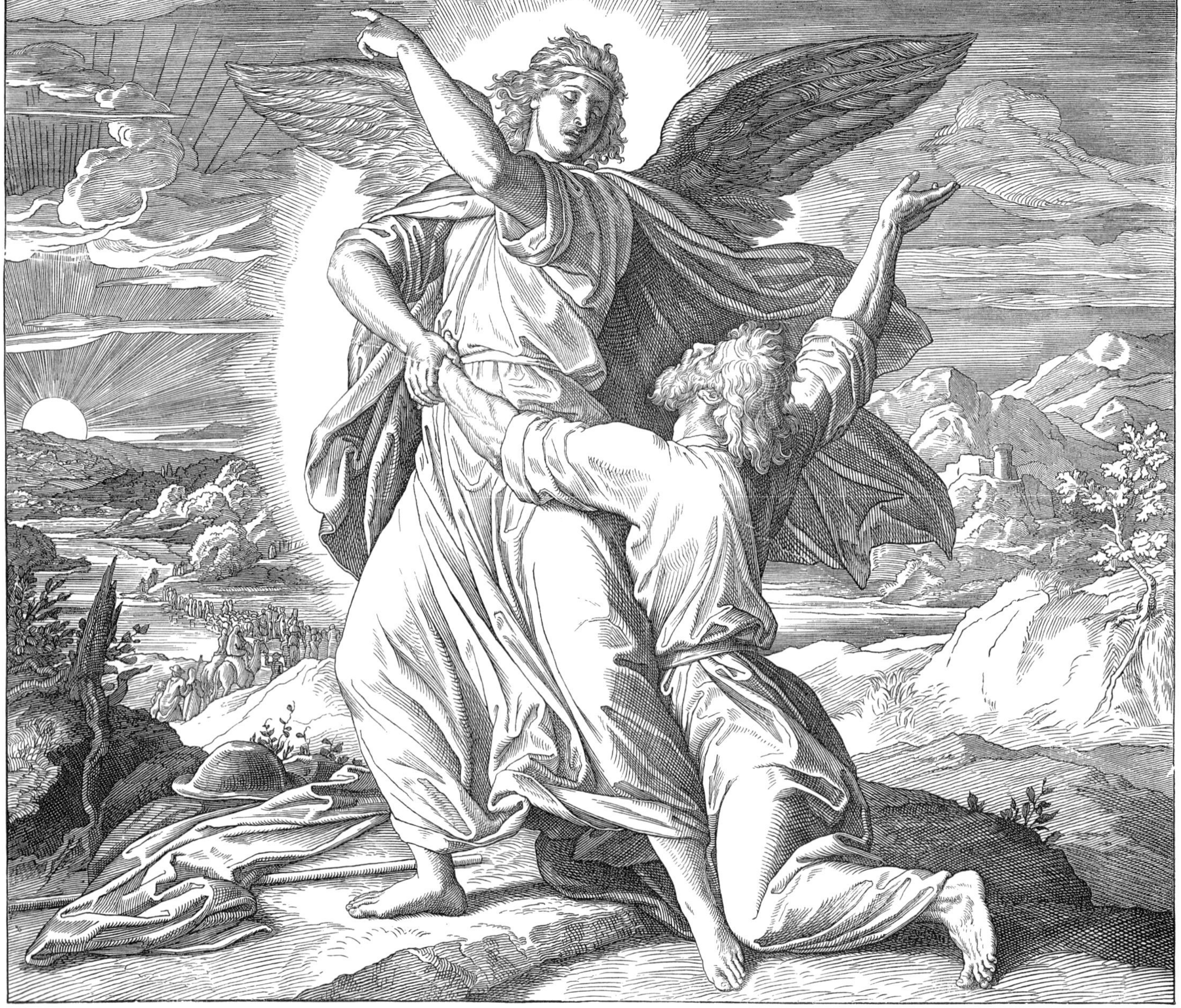

Jacob Wrestles with the Angel

Genesis. Chapter 32.

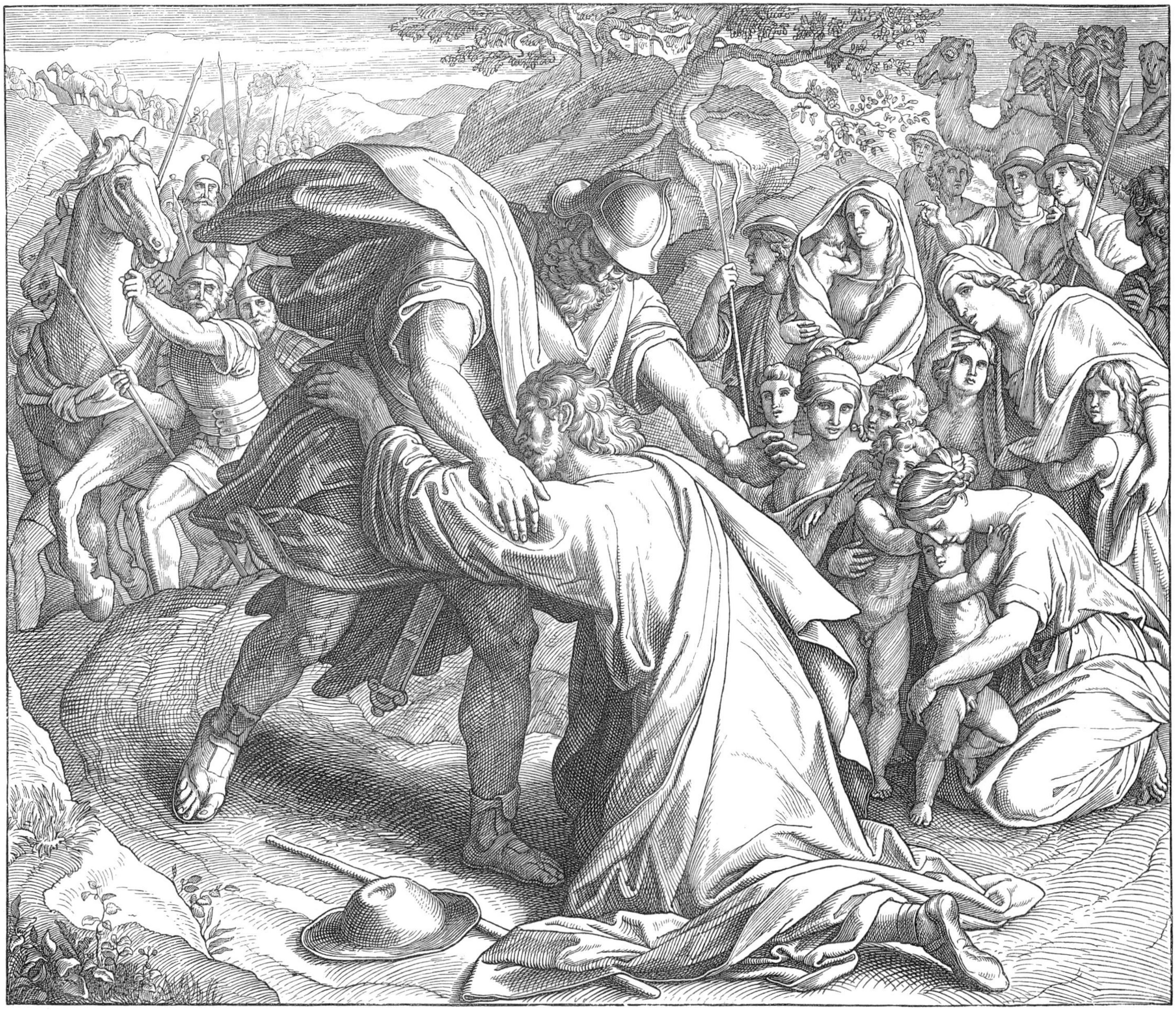

Jacob's Reconciliation with Esau

Genesis. Chapter 33.

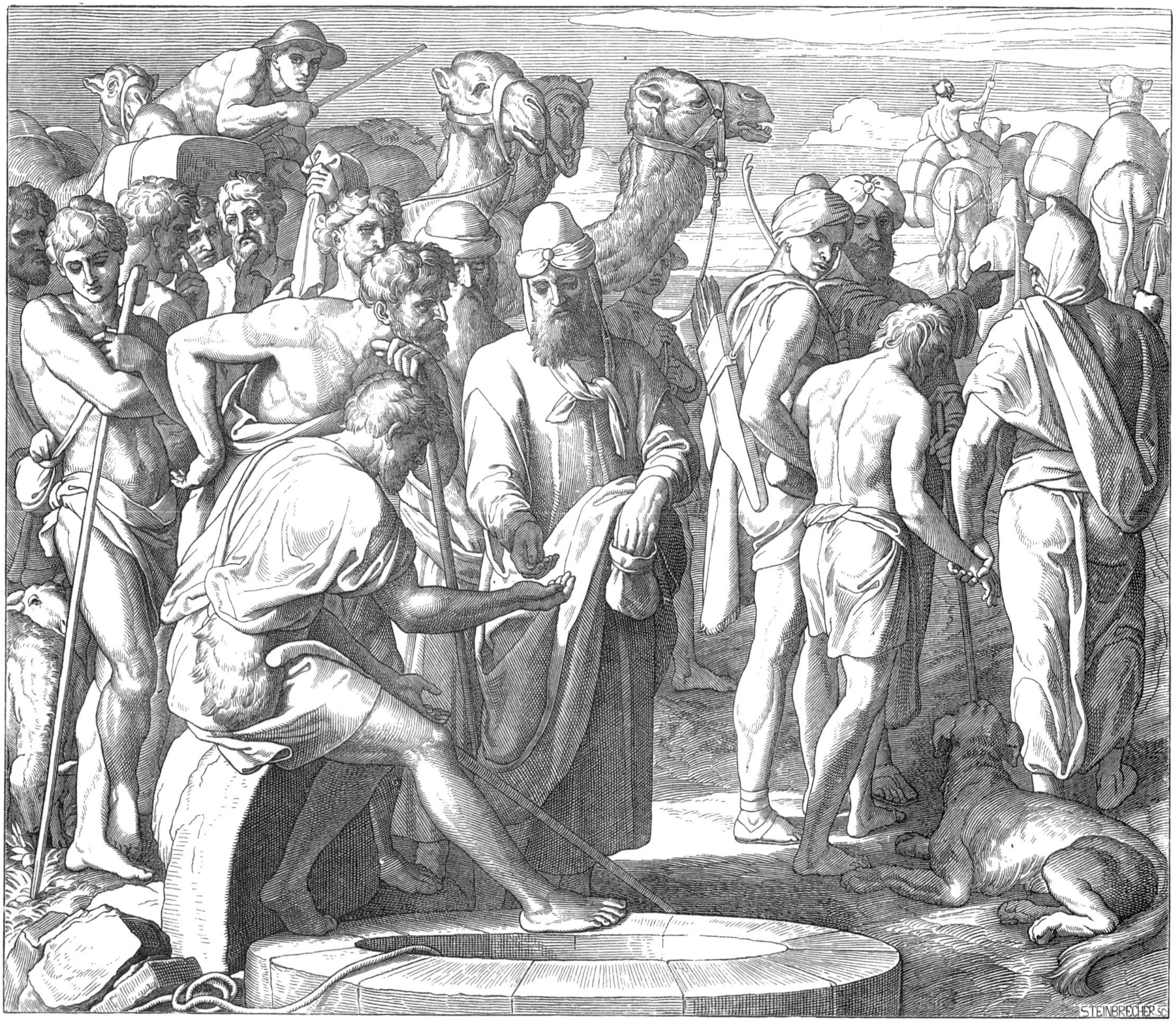

JOSEPH IS SOLD INTO EGYPT

Genesis. Chapter 37.

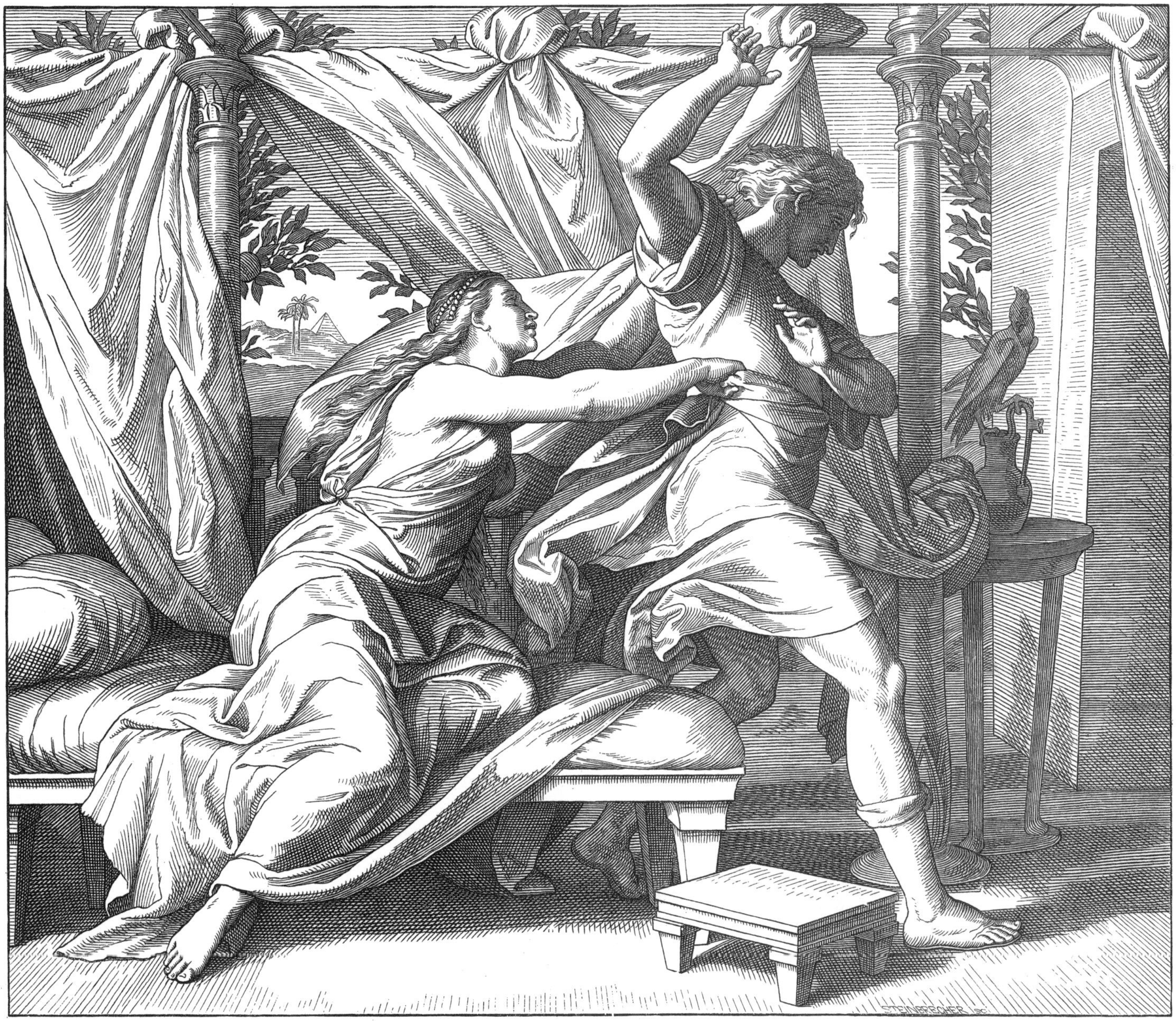

Joseph's Chastity and Potiphar's Unfaithful Wife

Genesis. Chapter 39.

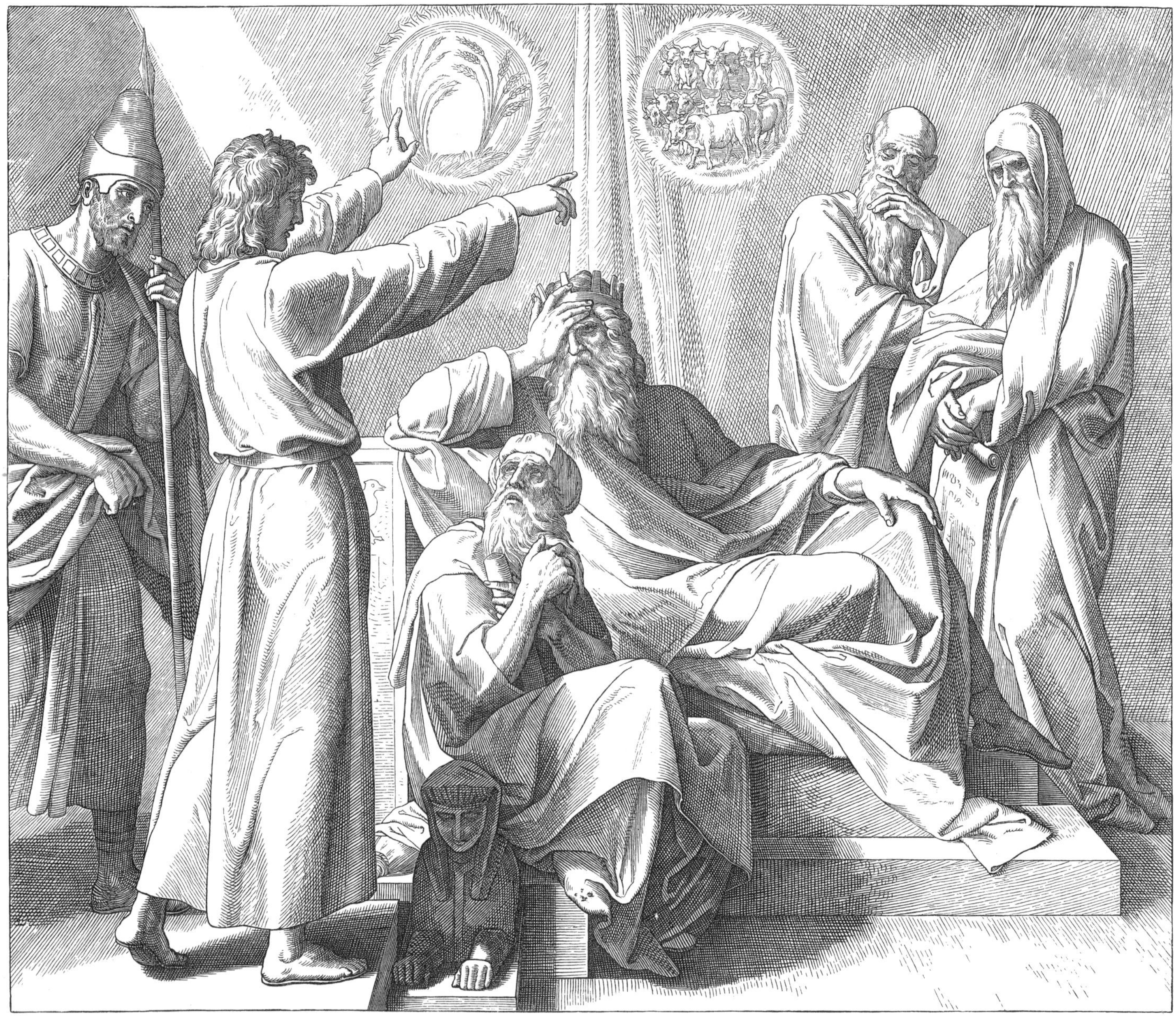

Joseph Interprets Pharaoh's Dream

Genesis. Chapter 41.

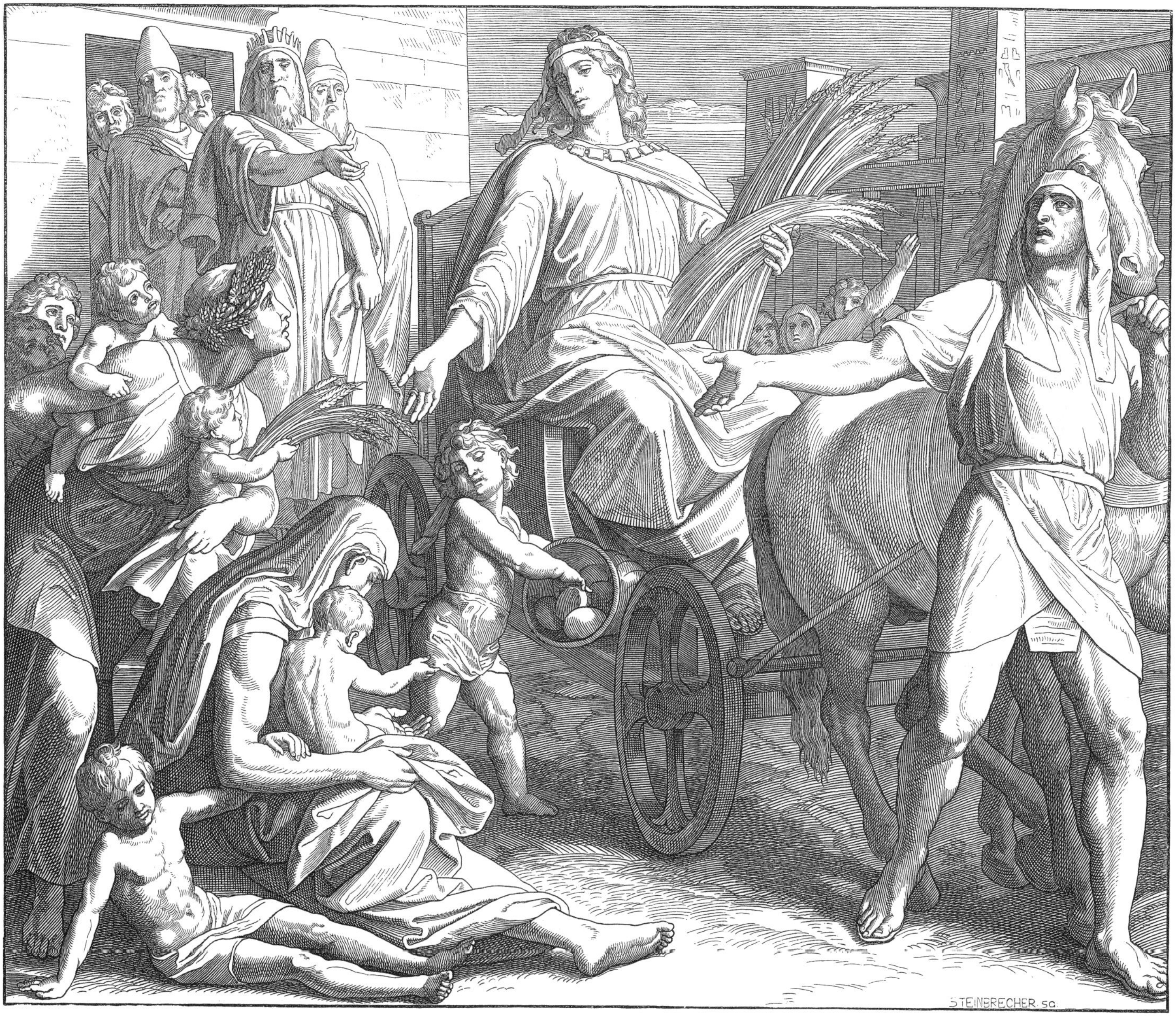

Joseph Is Ruler Over All Egypt

Genesis. Chapter 41.

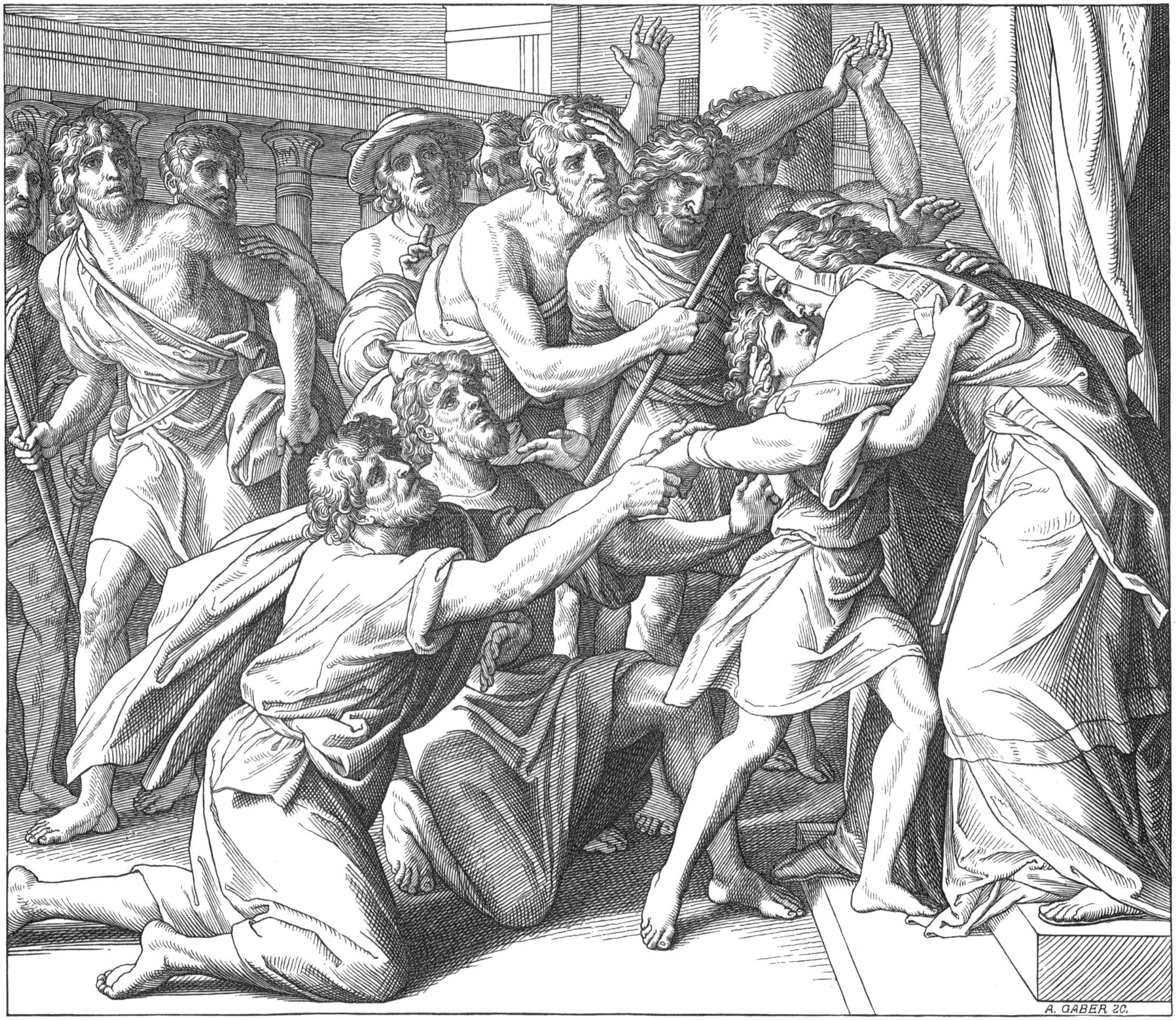

Joseph Reveals Himself to His Brothers

Genesis. Chapter 45.

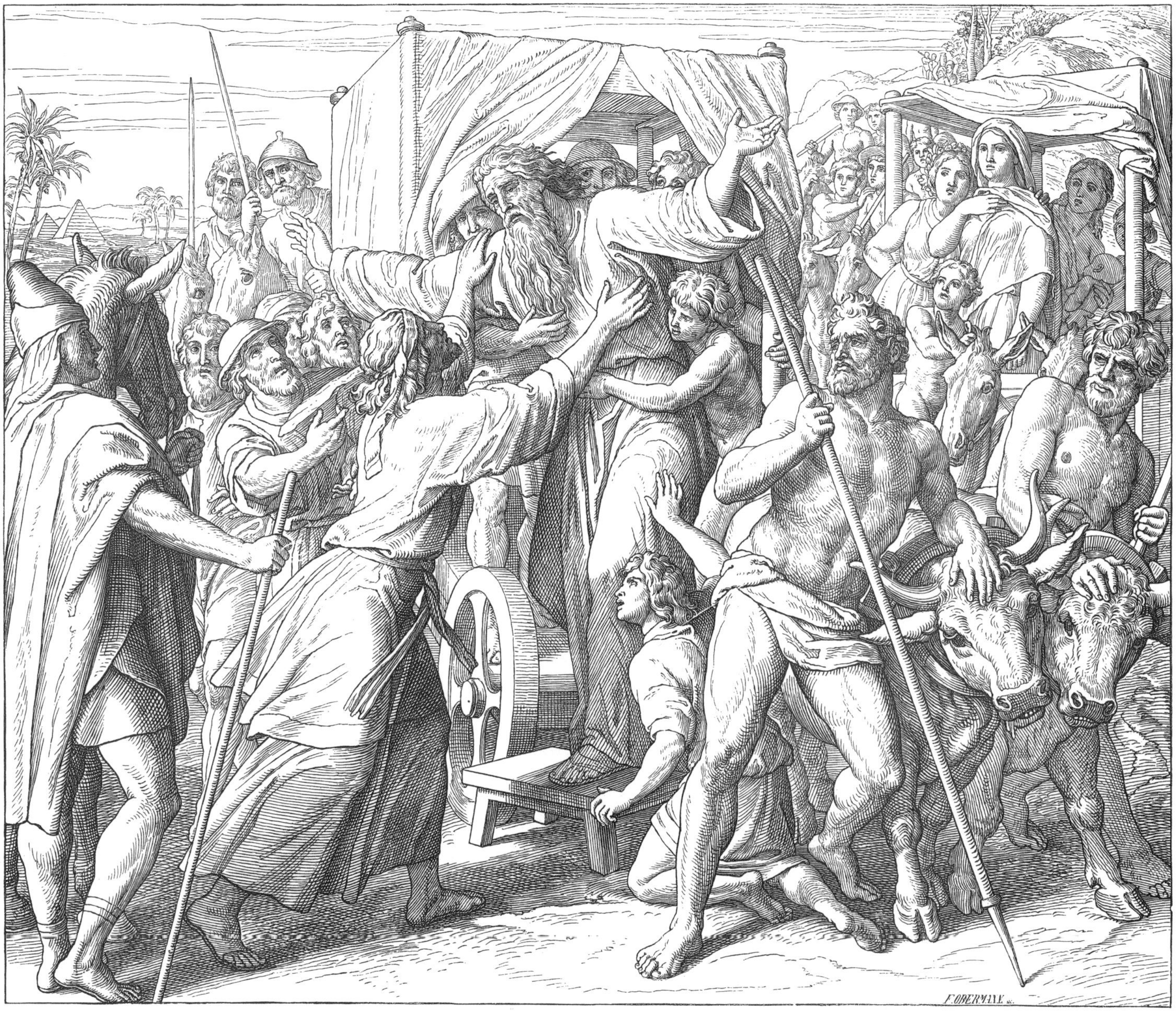

Jacob Comes Into Egypt

Genesis. Chapter 46.

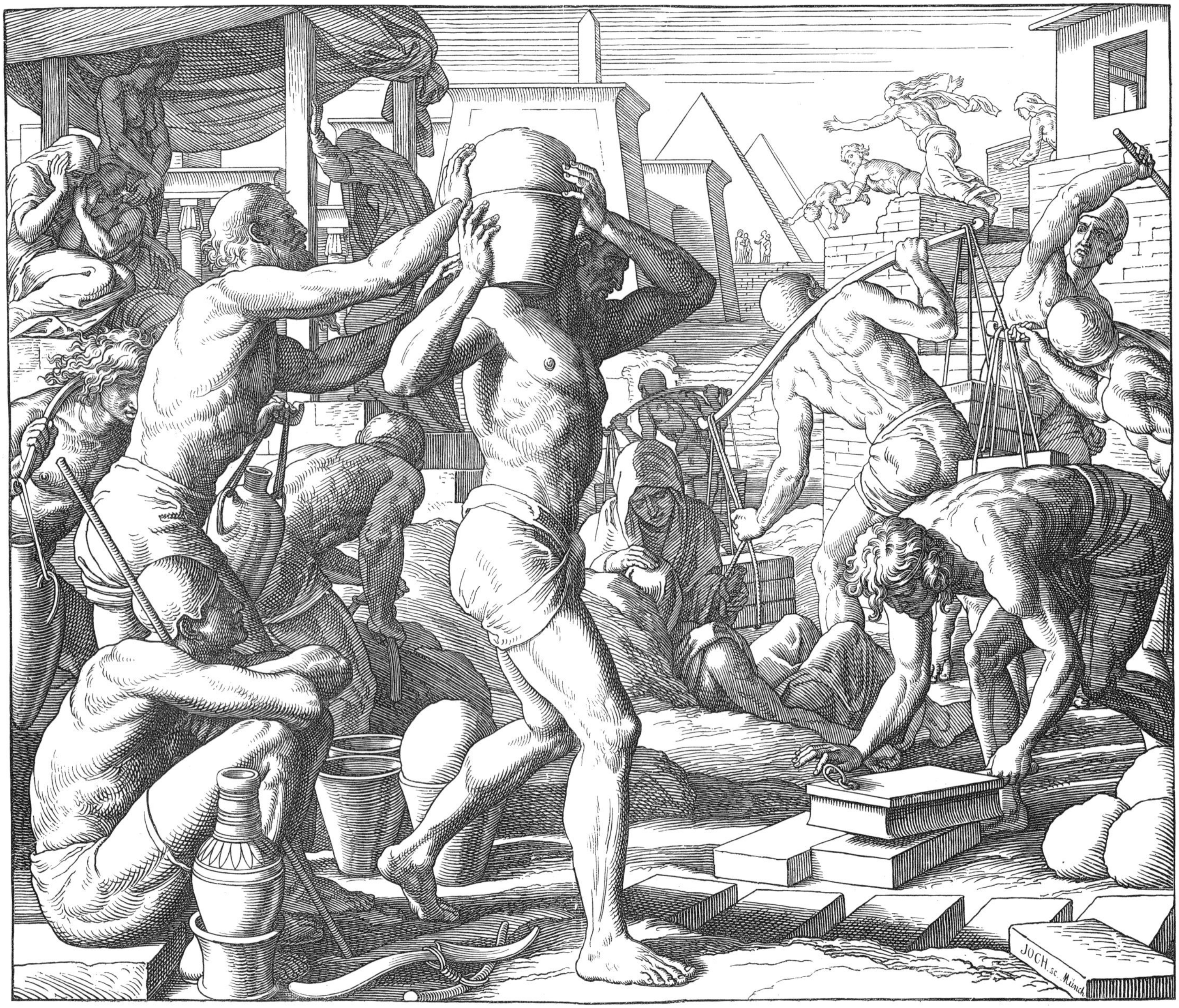

THE HARDSHIP AND SUBSERVIENCE OF THE ISRAELITES IN EGYPT

Exodus. Chapter 1.

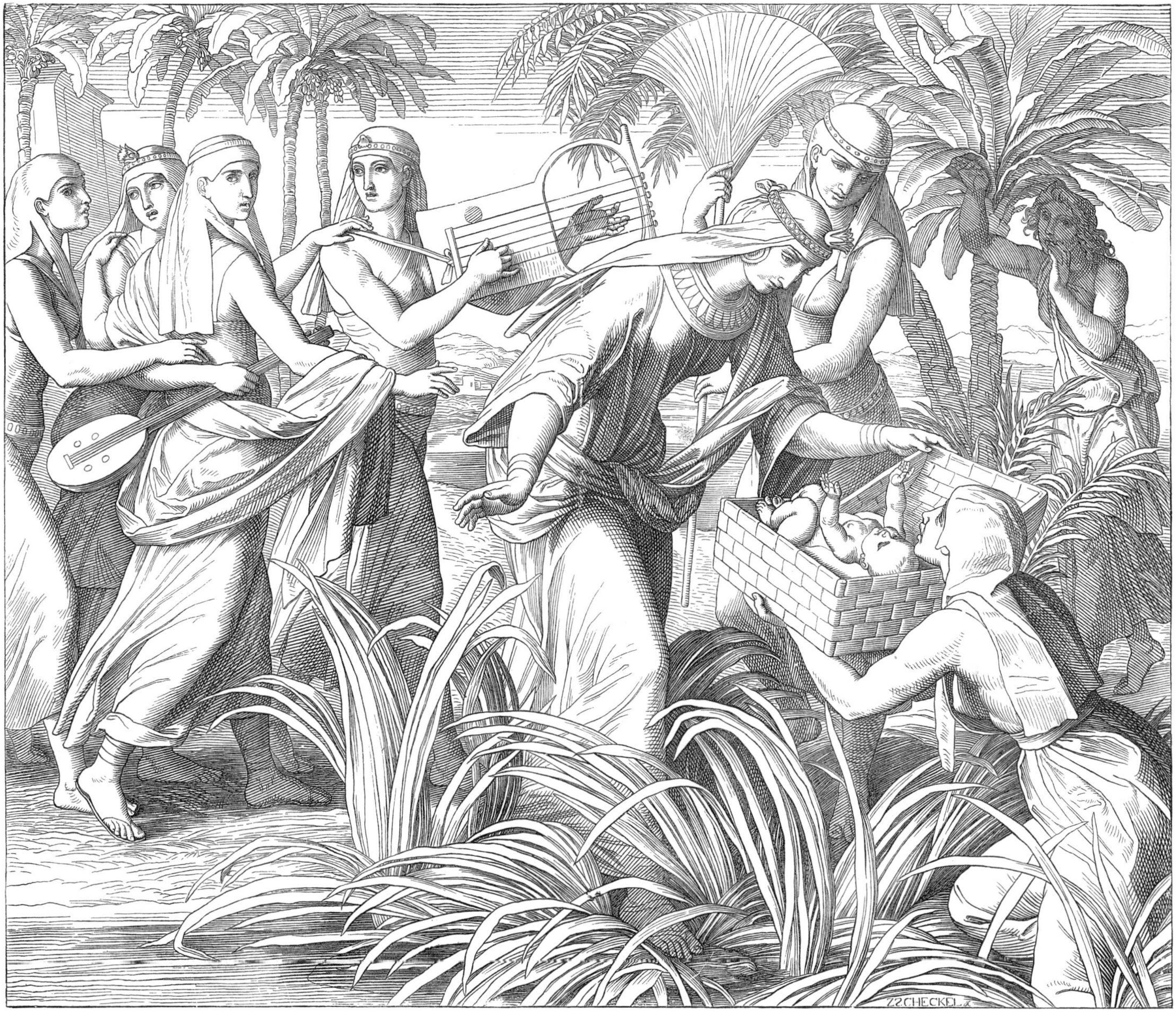

The Discovery of Moses

Exodus. Chapter 2.

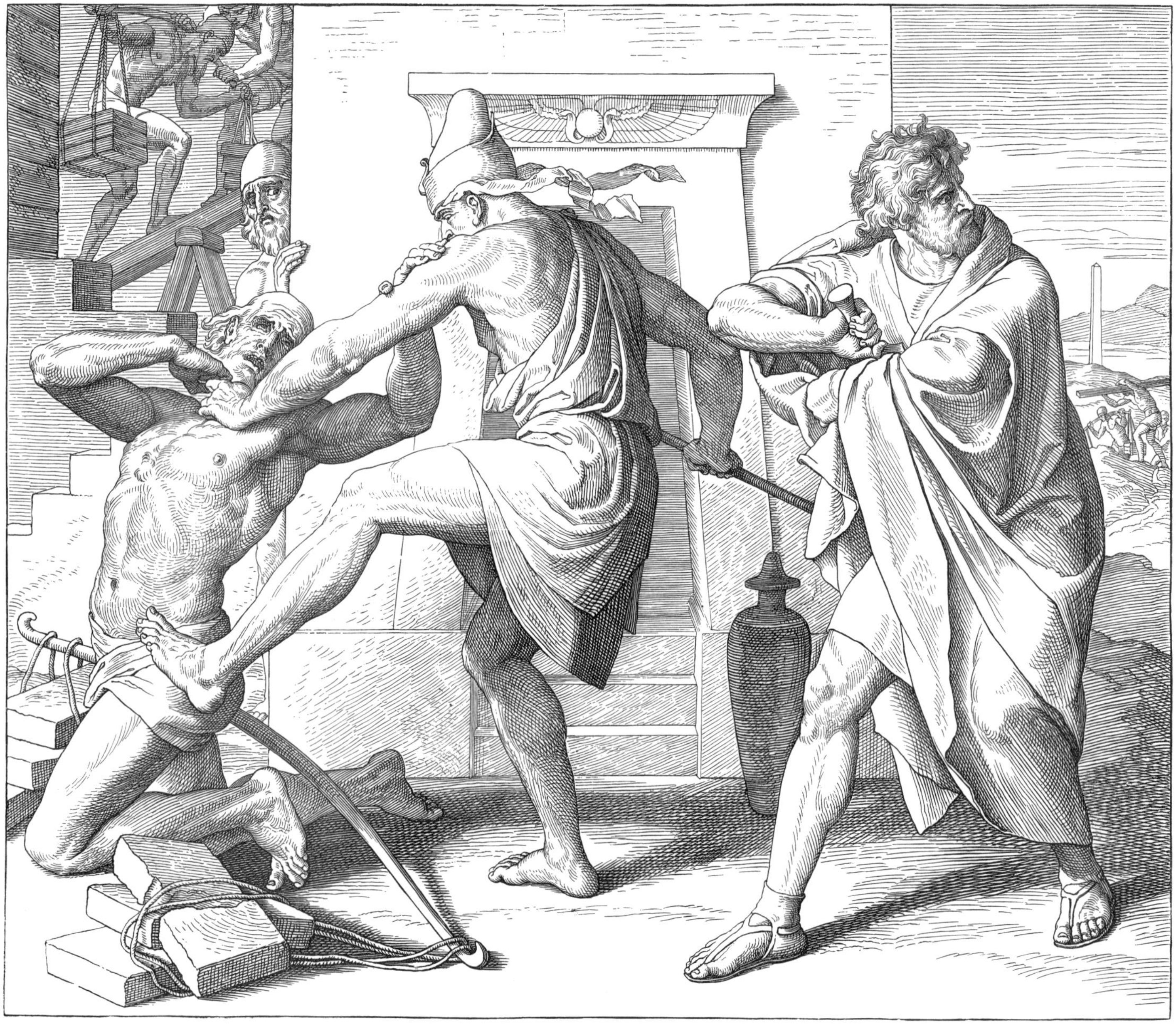

Moses Avenges the Mistreatment of a Fellow Hebrew

Exodus. Chapter 2.

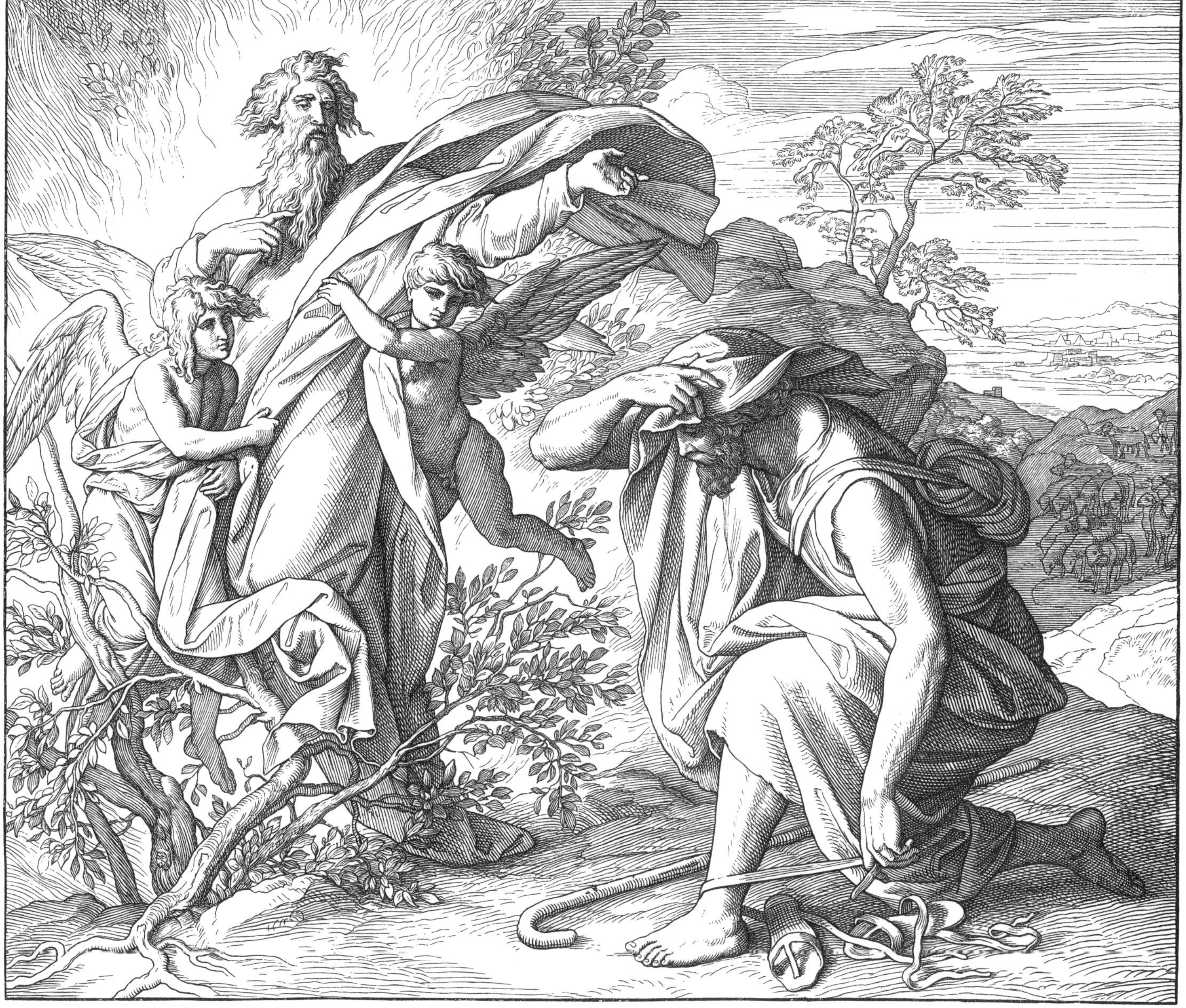

Moses Is Sent to Egypt
Exodus. Chapter 3.

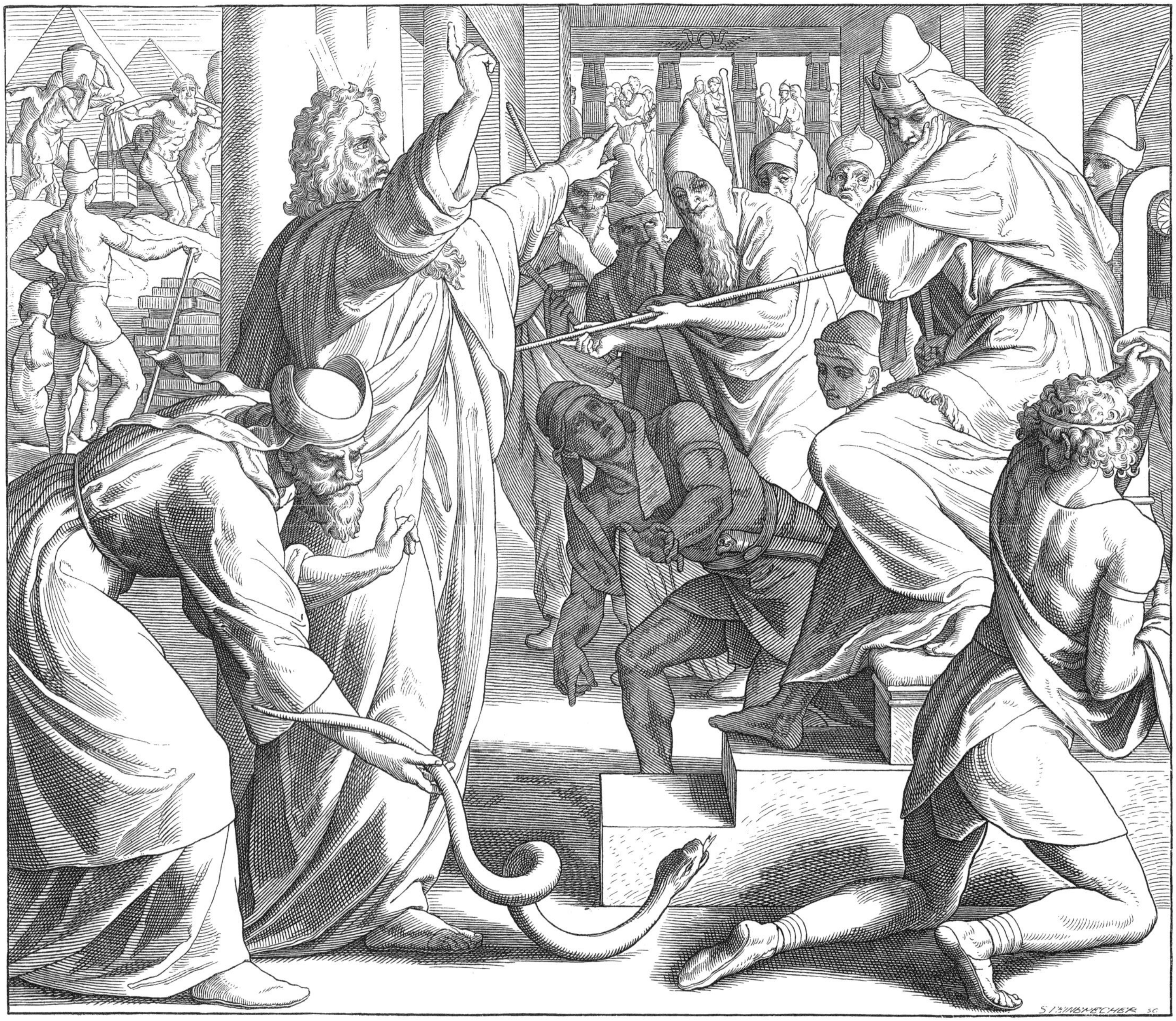

Moses Demands the Release of the Israelites

Exodus. Chapter 7.

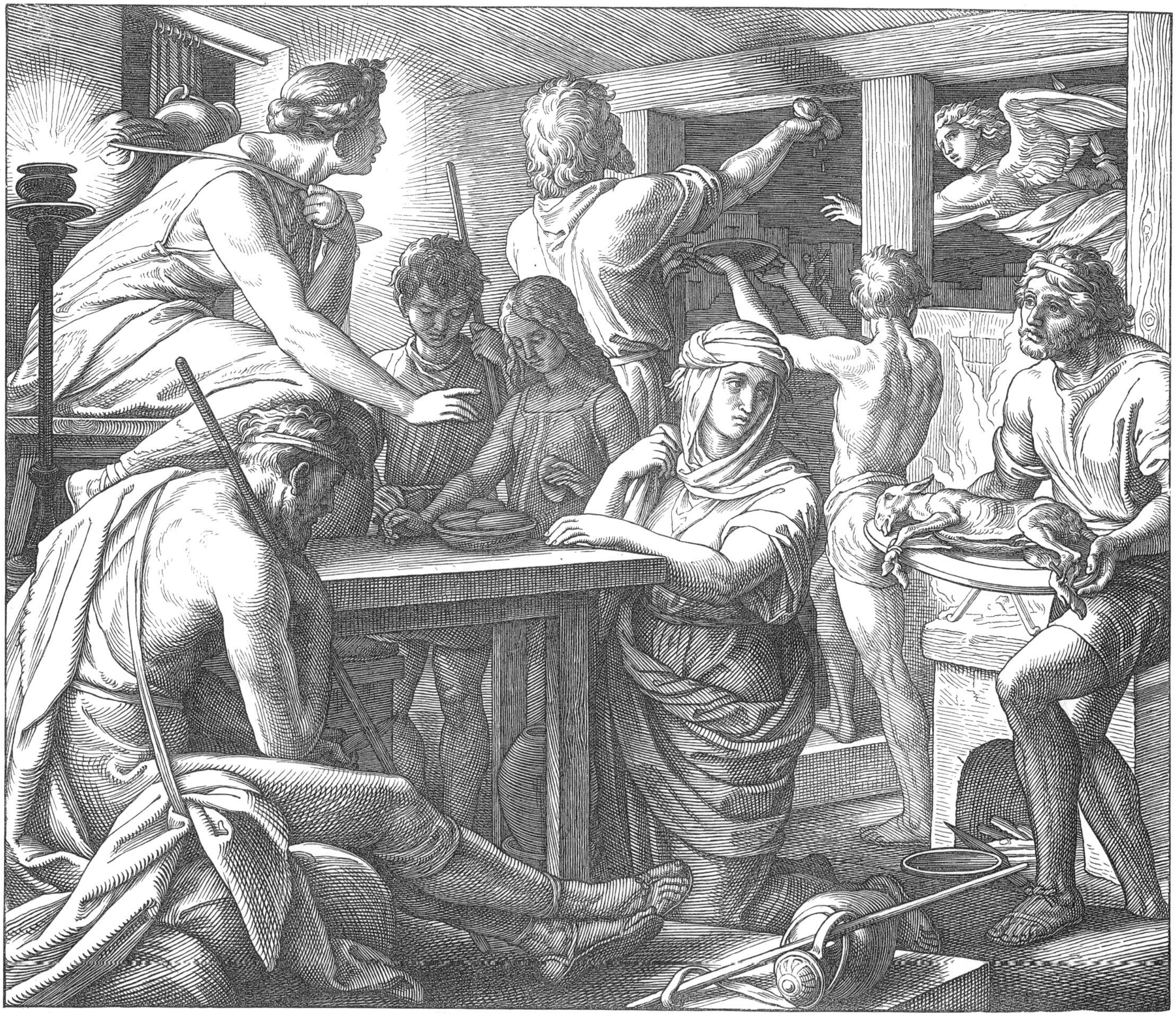

The Origin of the Paschal Lamb
Exodus. Chapter 12.

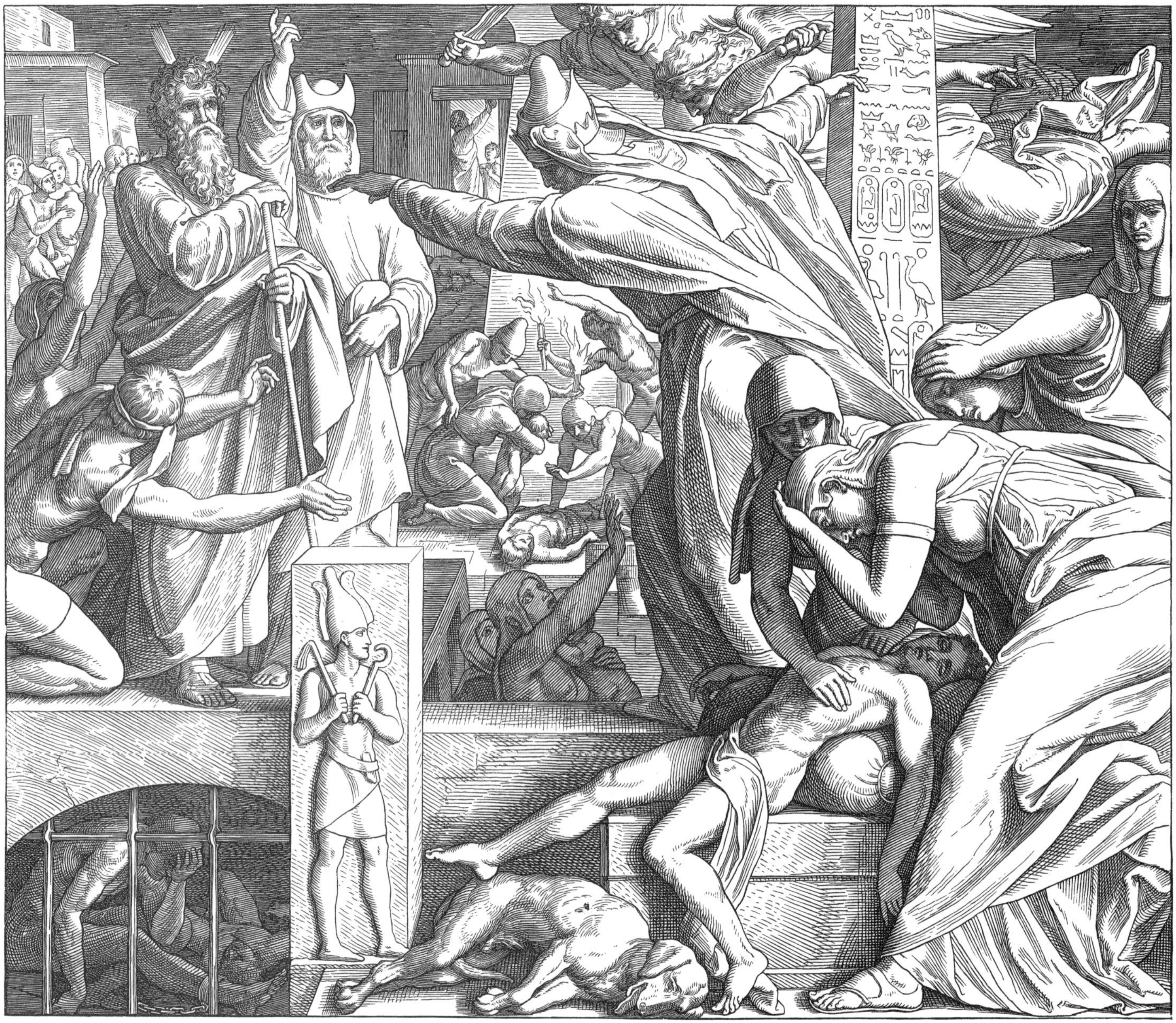

THE DEATH OF THE FIRSTBORN AND THE RELEASE OF THE ISRAELITES

Exodus. Chapter 12.

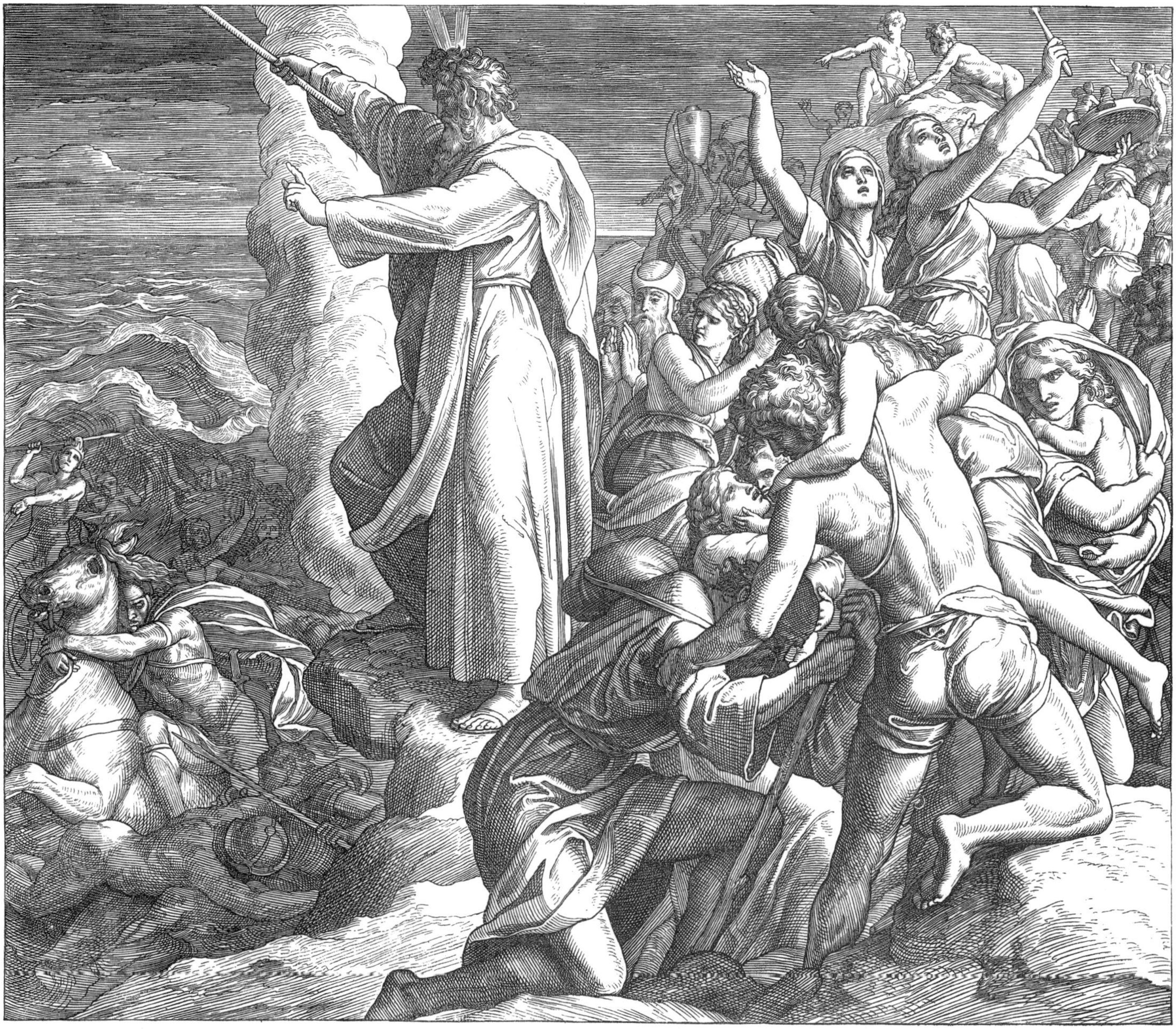

The Egyptians Drown in the Red Sea
Exodus. Chapter 14.

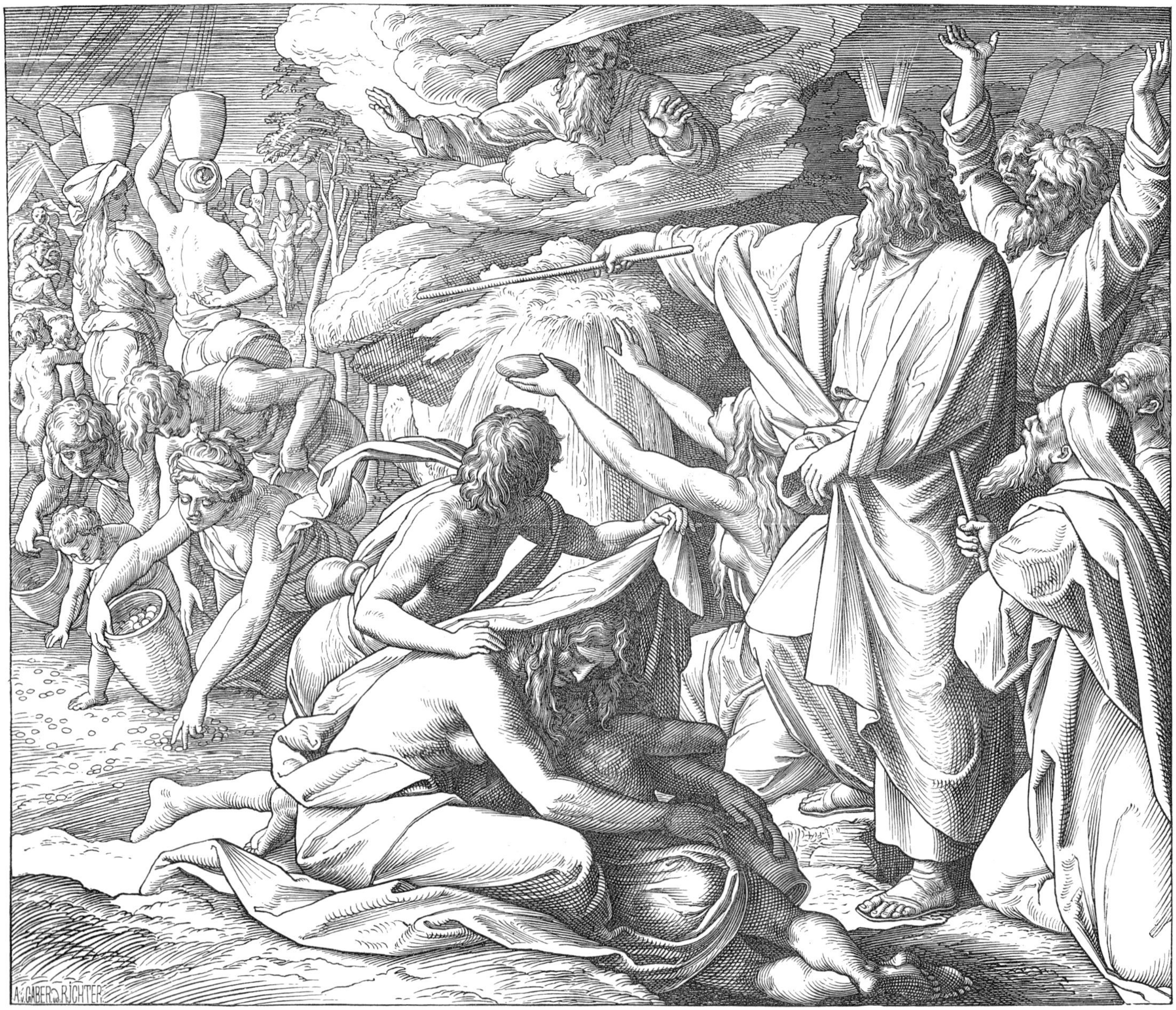

God Gives Israel Bread and Water in the Desert

Exodus. Chapters 16 and 17.

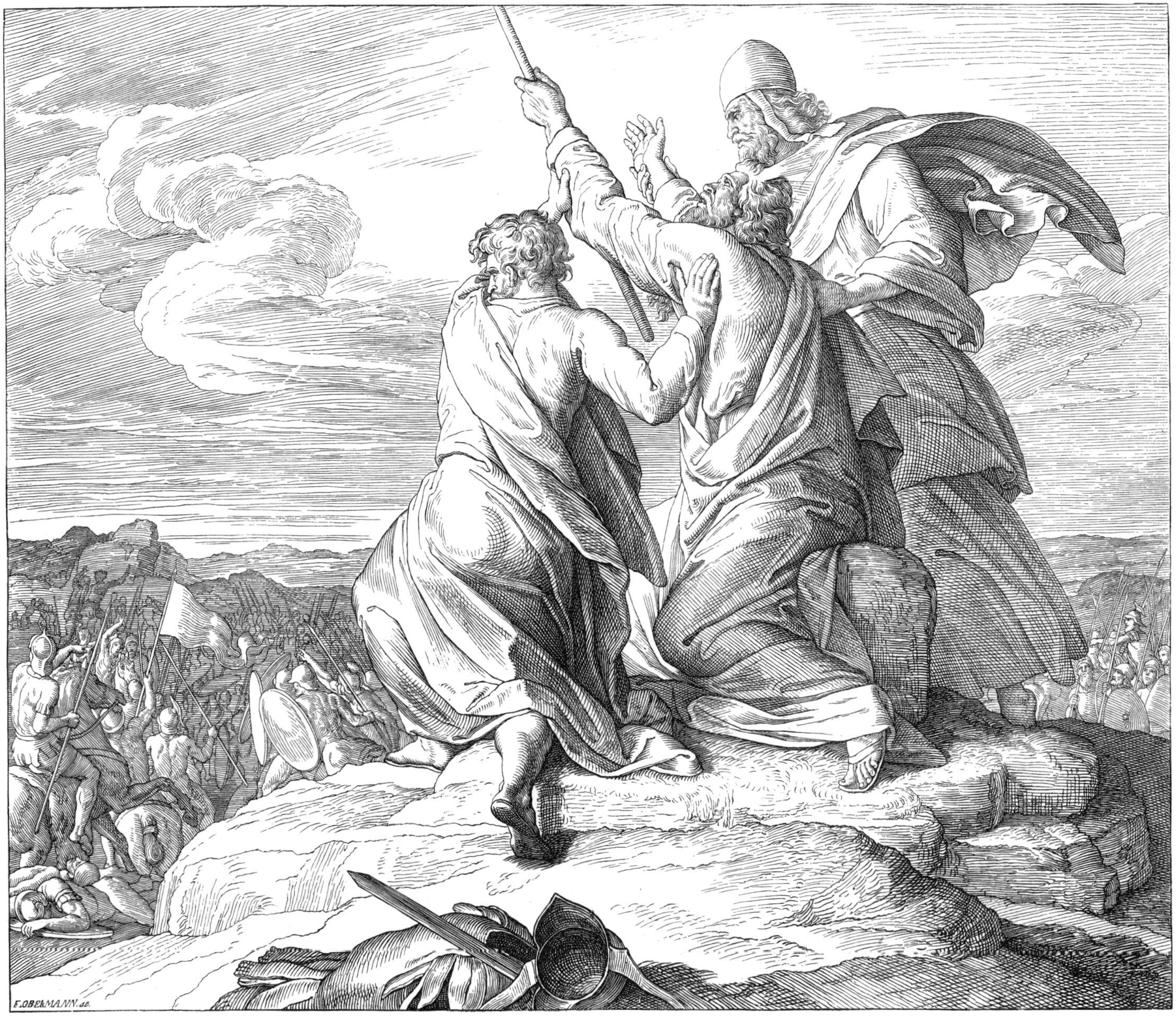

Moses Prays During the Battle Against Amalek

Exodus. Chapter 17.

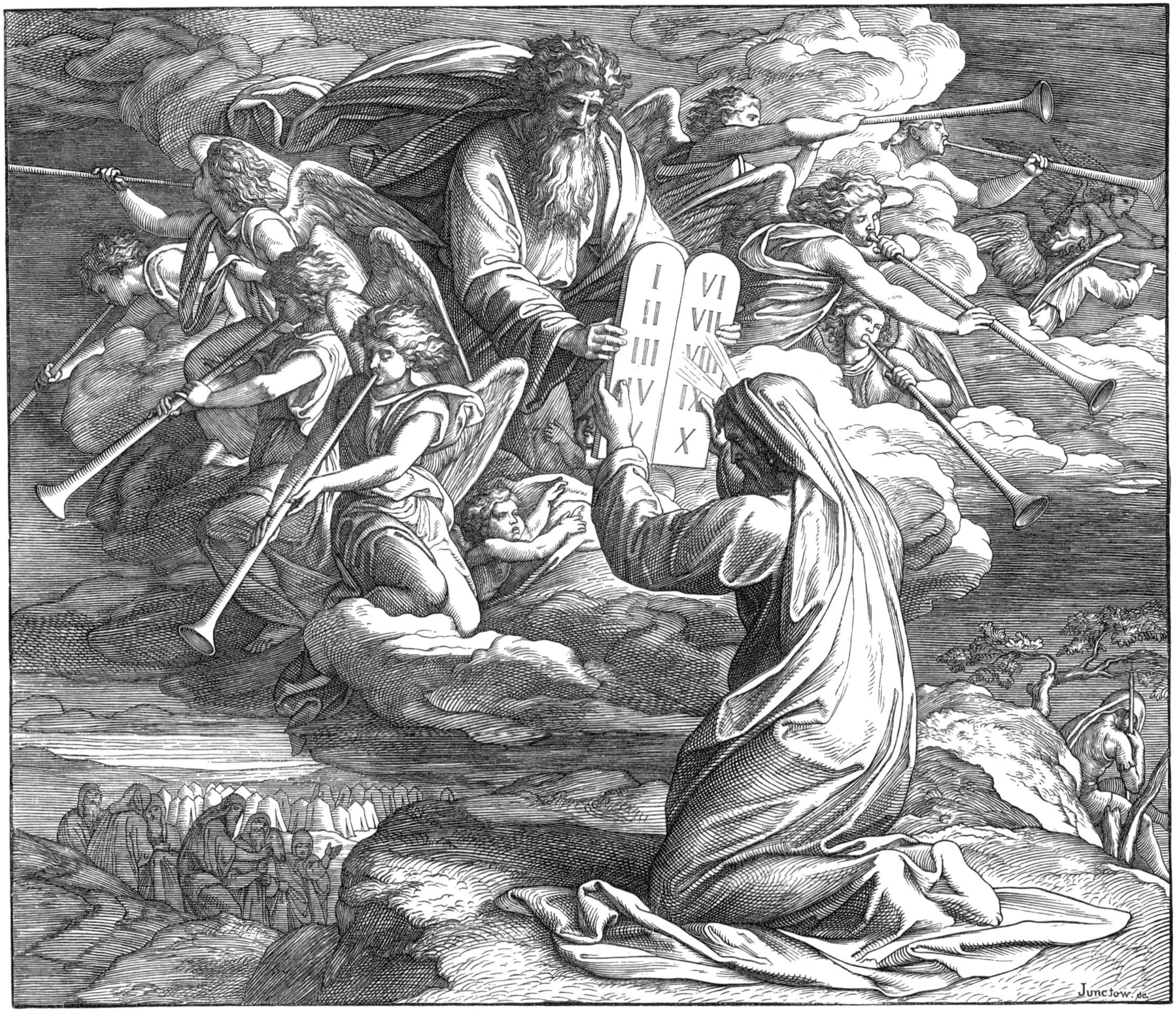

Moses Receives God's Holy Commandments

Exodus. Chapter 31.

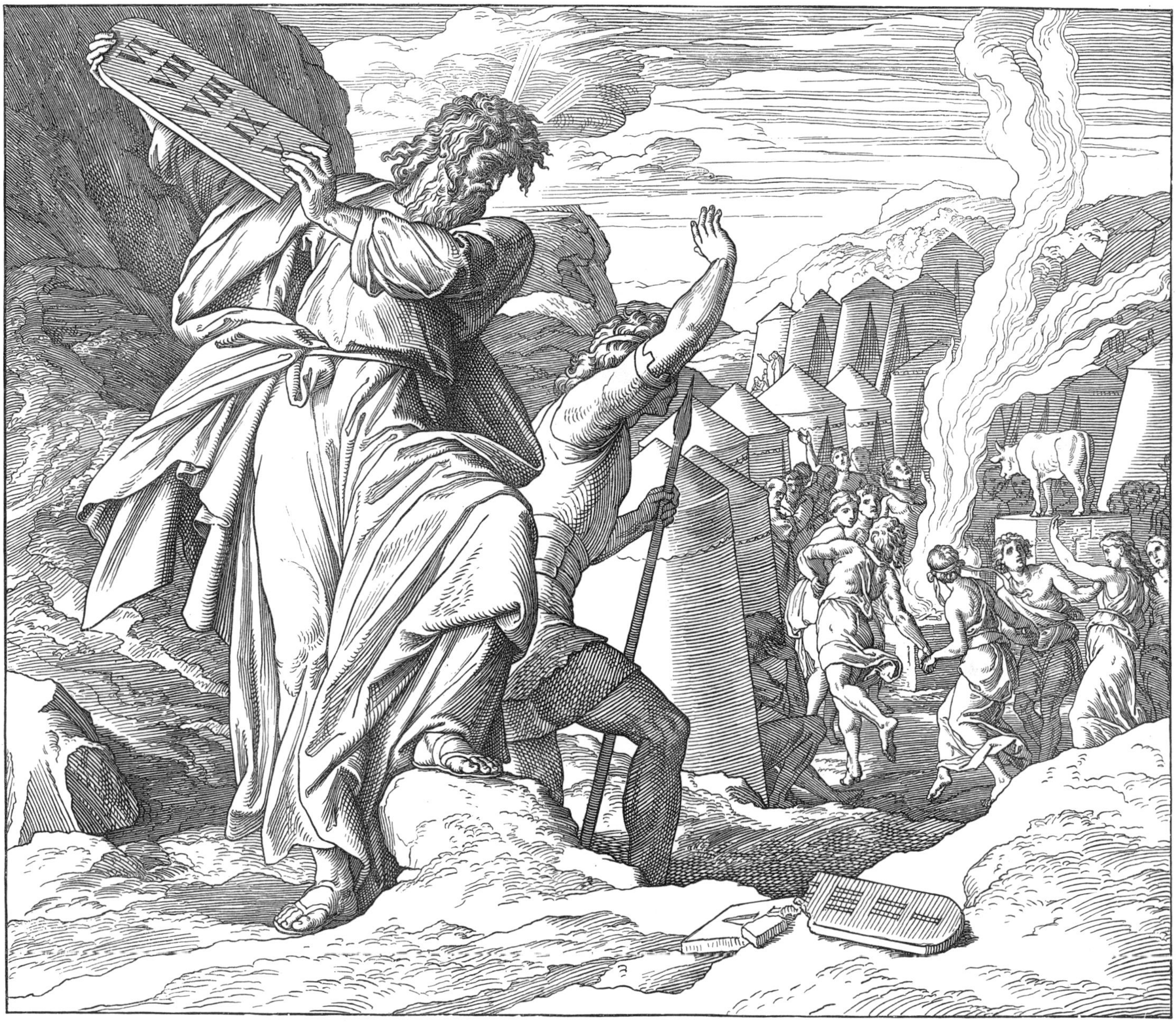

THE IDOLATRY OF THE GOLDEN CALF
Exodus. Chapter 32.

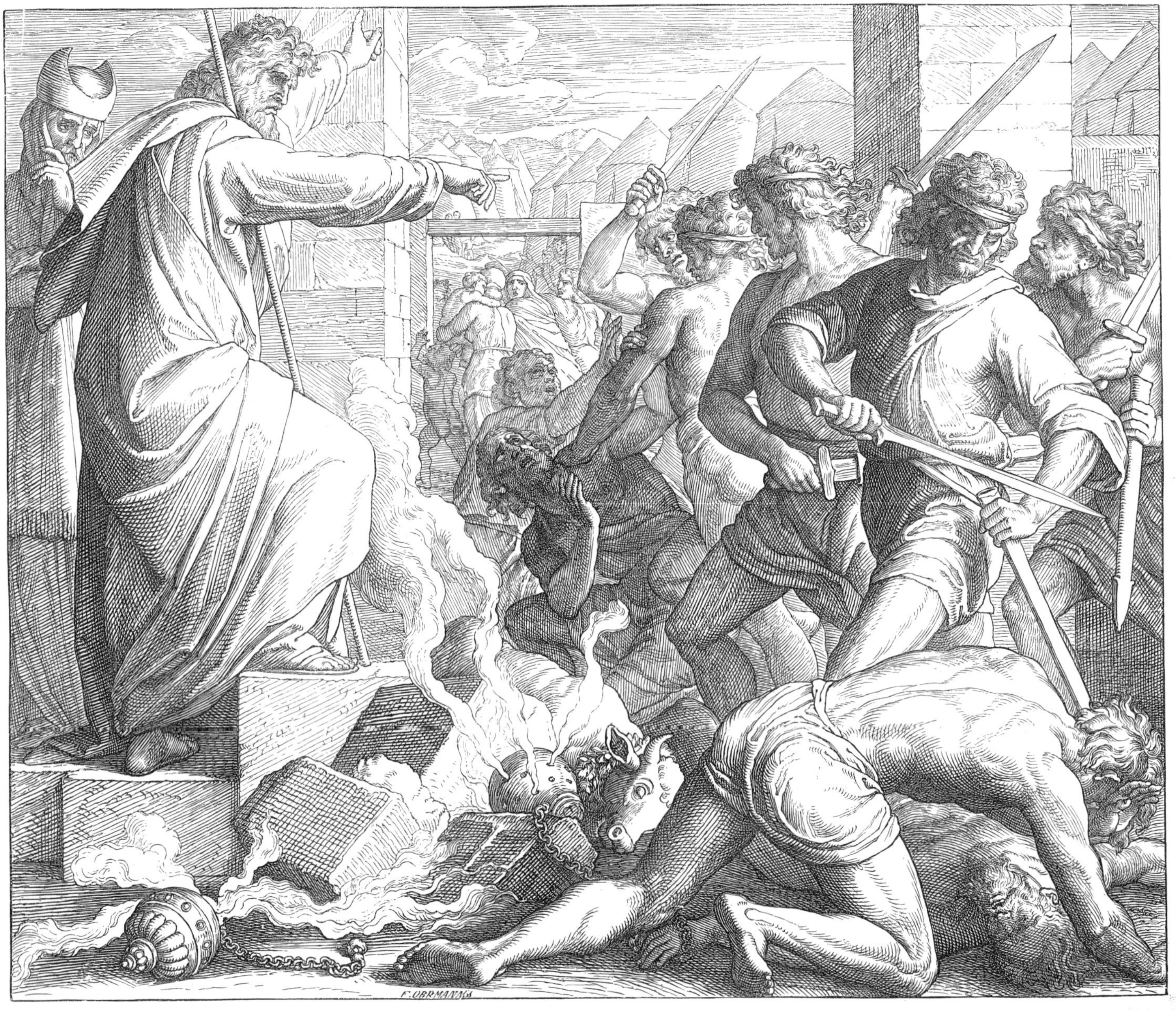

The Lord Orders Moses to Punish Idolatry of the People

Exodus. Chapter 32.

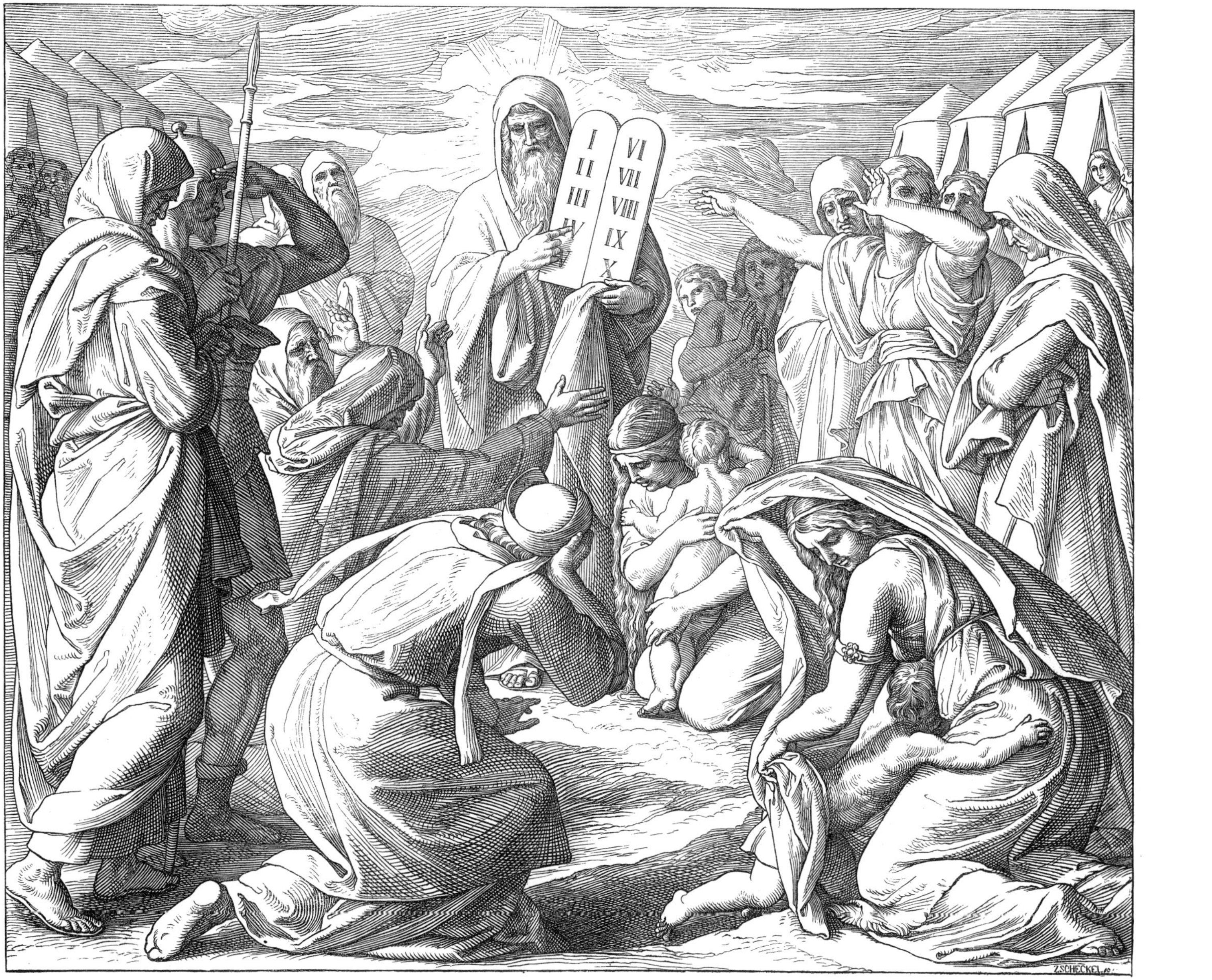

The Renewal of God's Covenant

Exodus. Chapter 34.

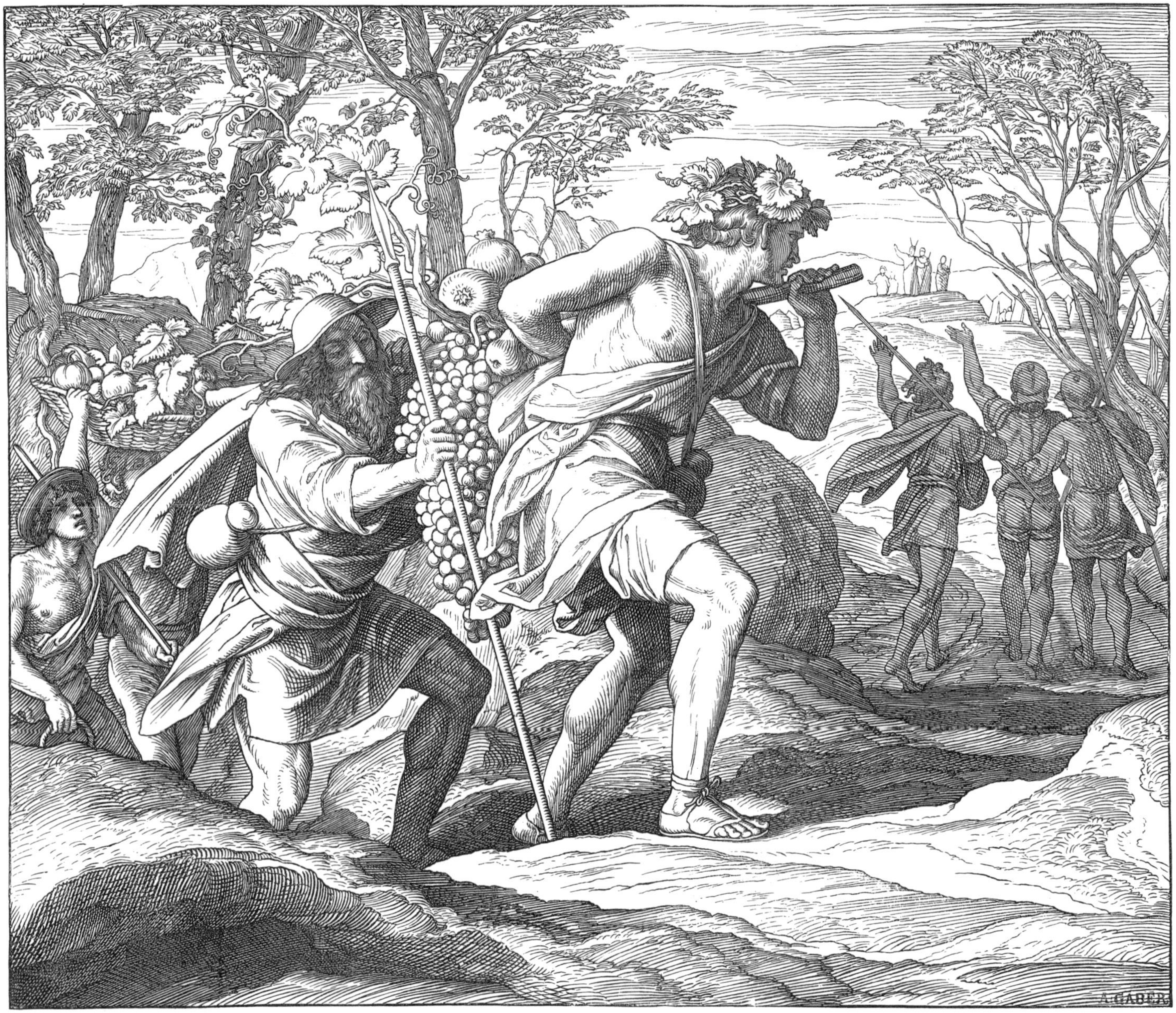

Spies Are Sent Into Canaan

Numbers. Chapter 13.

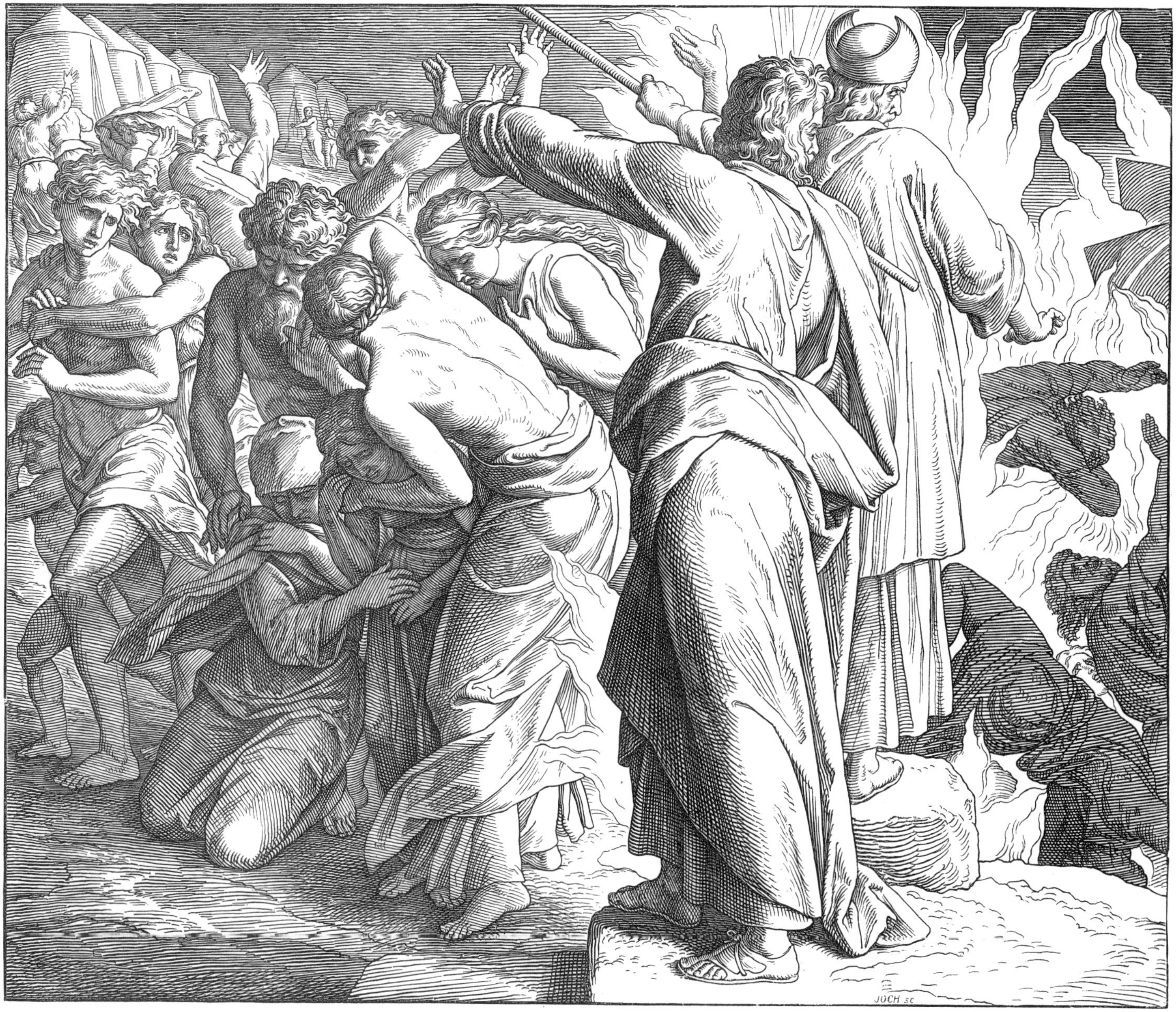

Korah and His Followers Are Punished

Numbers. Chapter 16.

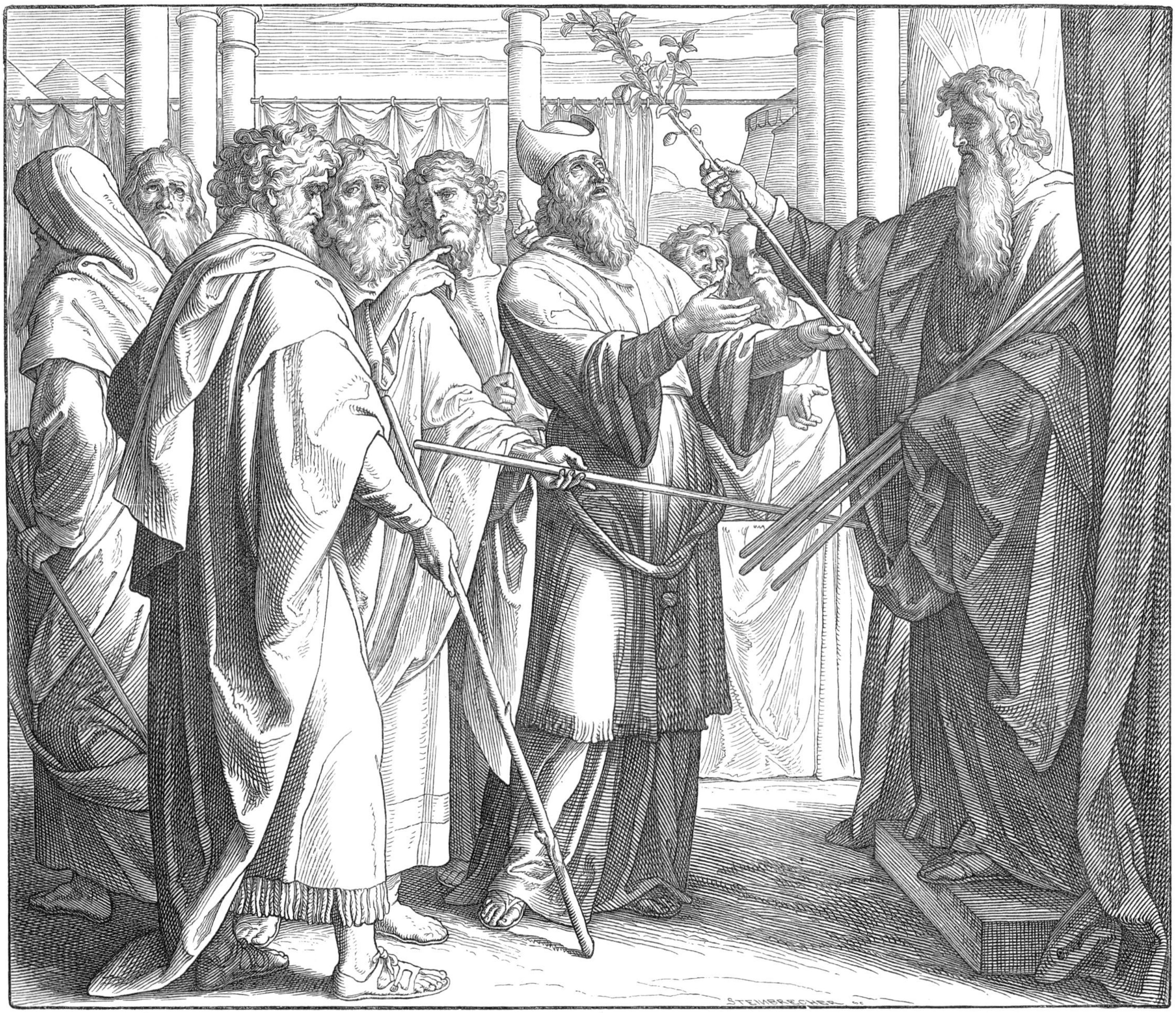

Aaron's Priesthood Is Confirmed by the Budding Rod

Numbers. Chapter 17.

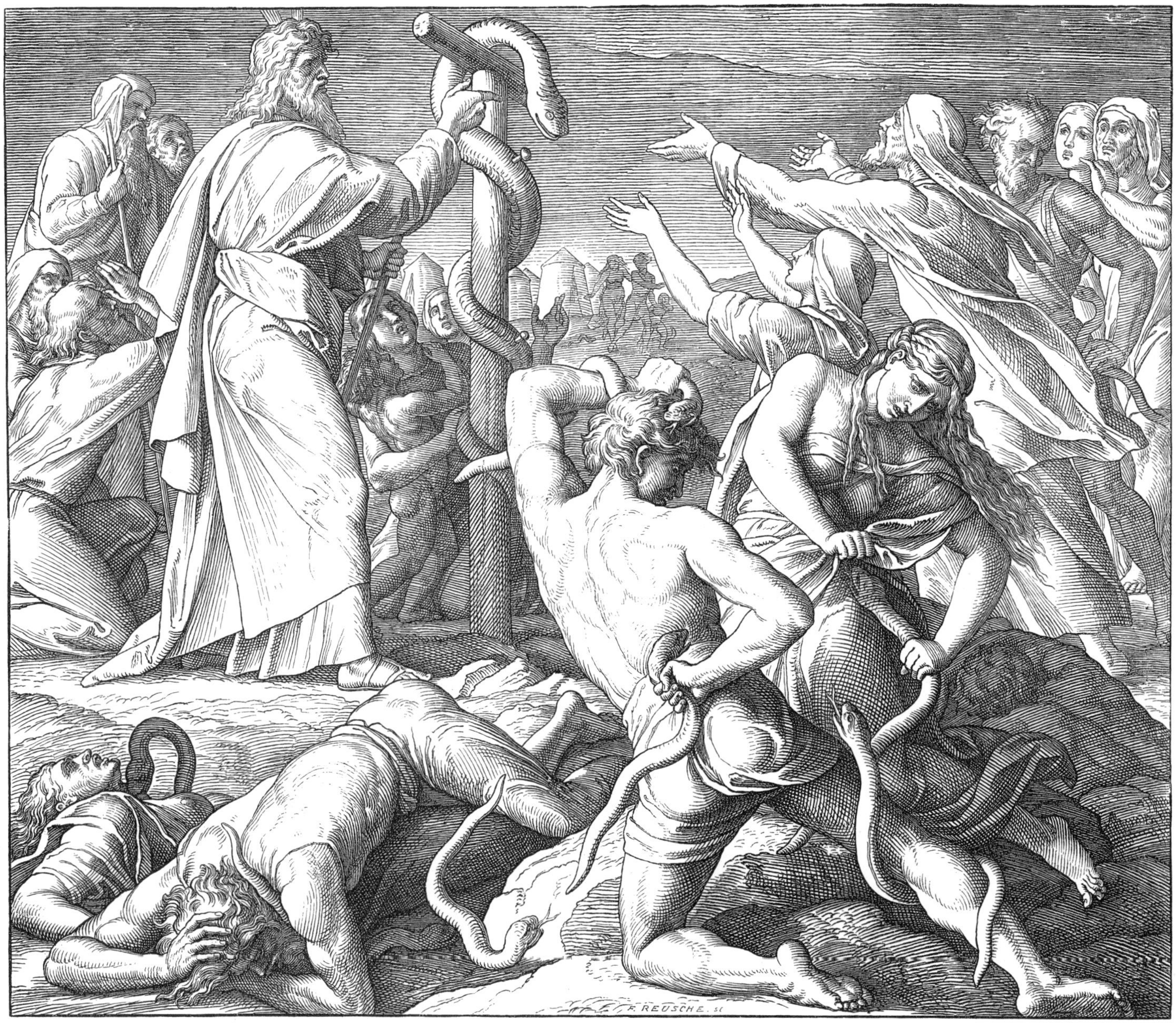

GOD SENDS FIERY SERPENTS AMONG THE PEOPLE

Numbers. Chapter 21.

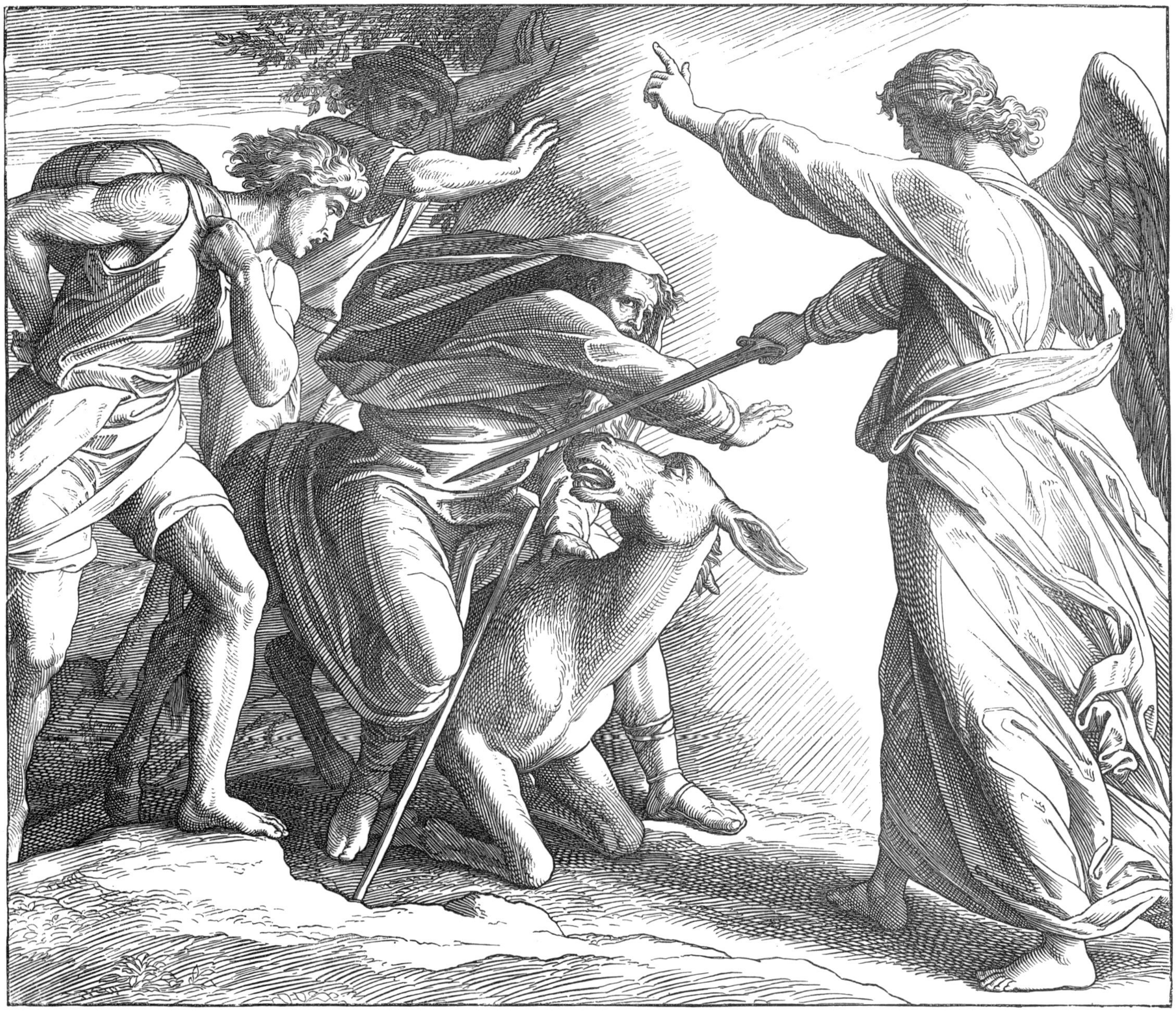

The Angel of the Lord Stands in the Way of Balaam
Numbers. Chapter 22.

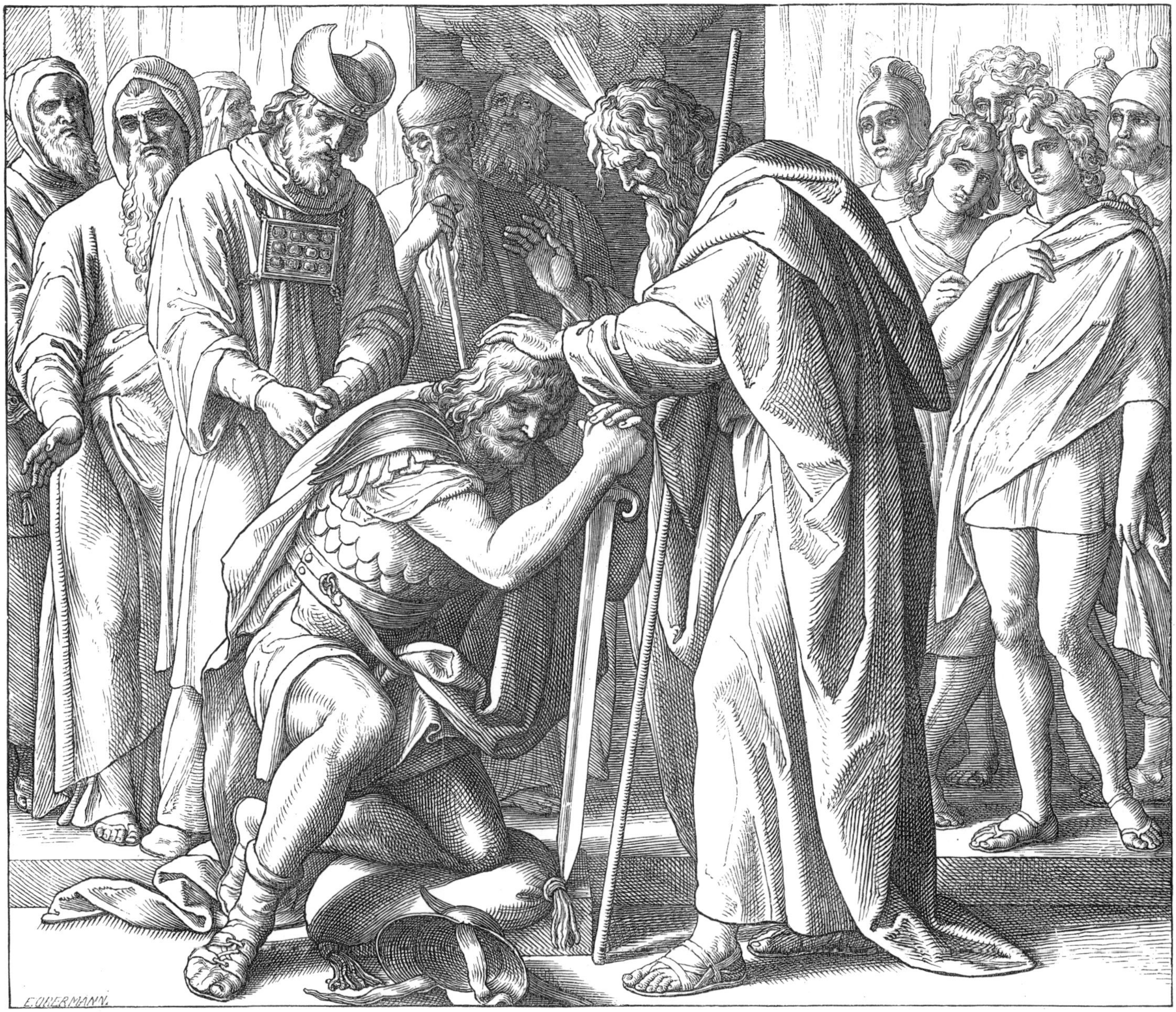

THE APPOINTMENT OF JOSHUA

Numbers. Chapter 27.

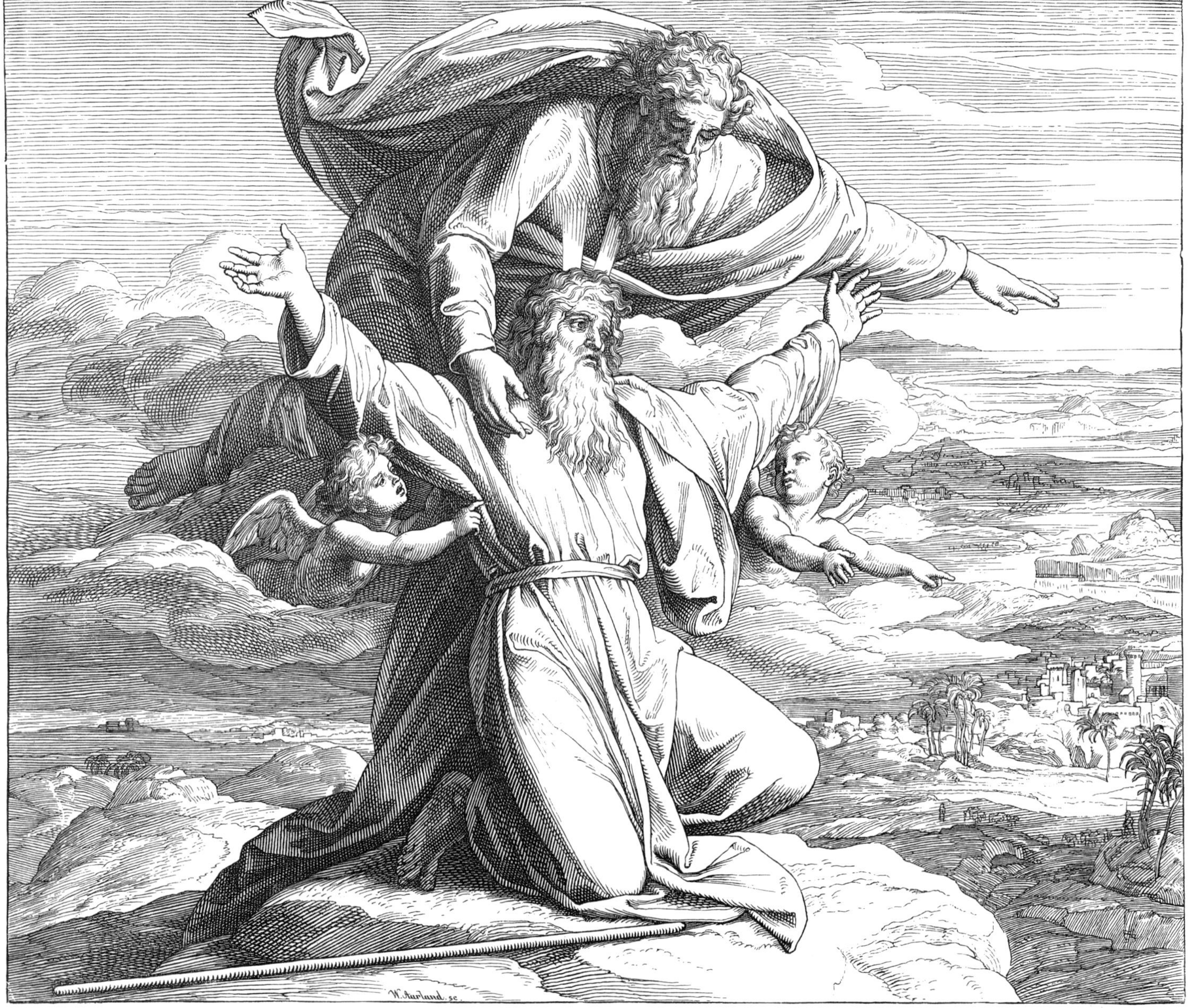

God Shows Moses the Promised Land

Deuteronomy. Chapter 34.

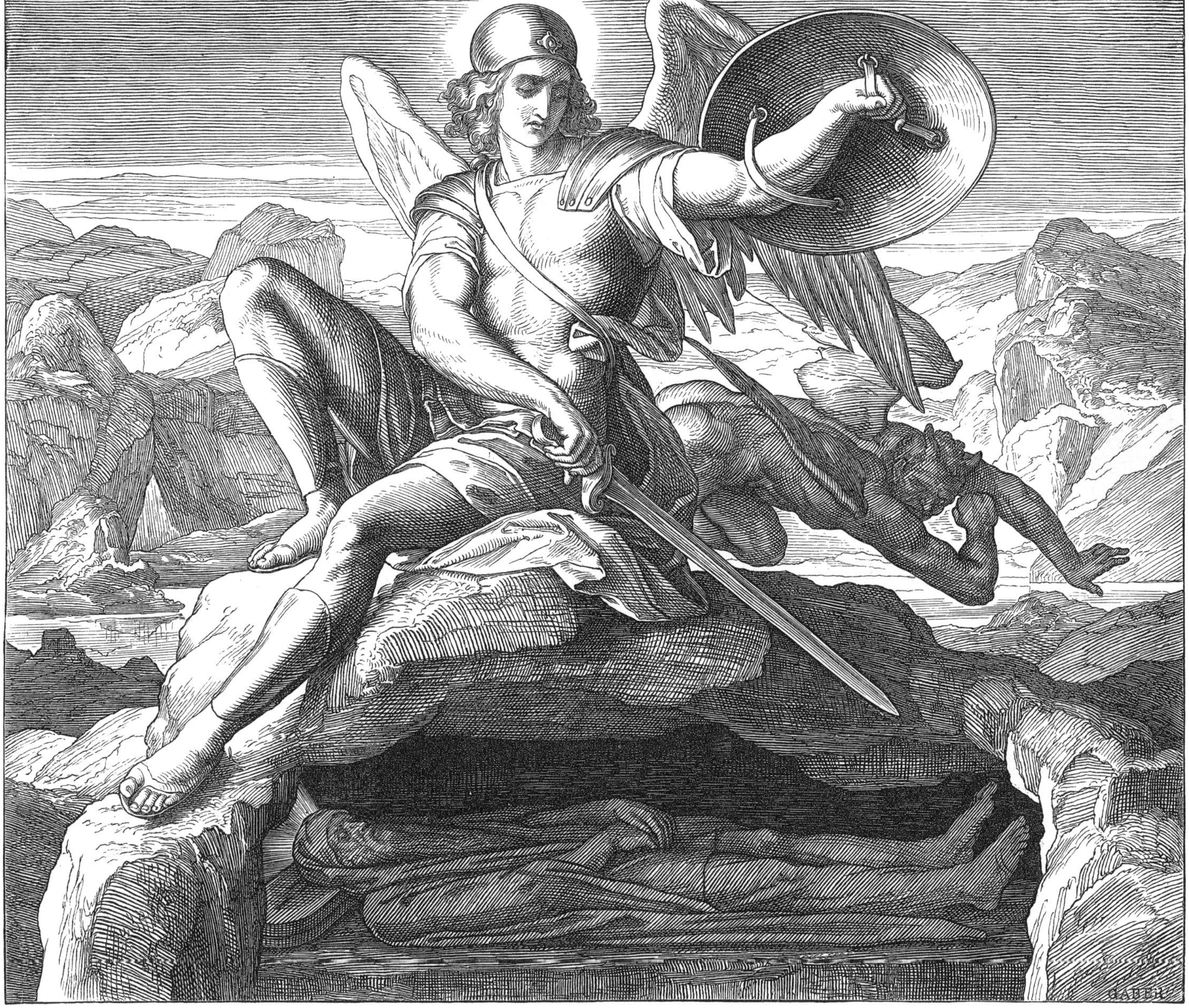

THE DEATH OF MOSES
Deuteronomy. Chapter 34.

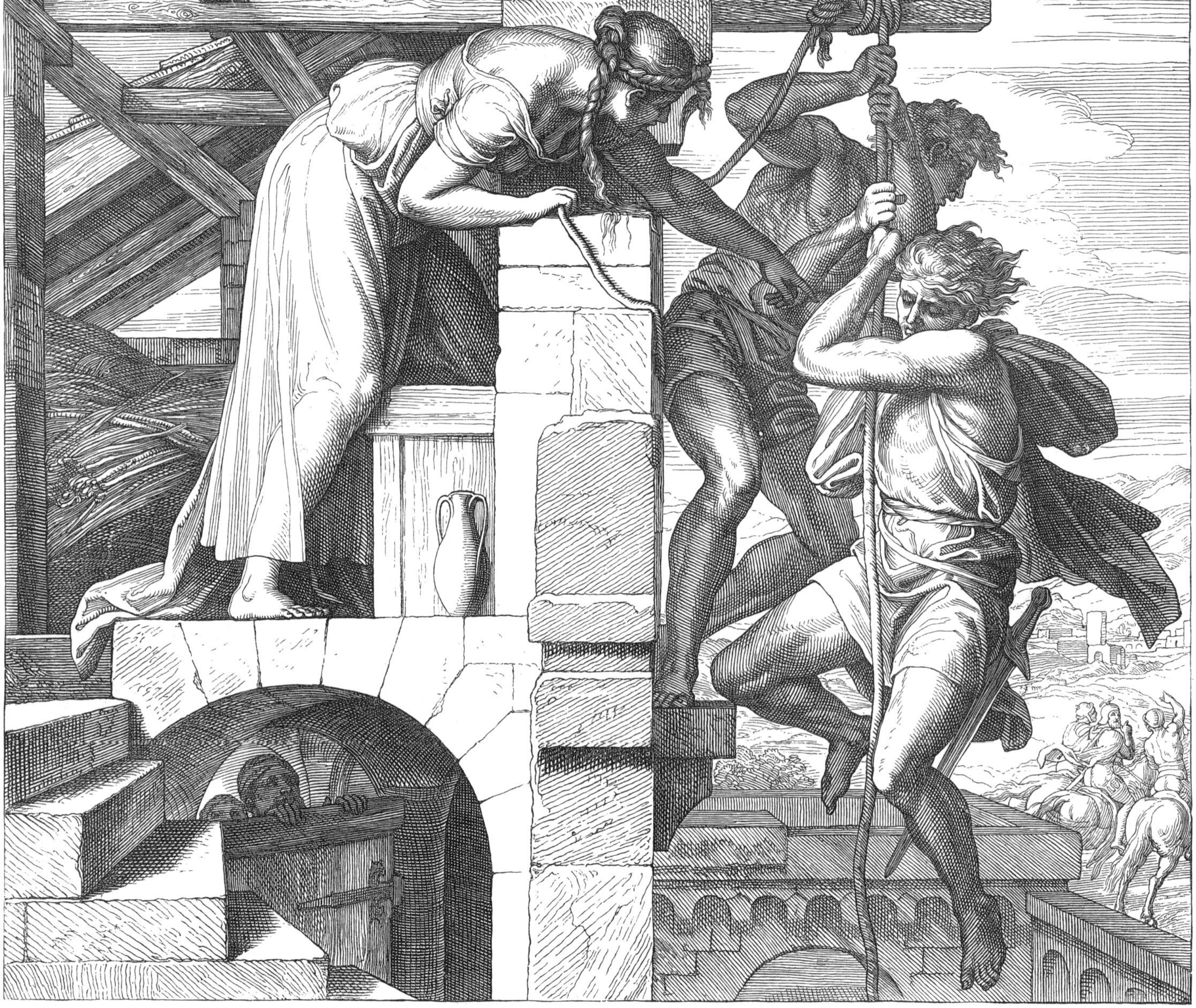

Rahab Rescues Two Israeli Spies

Joshua. Chapter 2.

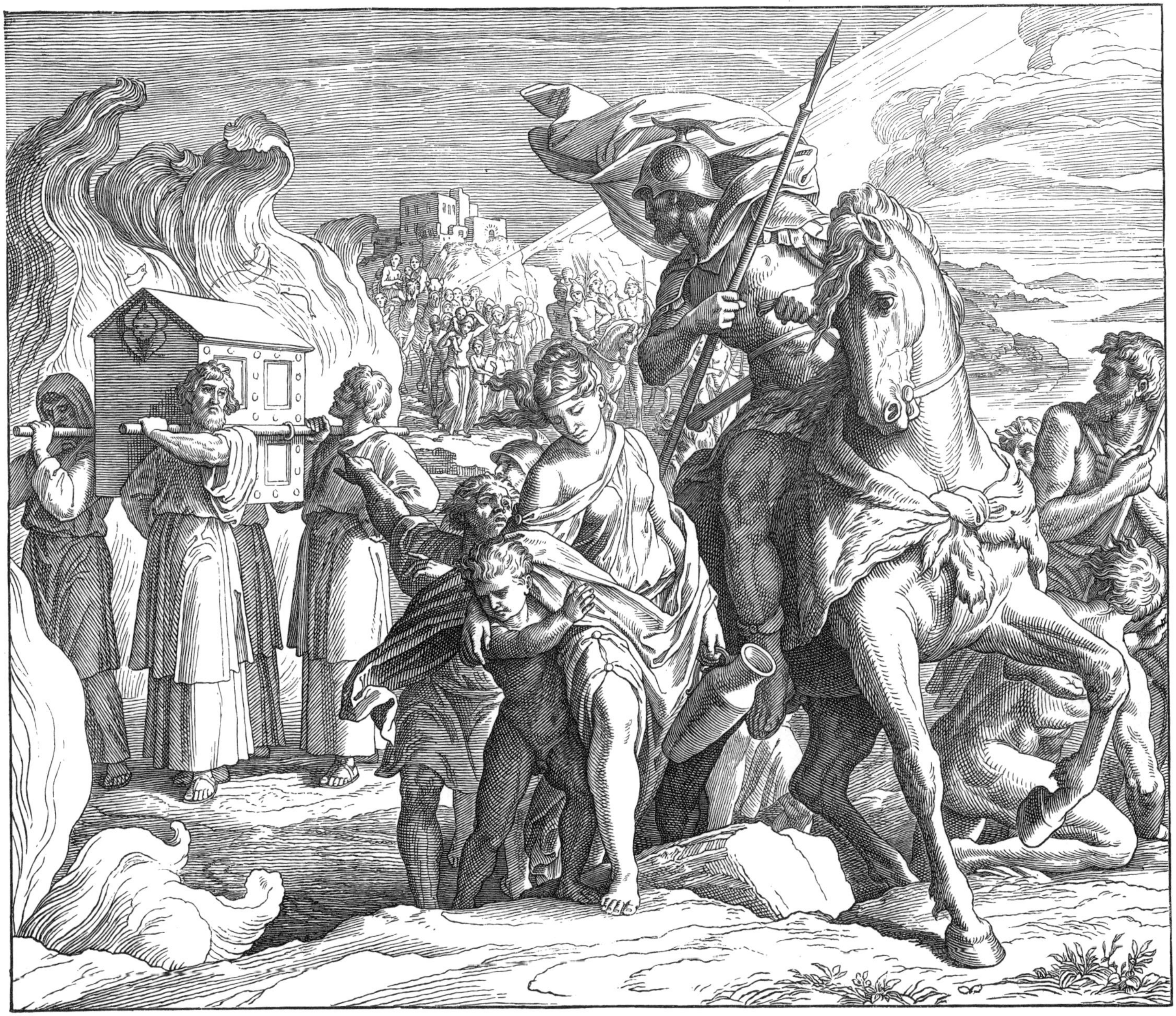

The Israelites Pass Over Jordan
Joshua. Chapter 3.

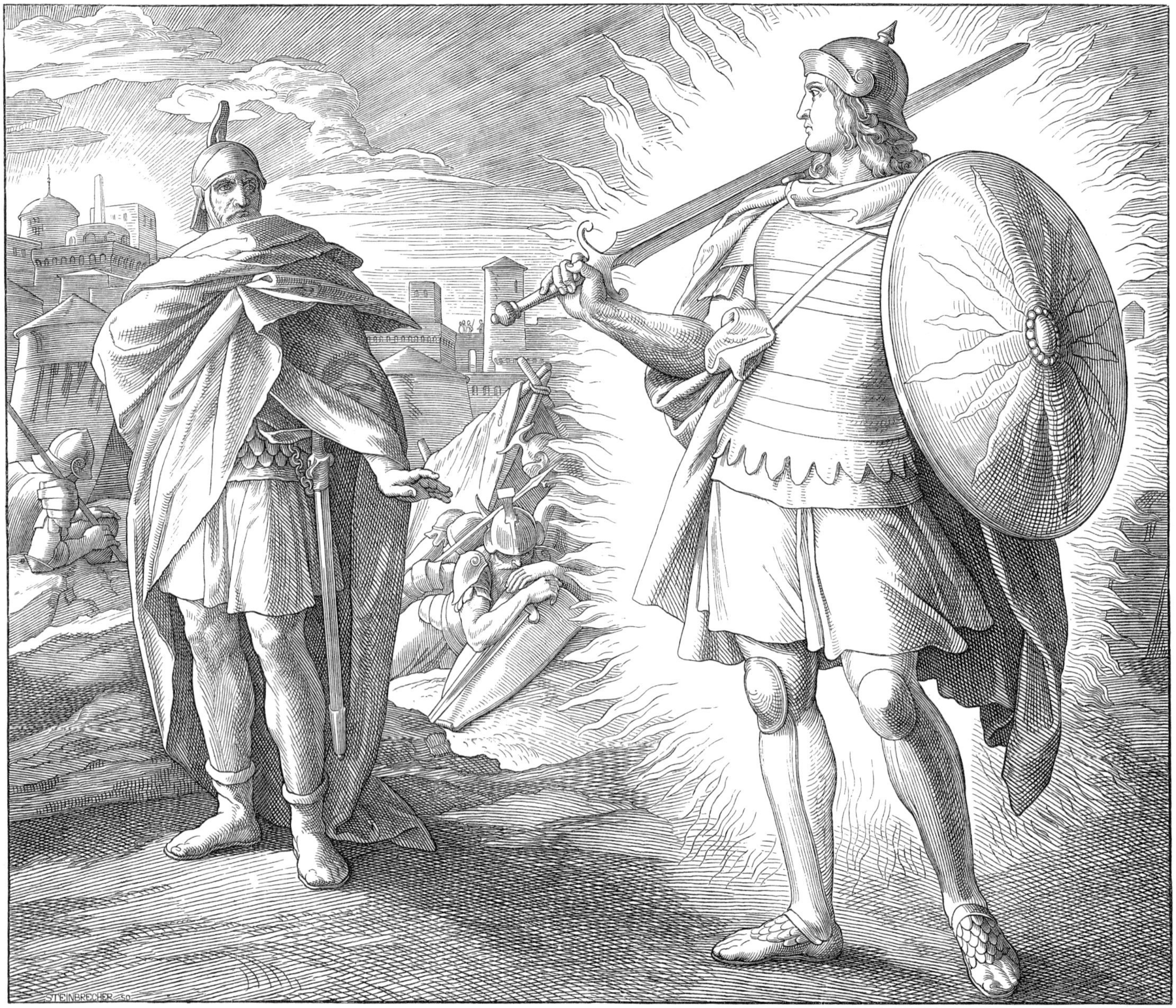

Joshua and the Captain of the Host of the Lord

Joshua. Chapter 5.

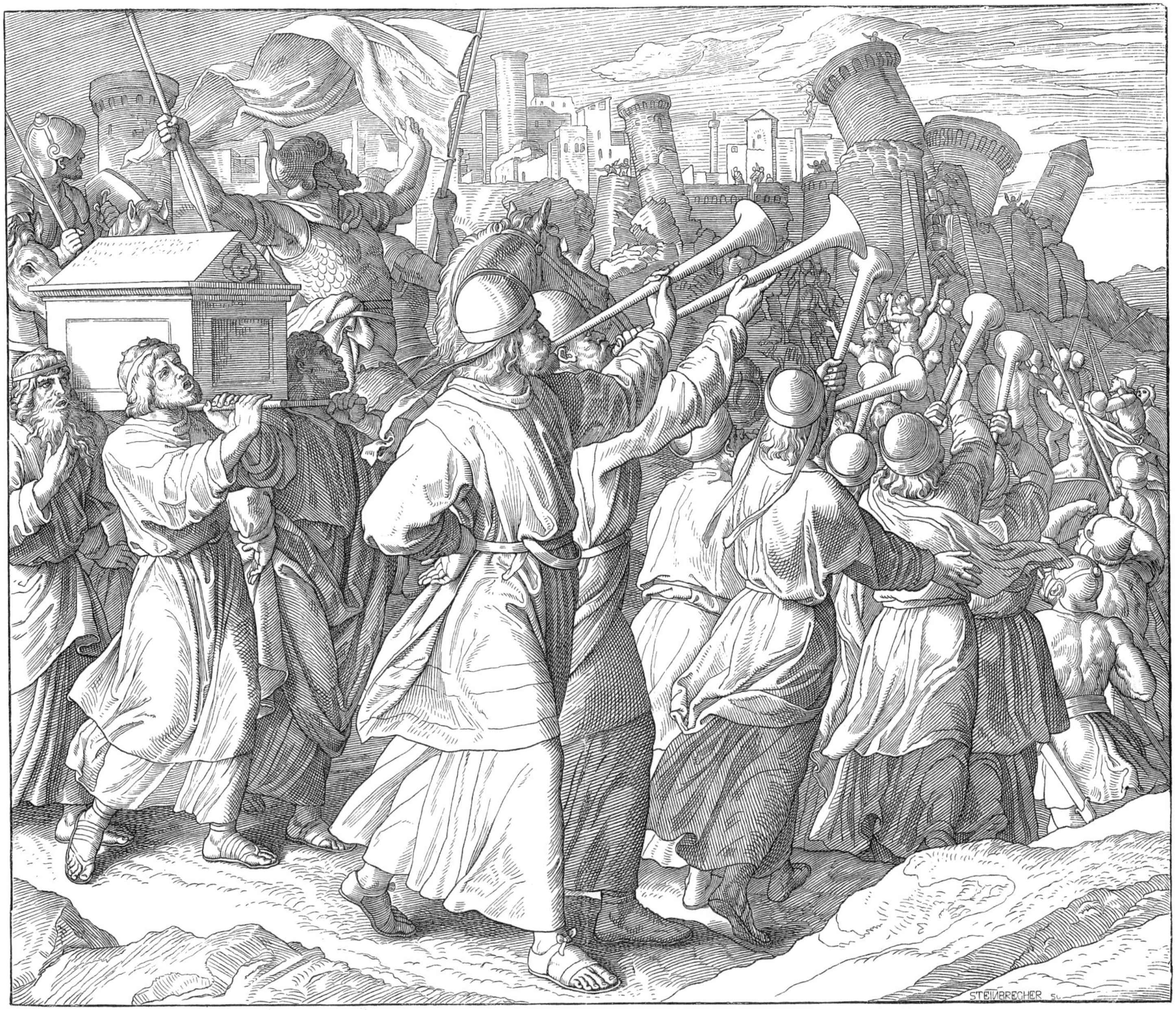

The Walls of Jericho Fall

Joshua. Chapter 6.

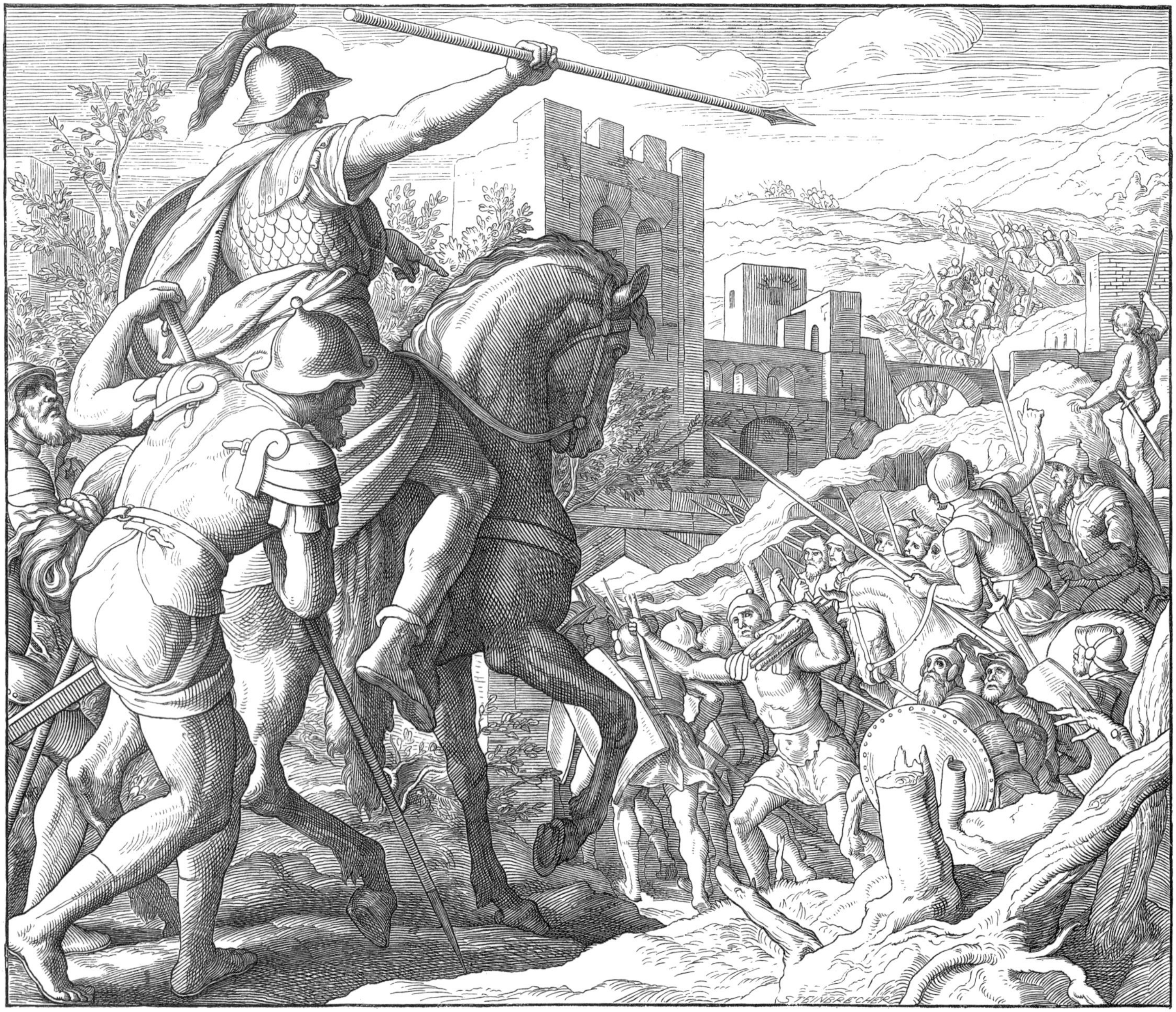

Conquering the City of Ai
Joshua. Chapter 8.

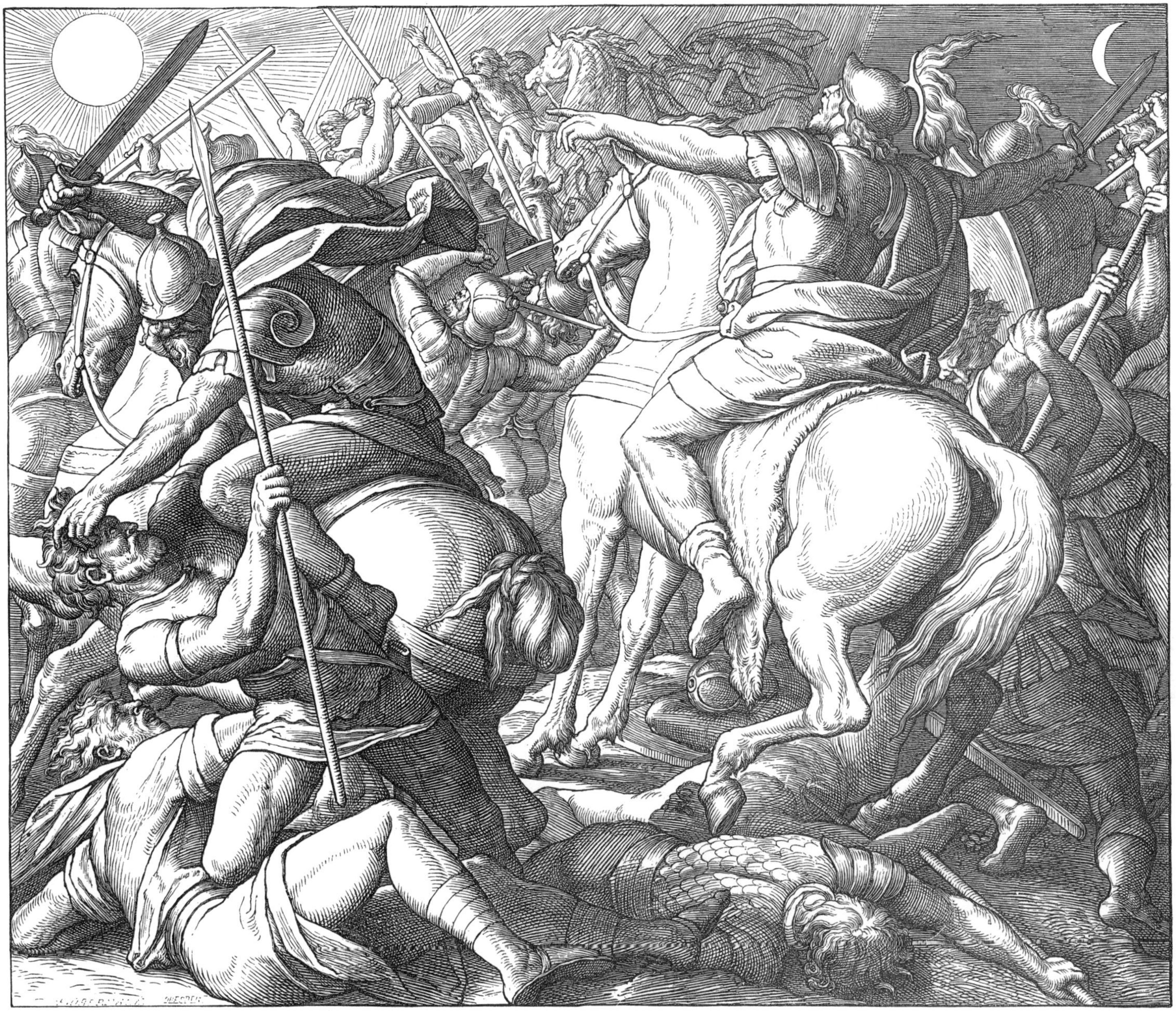

The Sun and the Moon Stand Still
Joshua. Chapter 10.

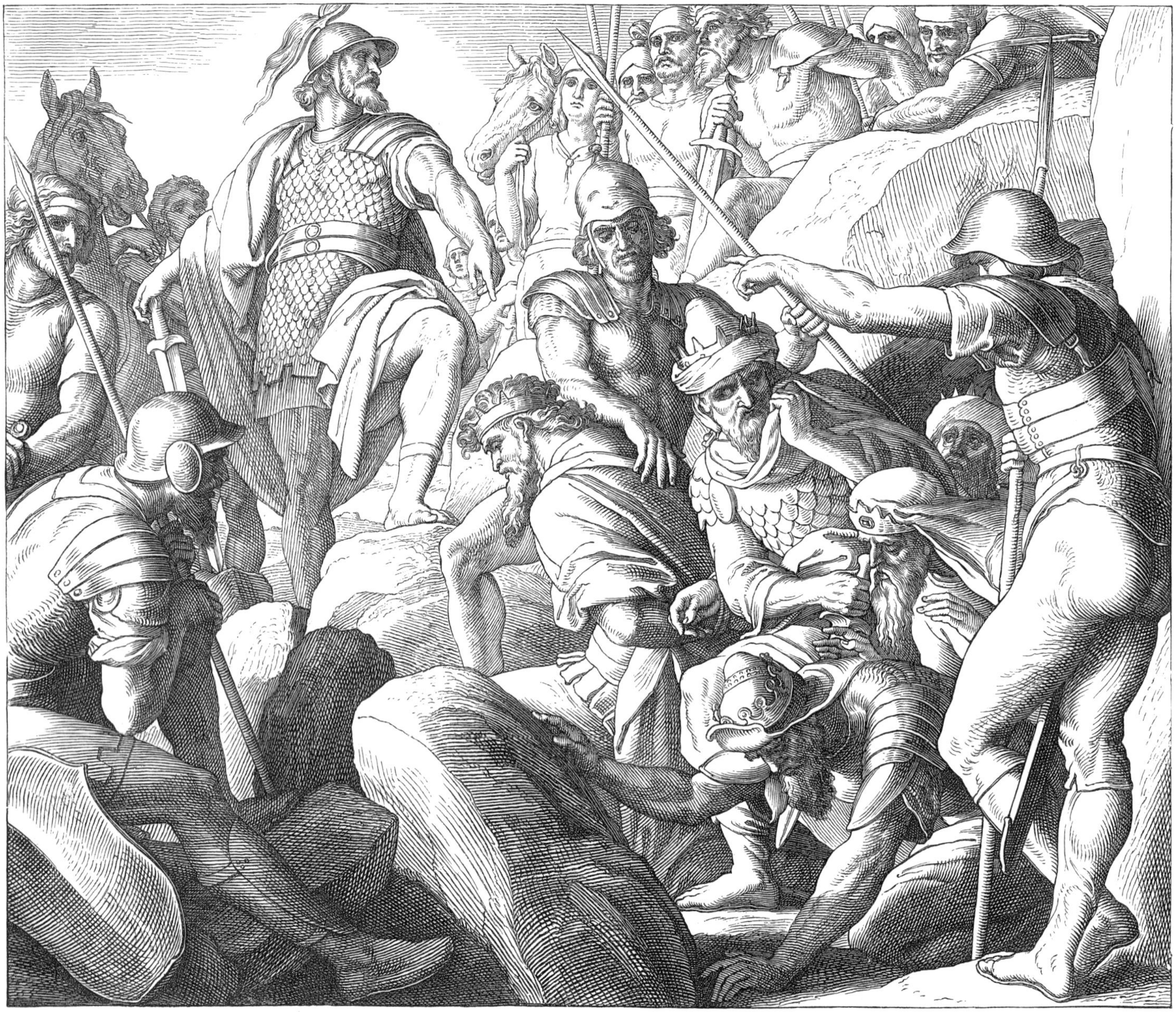

Joshua Holds Five Kings in the Cave at Makkedah
Joshua. Chapter 10.

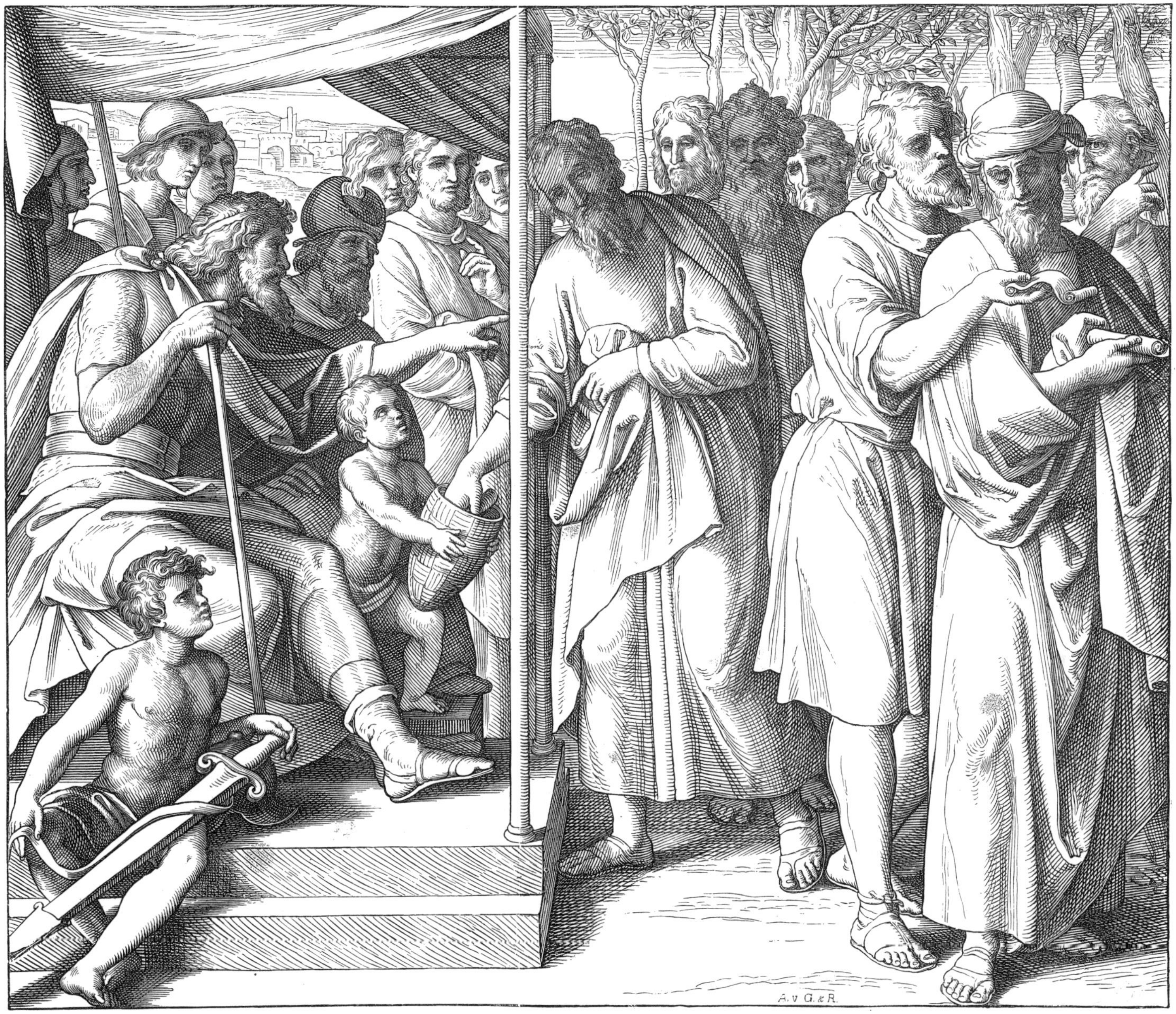

The Division of the Land

Joshua. Chapter 13.

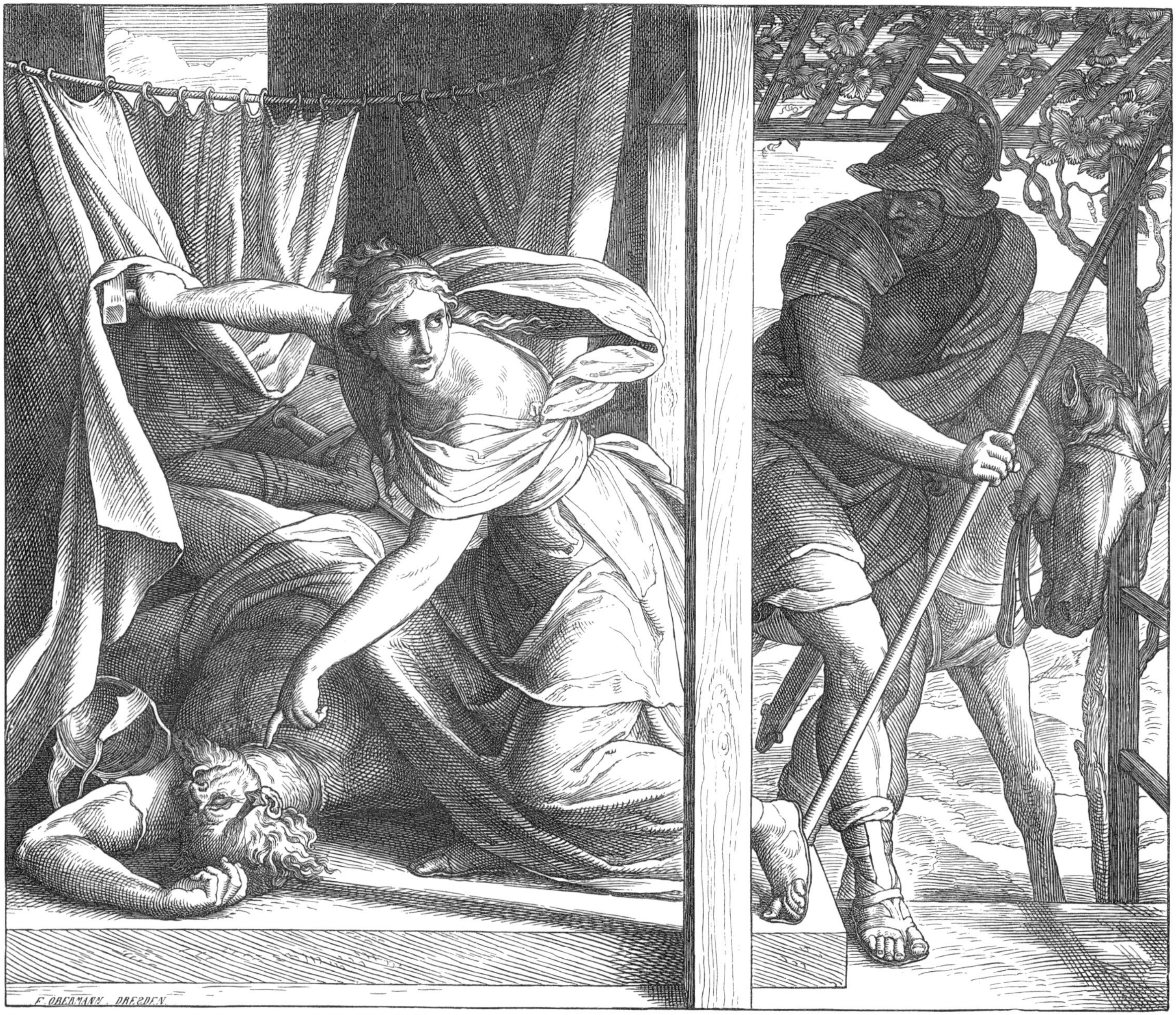

SISERA, CAPTAIN OF JABIN'S ARMY, DIES AT THE HAND OF JAEL

Judges. Chapter 4.

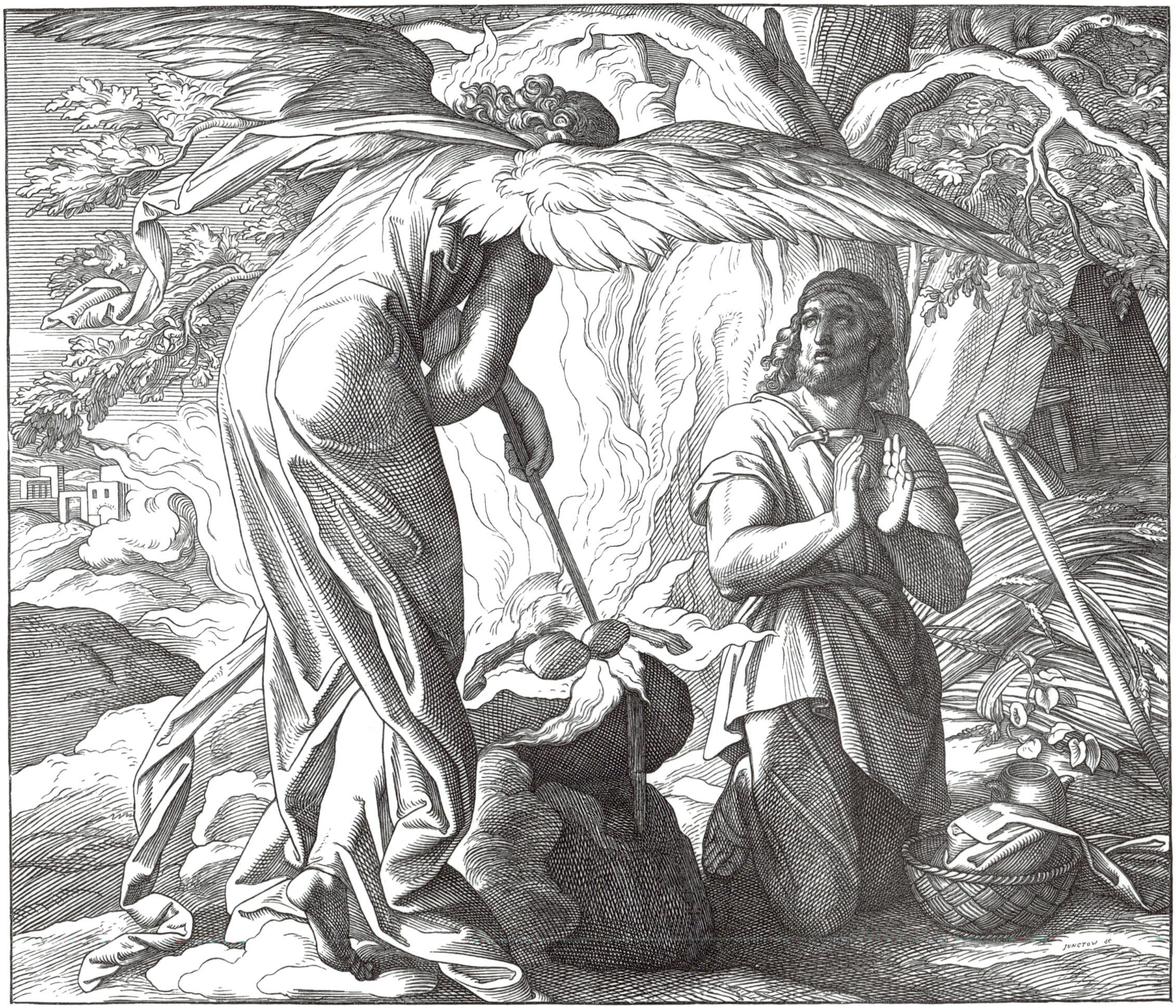

THE CALL OF GIDEON
Judges. Chapter 6.

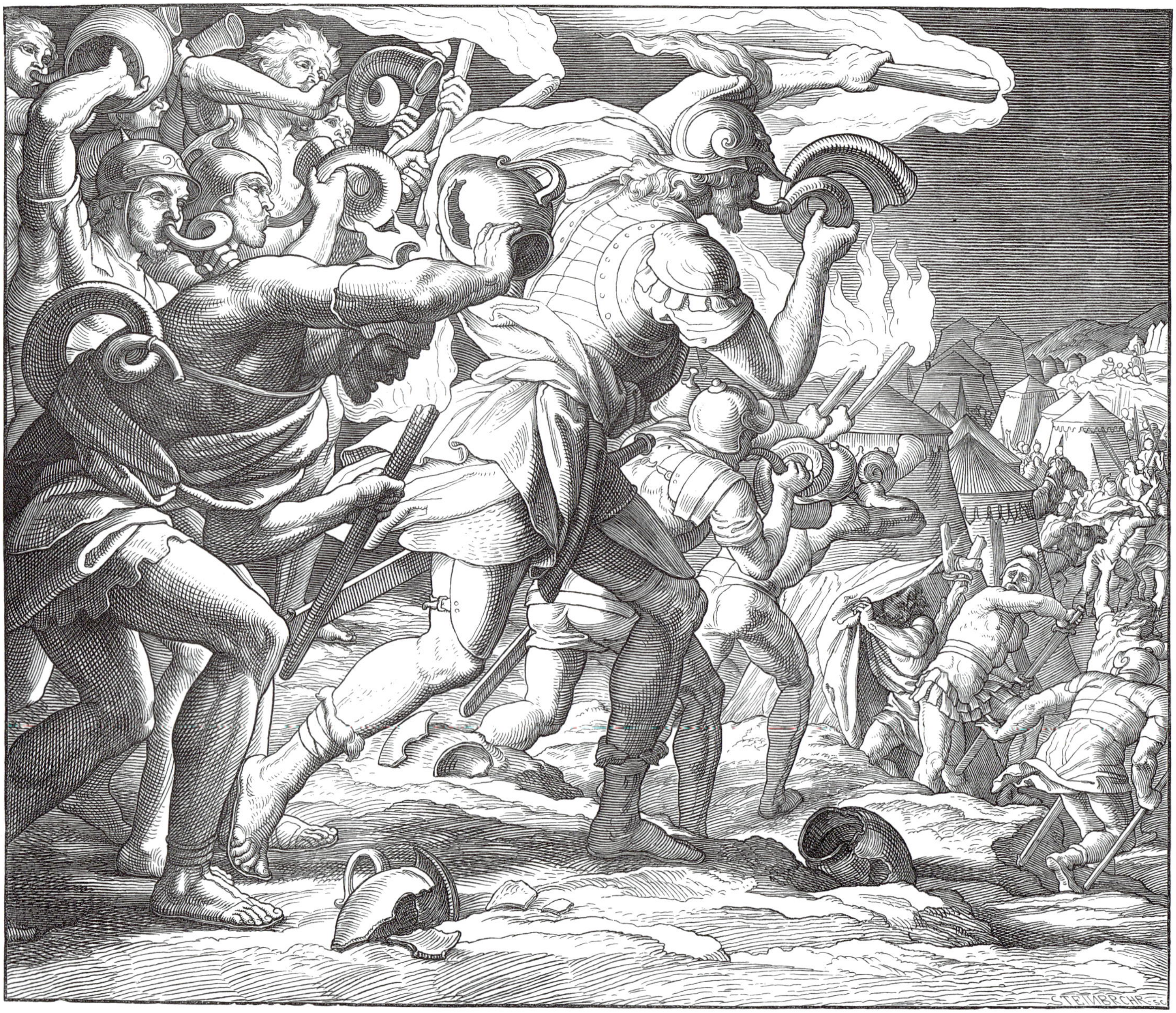

GIDEON'S ARMY DEFEATS MIDIAN

Judges. Chapter 7.

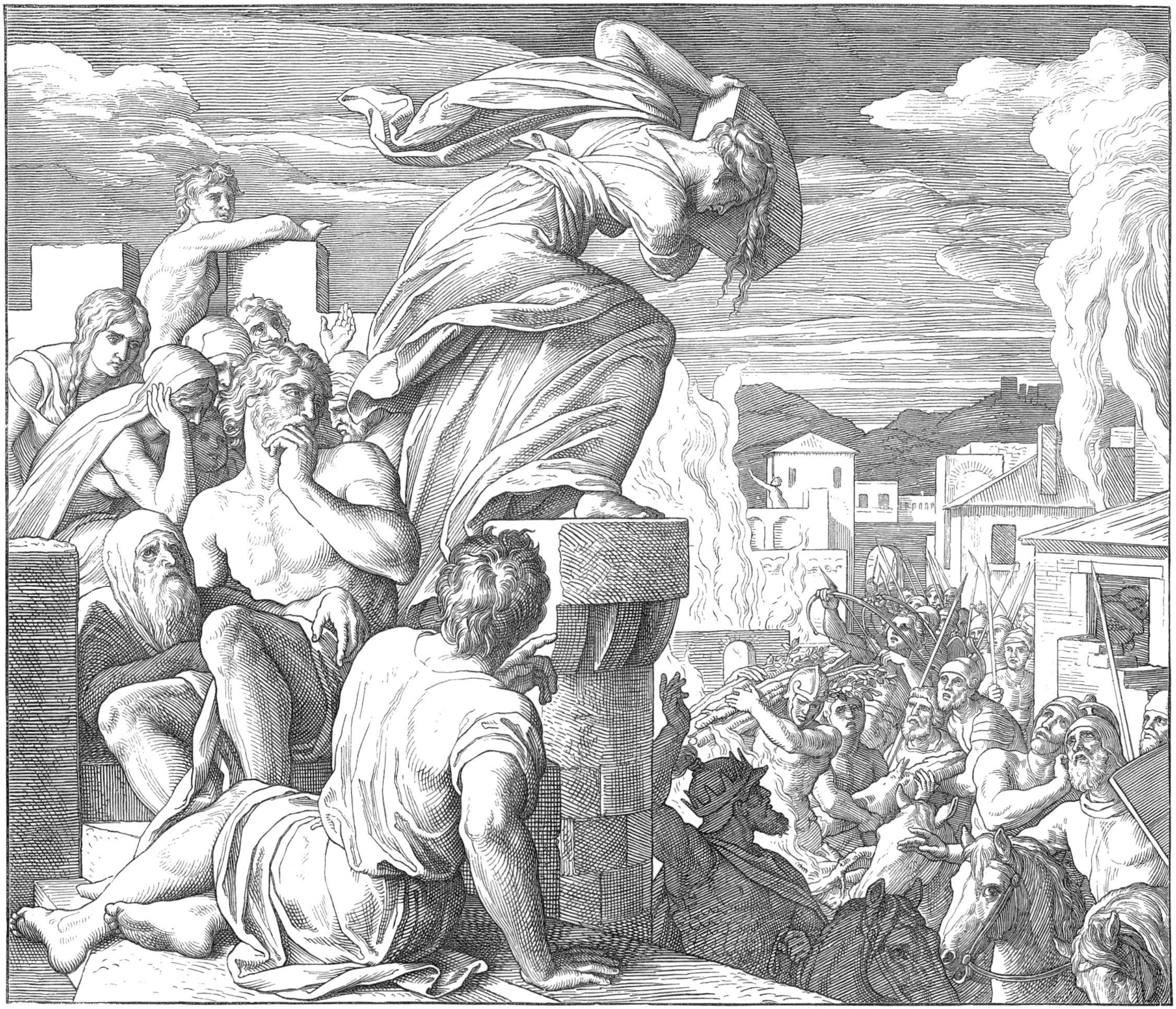

The Death of Abimelech
Judges. Chapter 9.

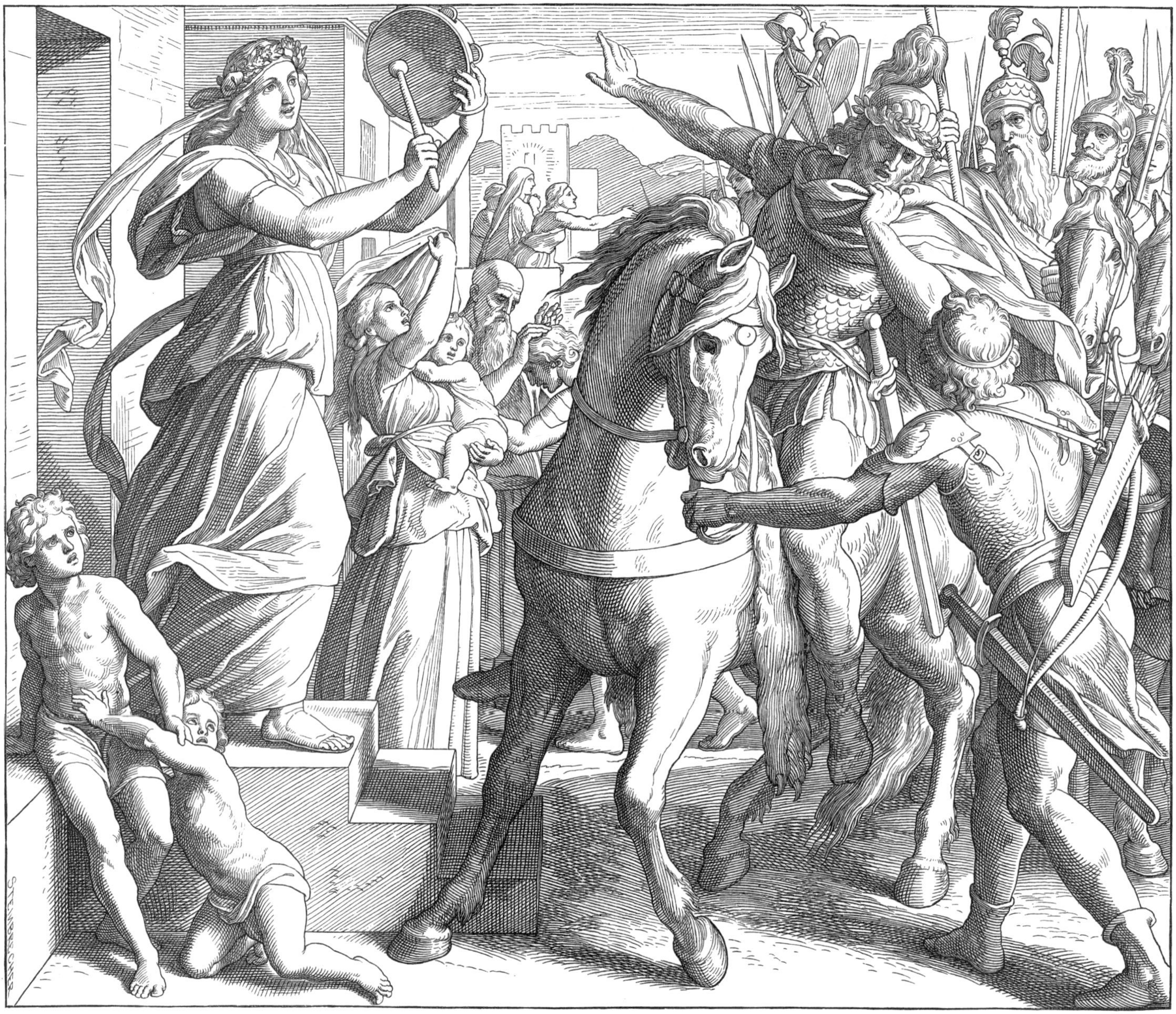

Jephthah's Conquest and Vow

Judges. Chapter 11.

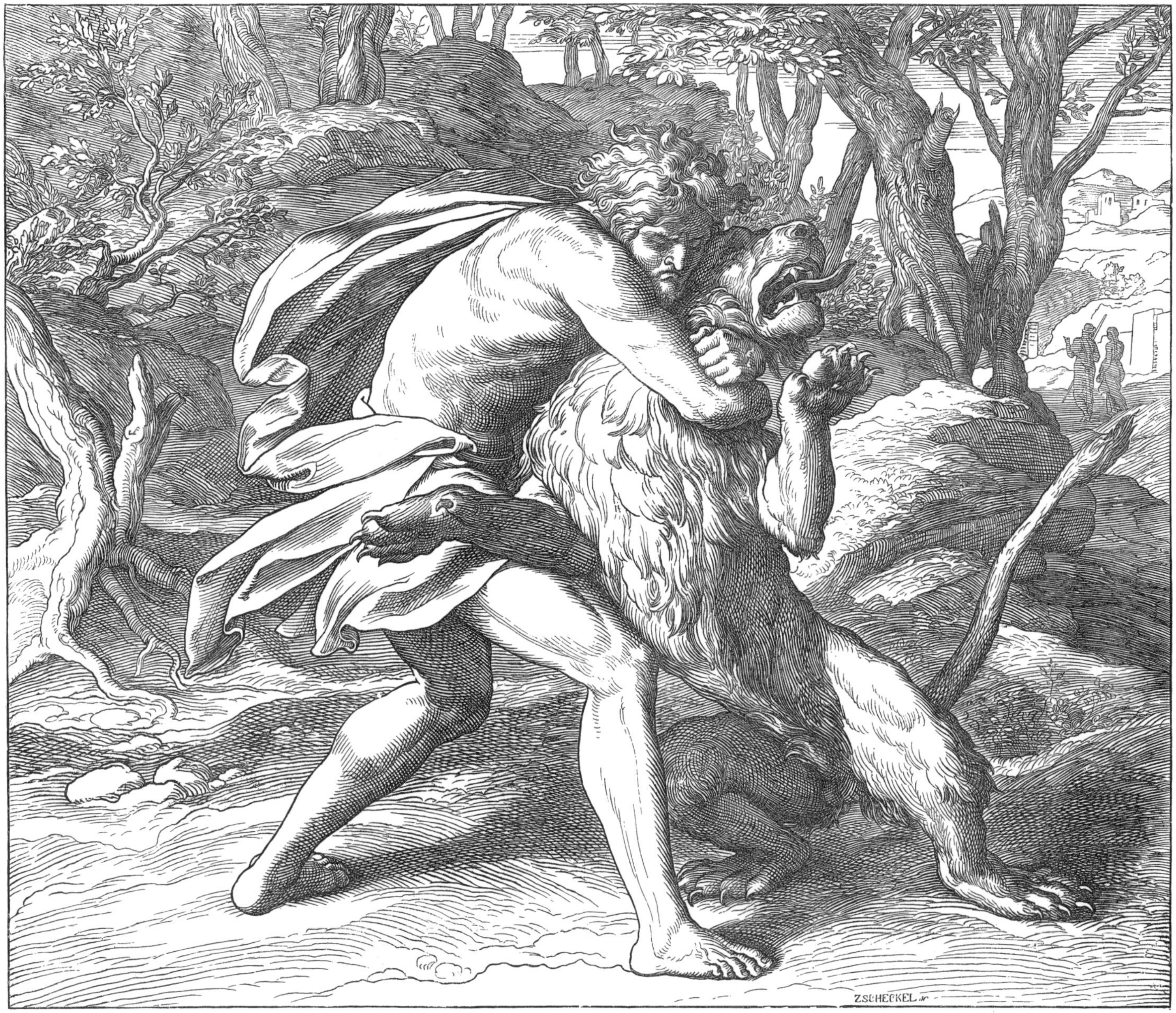

Samson's Heroic Act
Judges. Chapter 14.

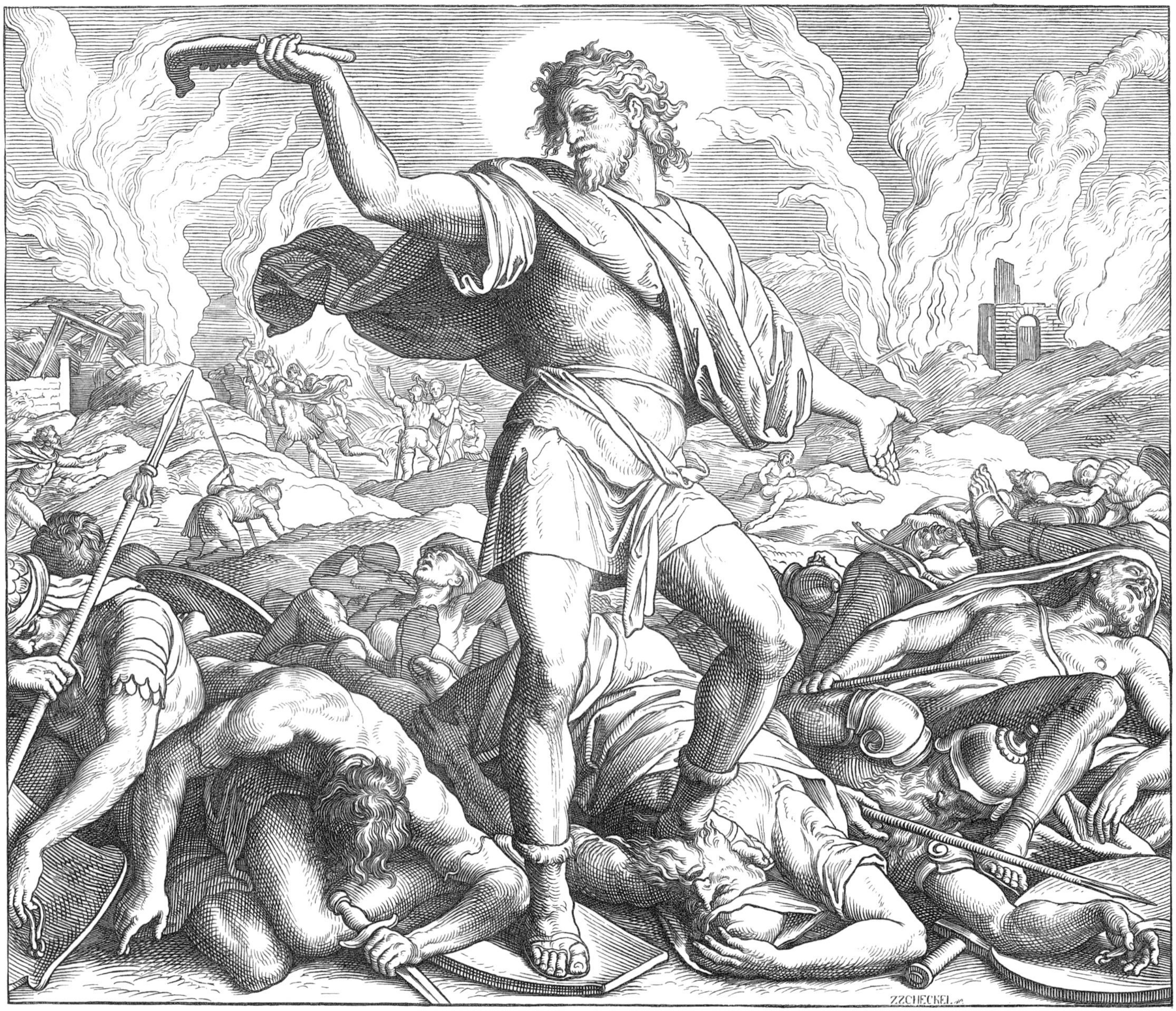

Samson Slays One Thousand Philistines with the Jawbone of an Ass
Judges. Chapter 15.

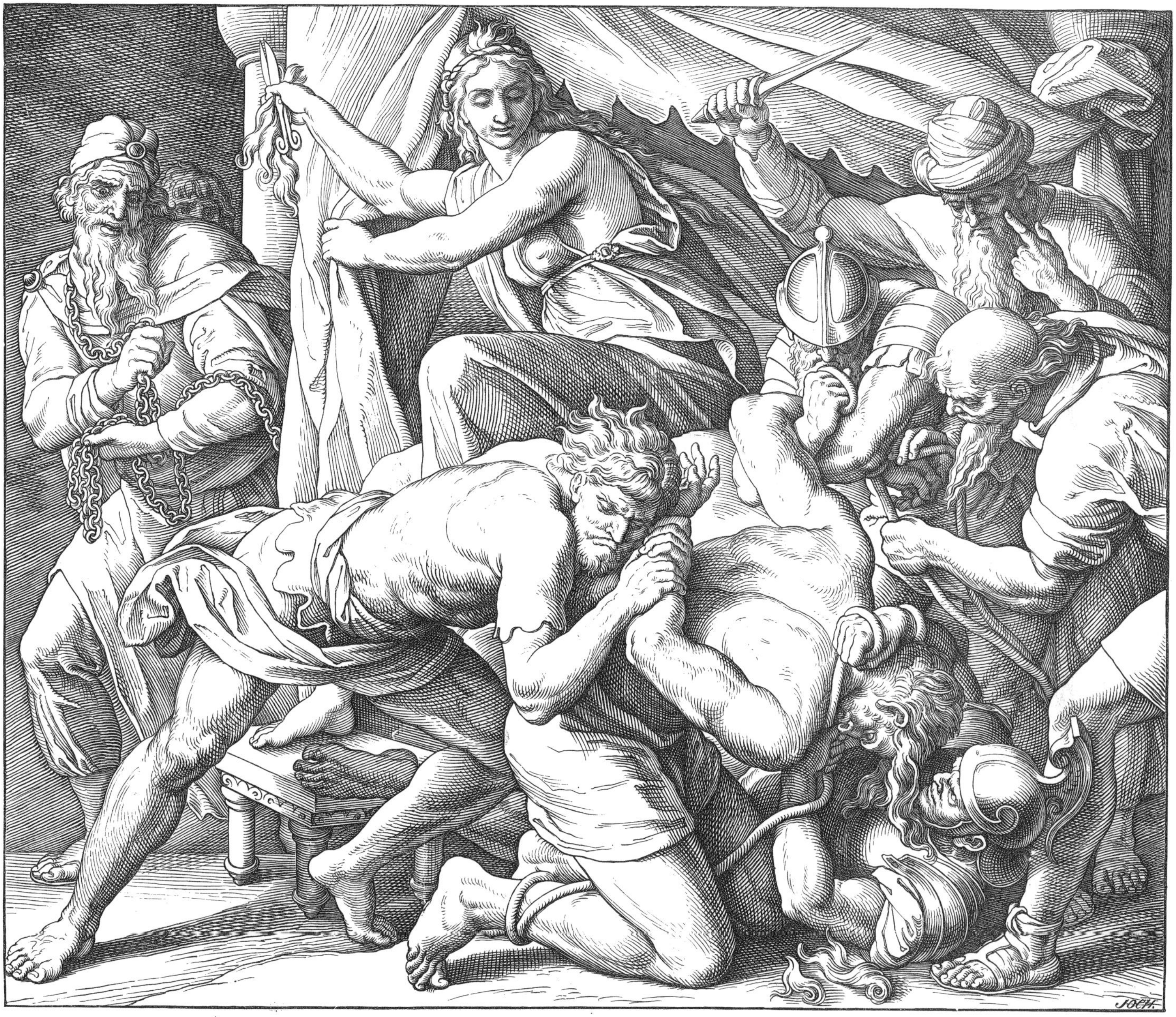

The Demise of Samson
Judges. Chapter 16.

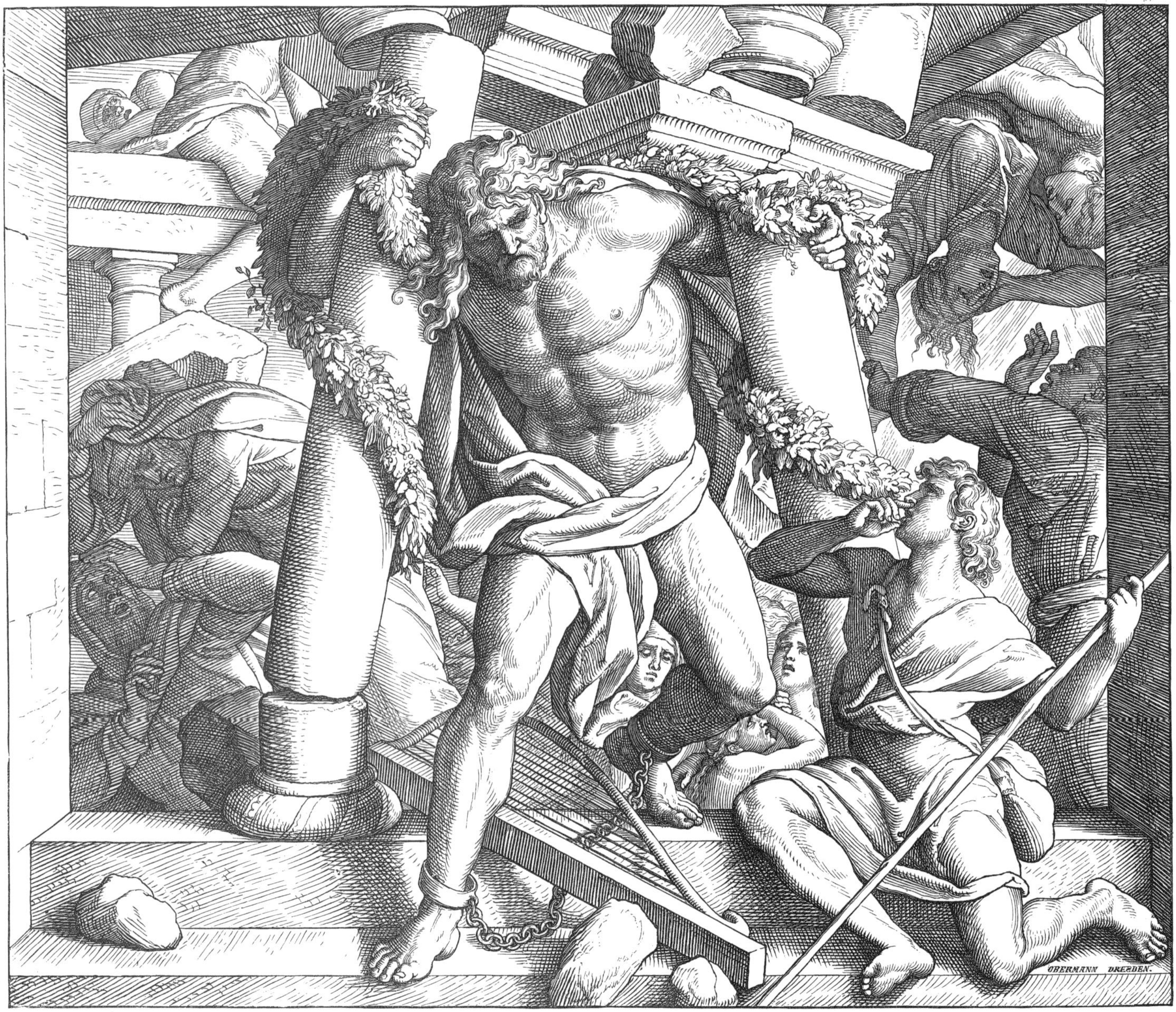

SAMSON'S VENGEANCE AND DEATH
Judges. Chapter 16.

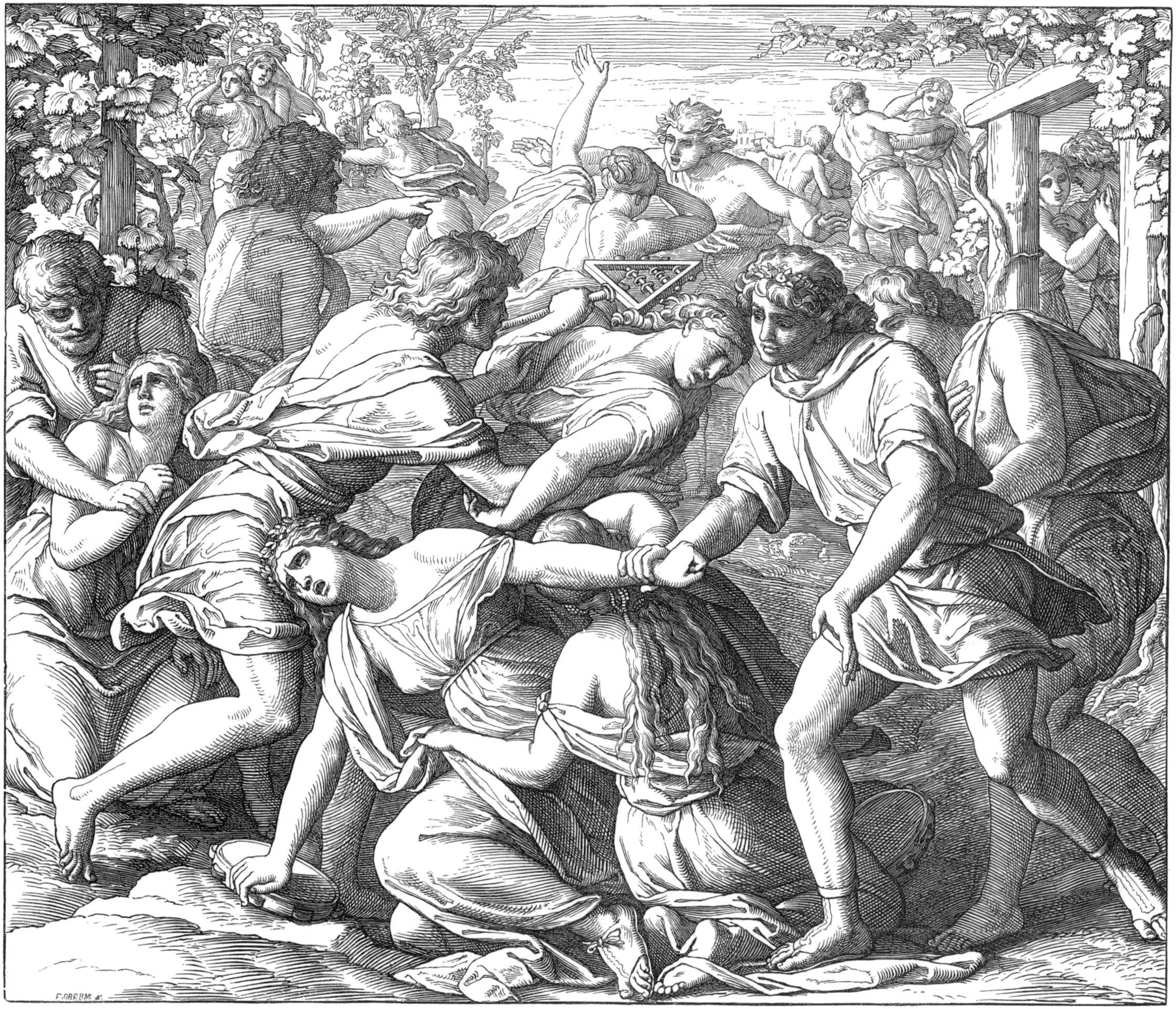

Wives for the Benjamites
Judges. Chapter 21.

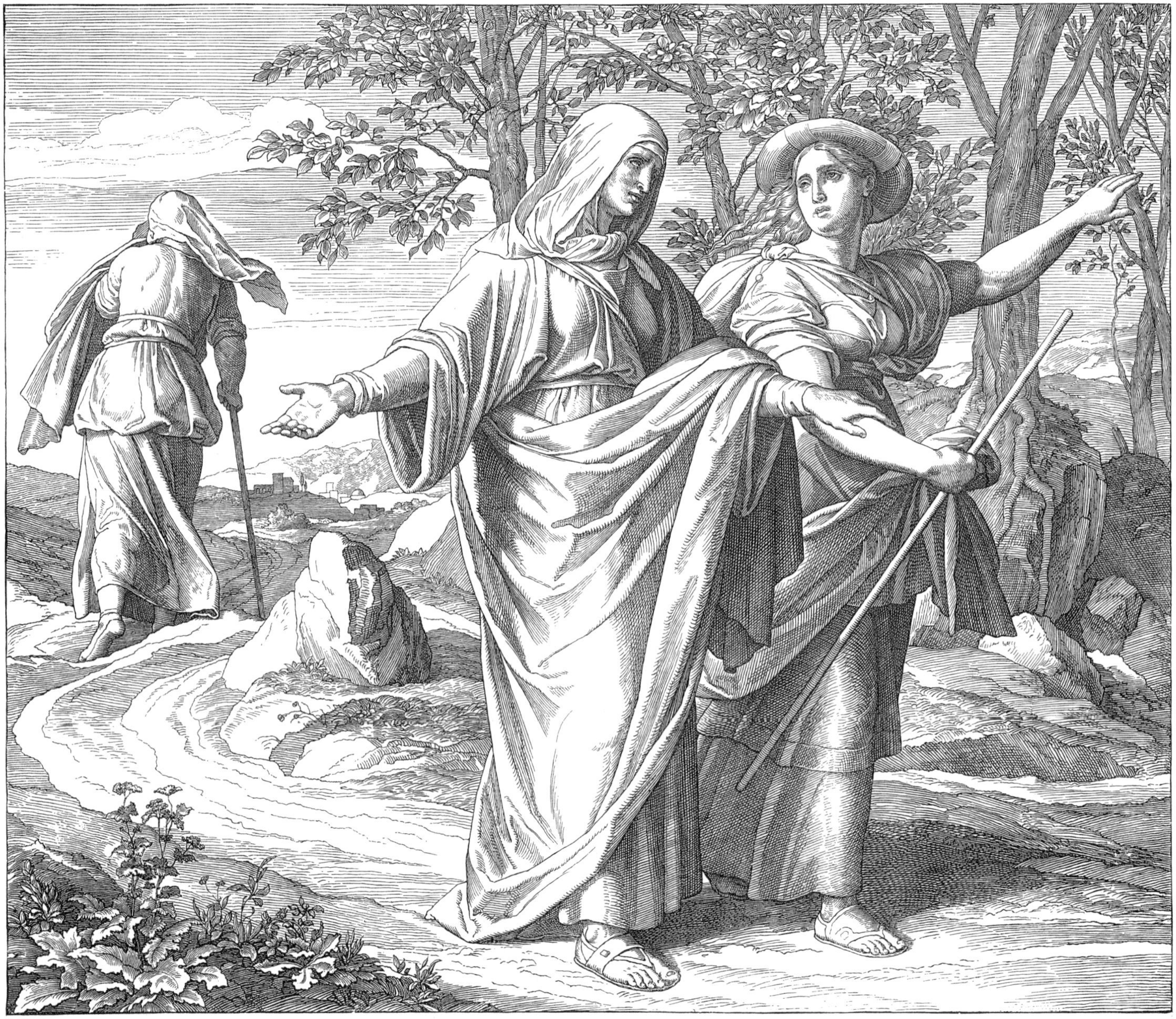

Ruth Travels with Naomi to Bethlehem

The Book of Ruth. Chapter 1.

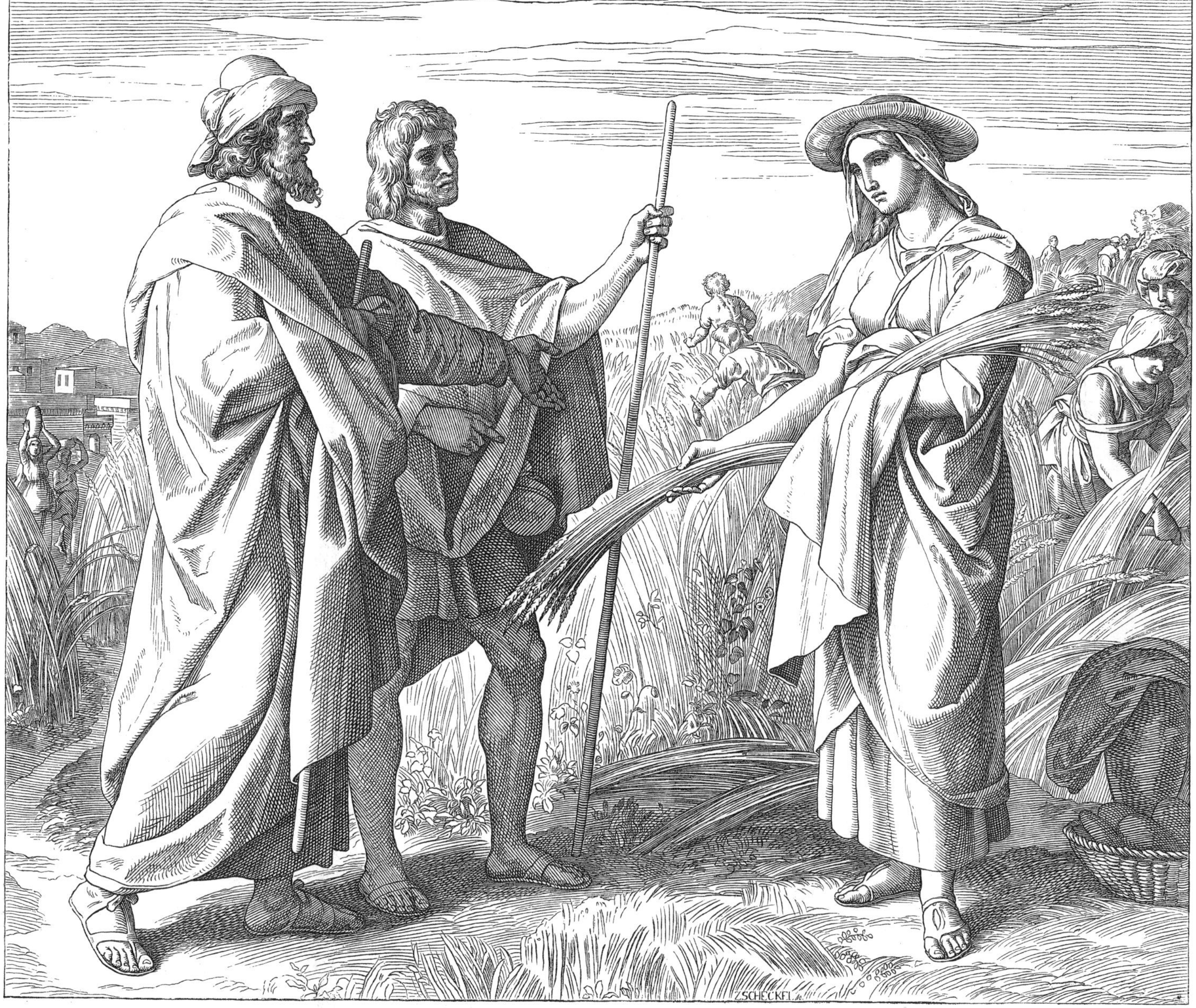

Ruth Gleans in the Field of Boaz

The Book of Ruth. Chapter 2.

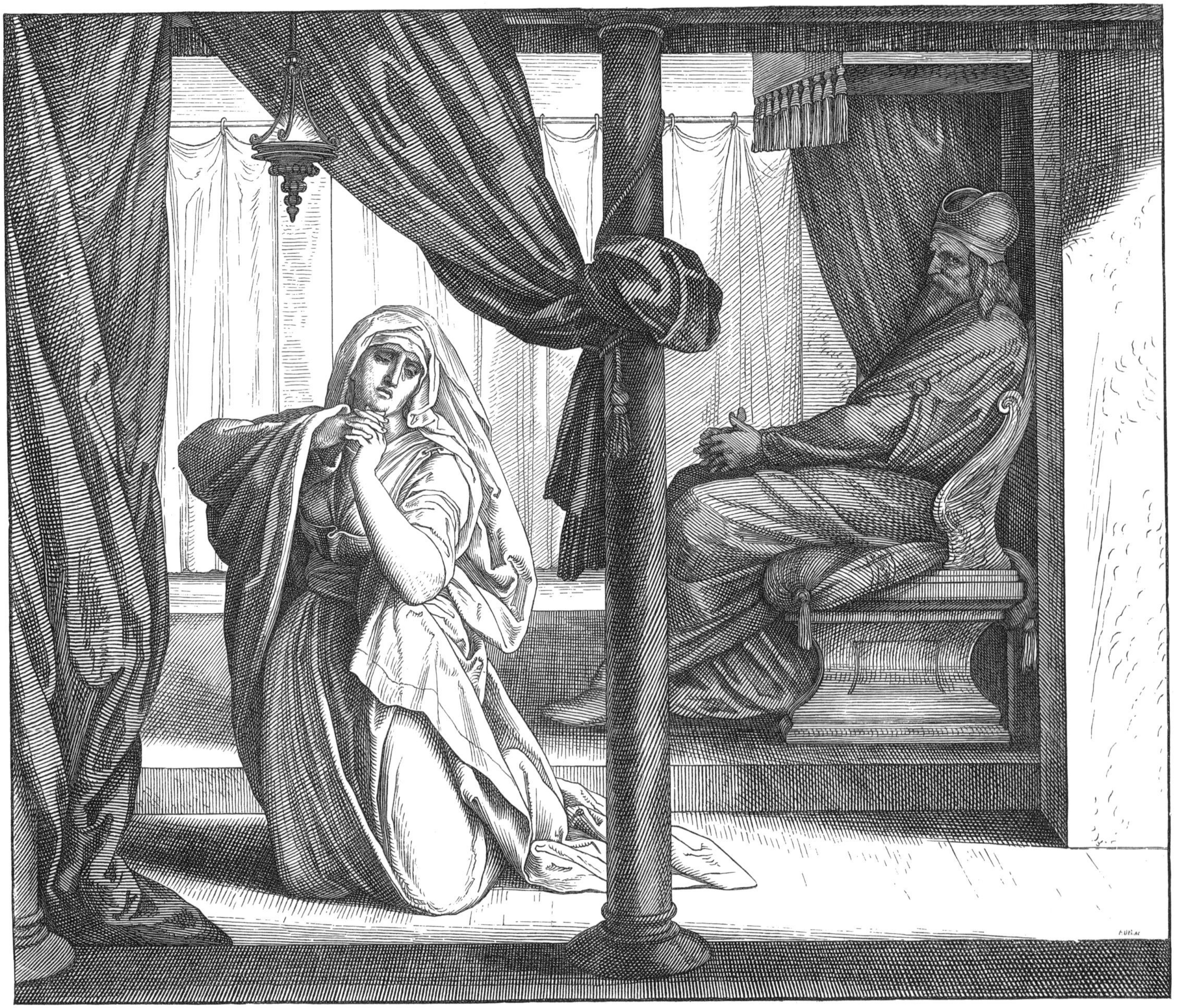

HANNAH'S PRAYER

The First Book of Samuel. Chapter 1.

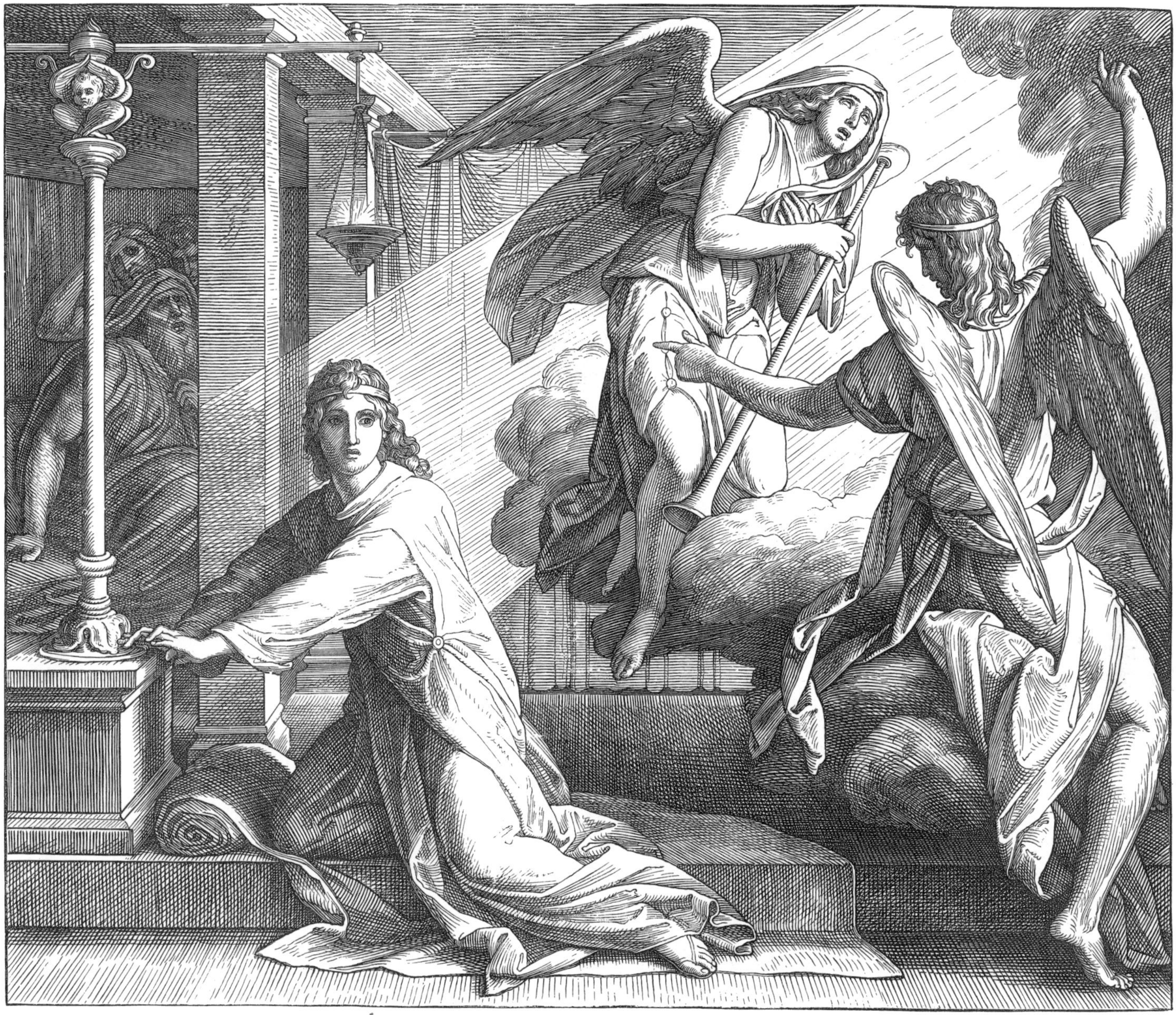

The Word of the Lord to Samuel

The First Book of Samuel. Chapter 3.

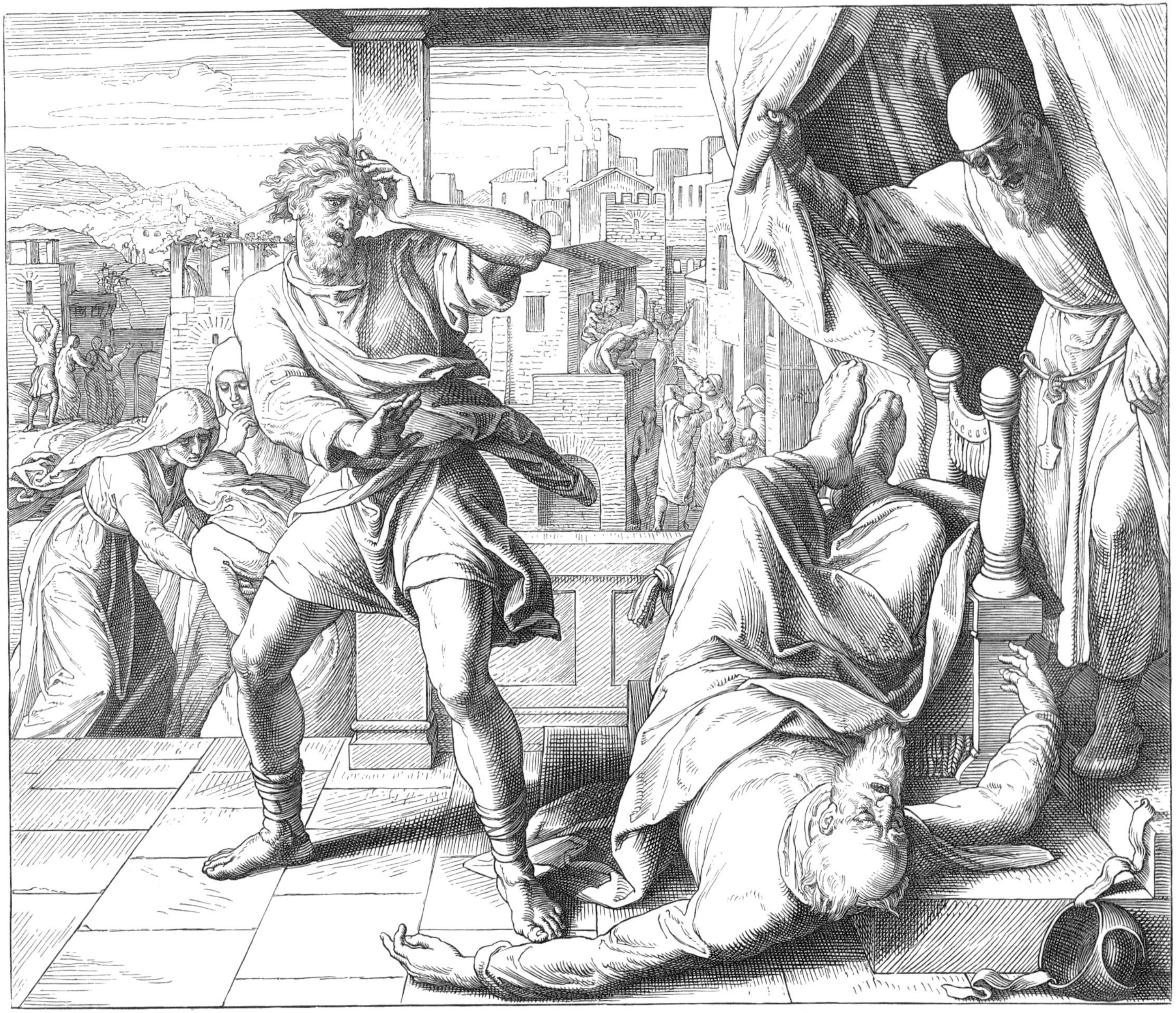

Eli's Death

The First Book of Samuel. Chapter 4.

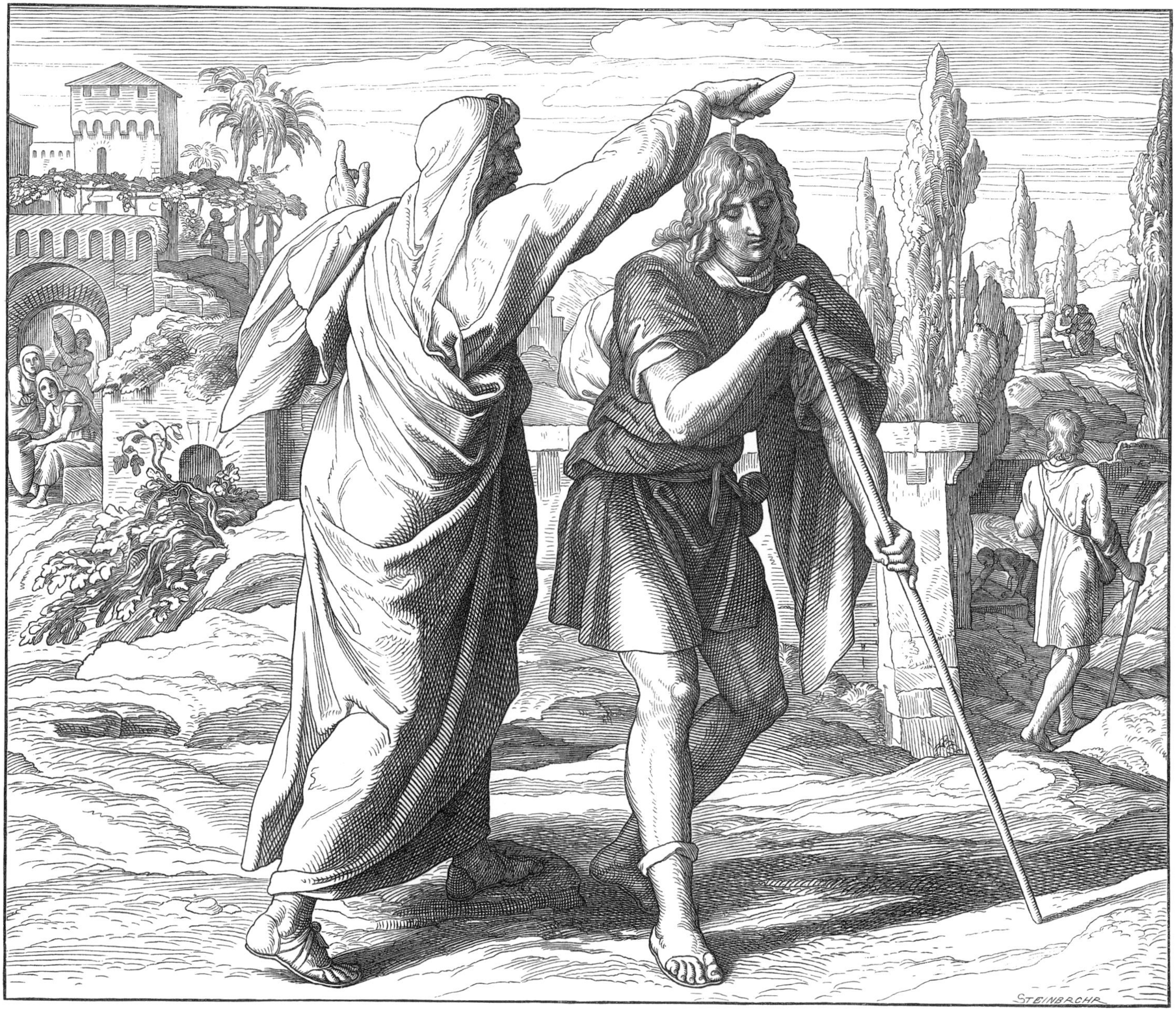

Samuel Anoints Saul As King

The First Book of Samuel. Chapter 10.

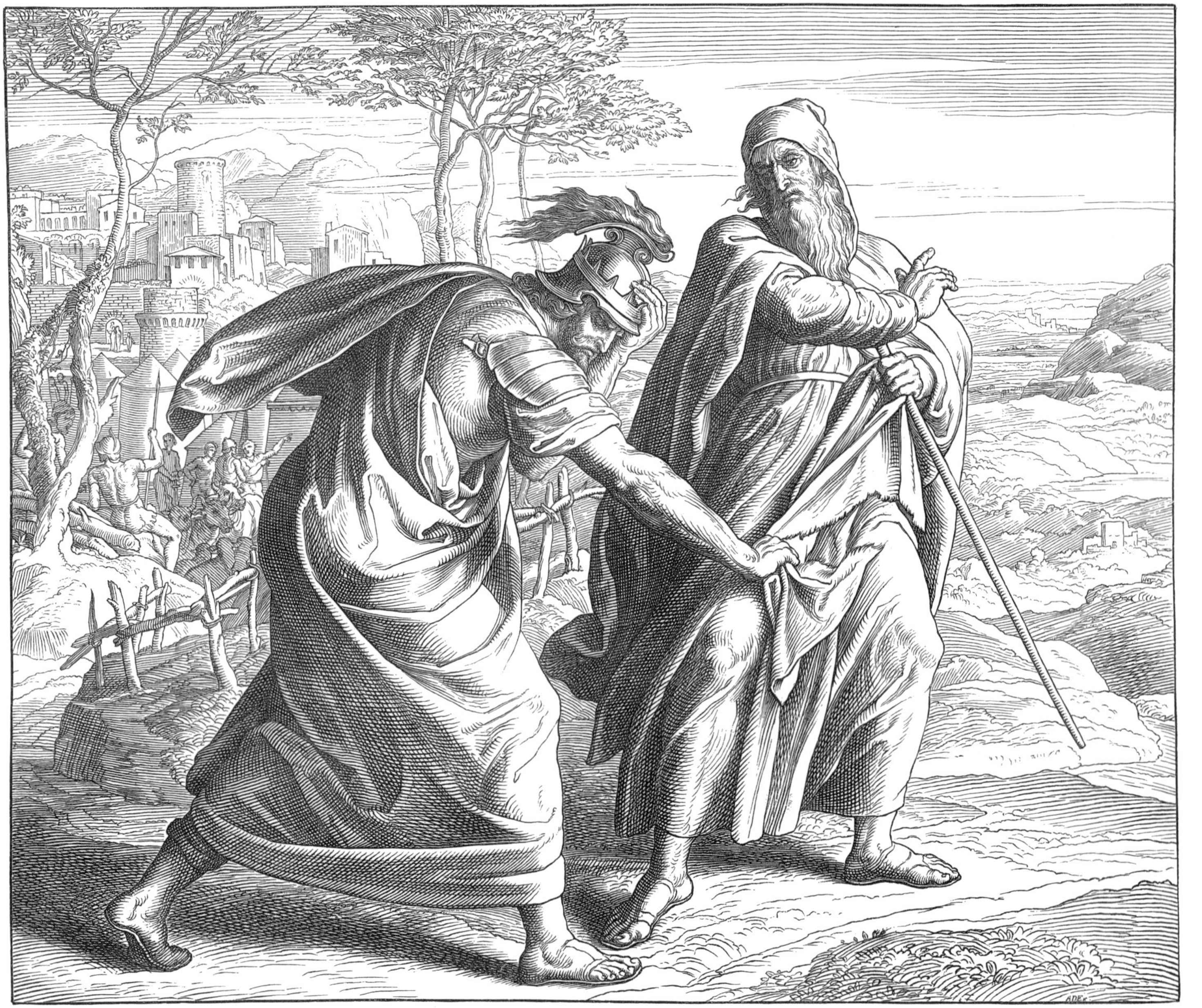

Saul Is Rejected As King

The First Book of Samuel. Chapter 15.

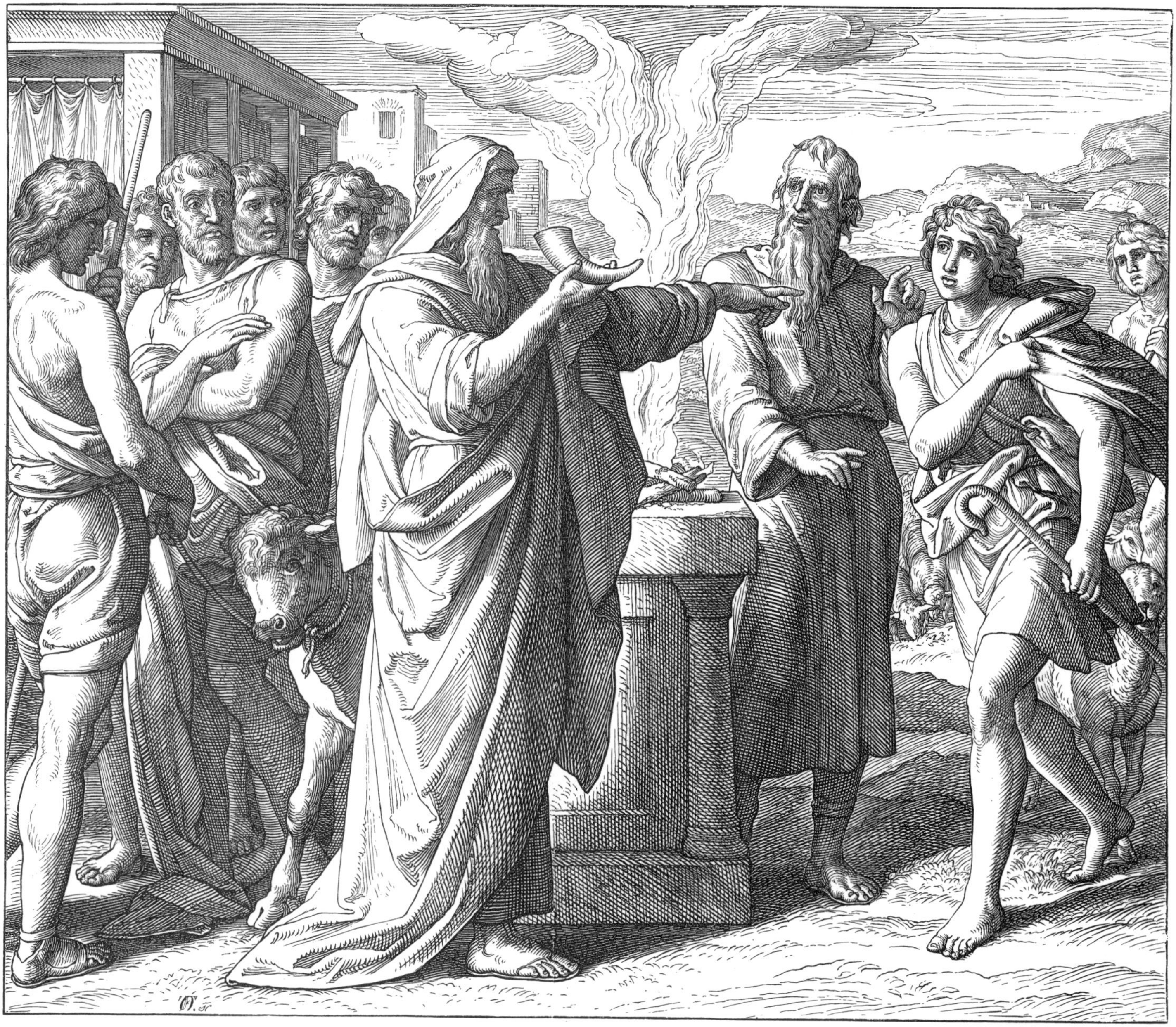

David Is Anointed King

The First Book of Samuel. Chapter 16.

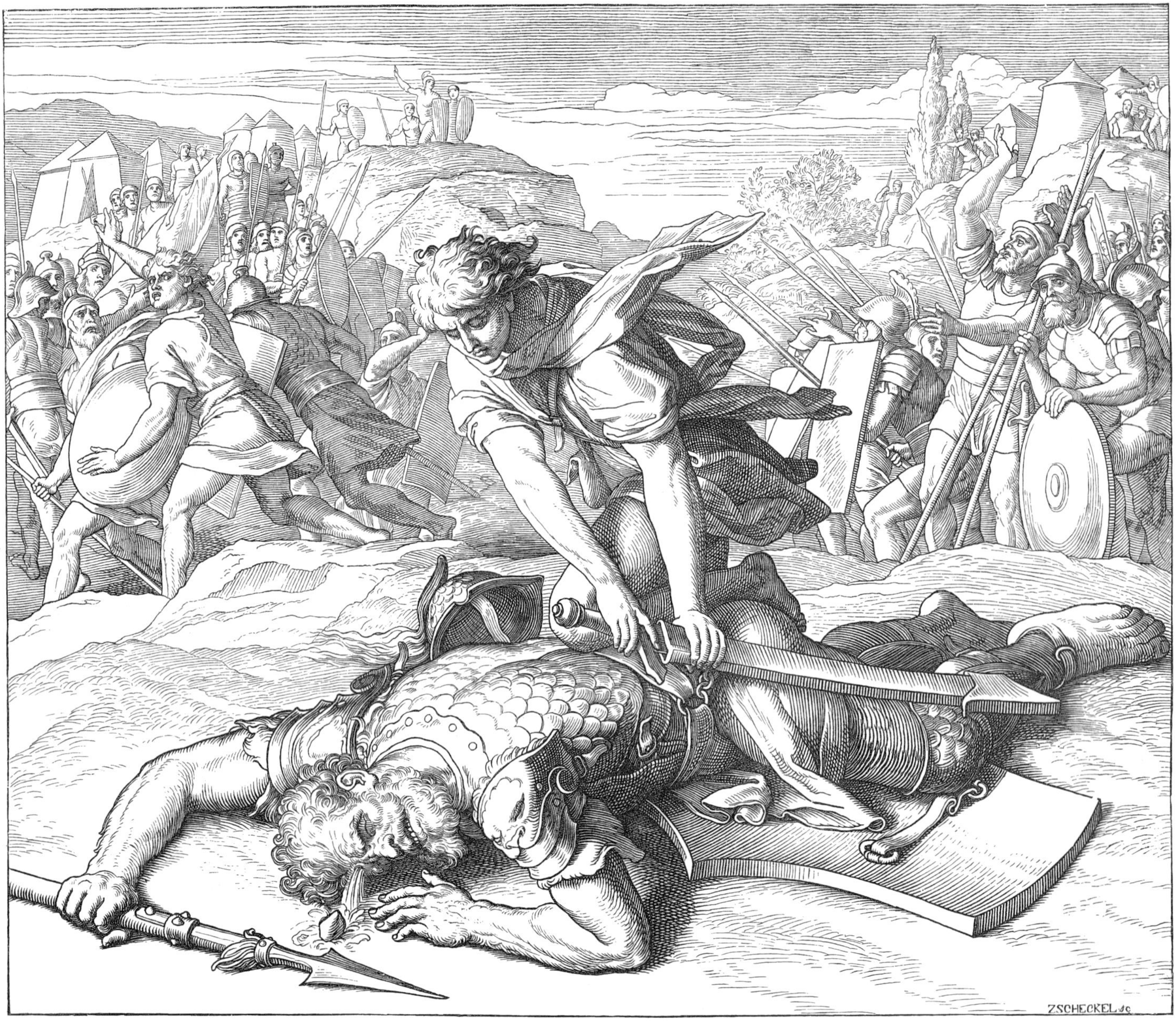

David Slays Goliath

The First Book of Samuel. Chapter 17.

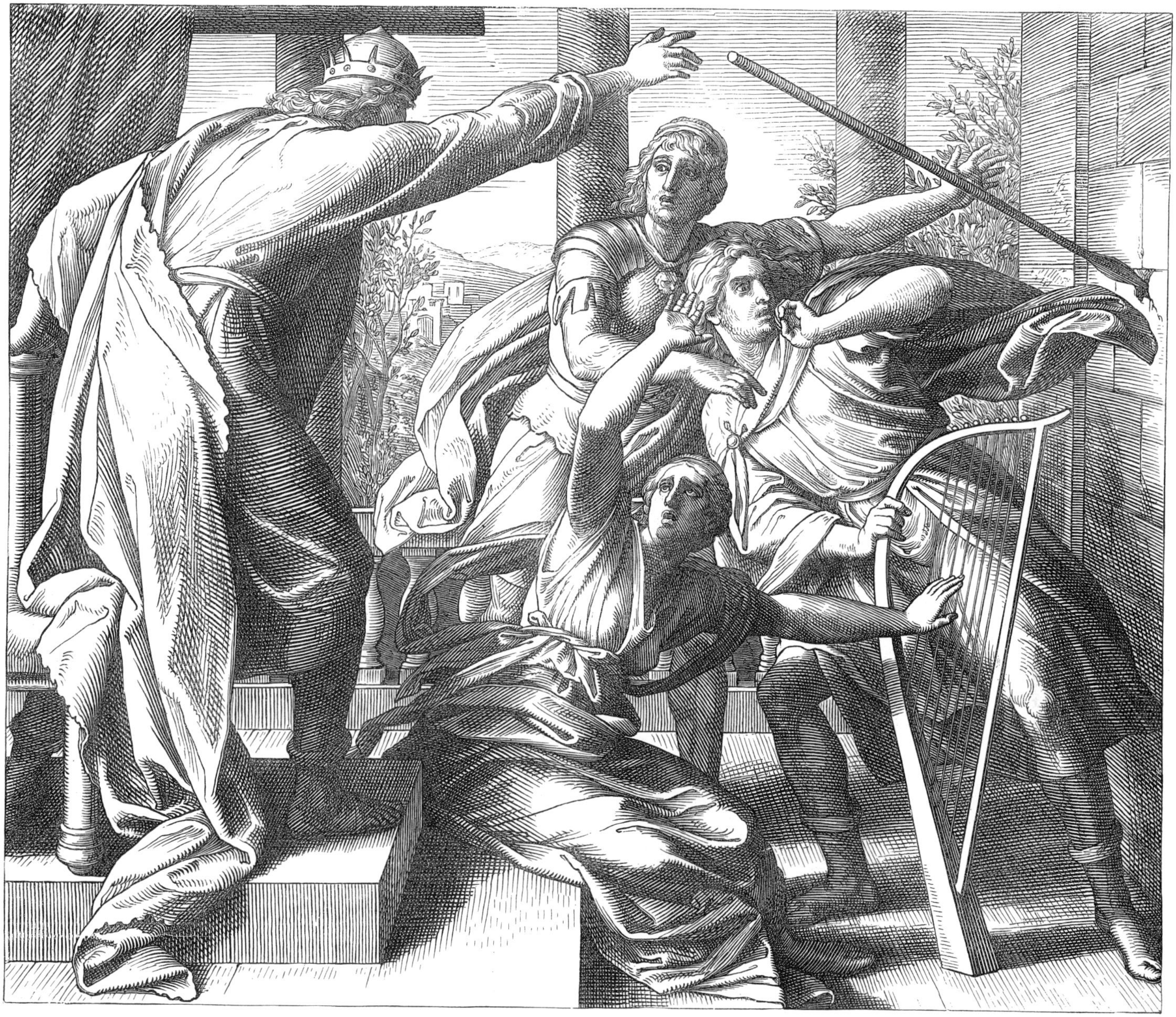

Saul Tries to Kill David

The First Book of Samuel. Chapter 19.

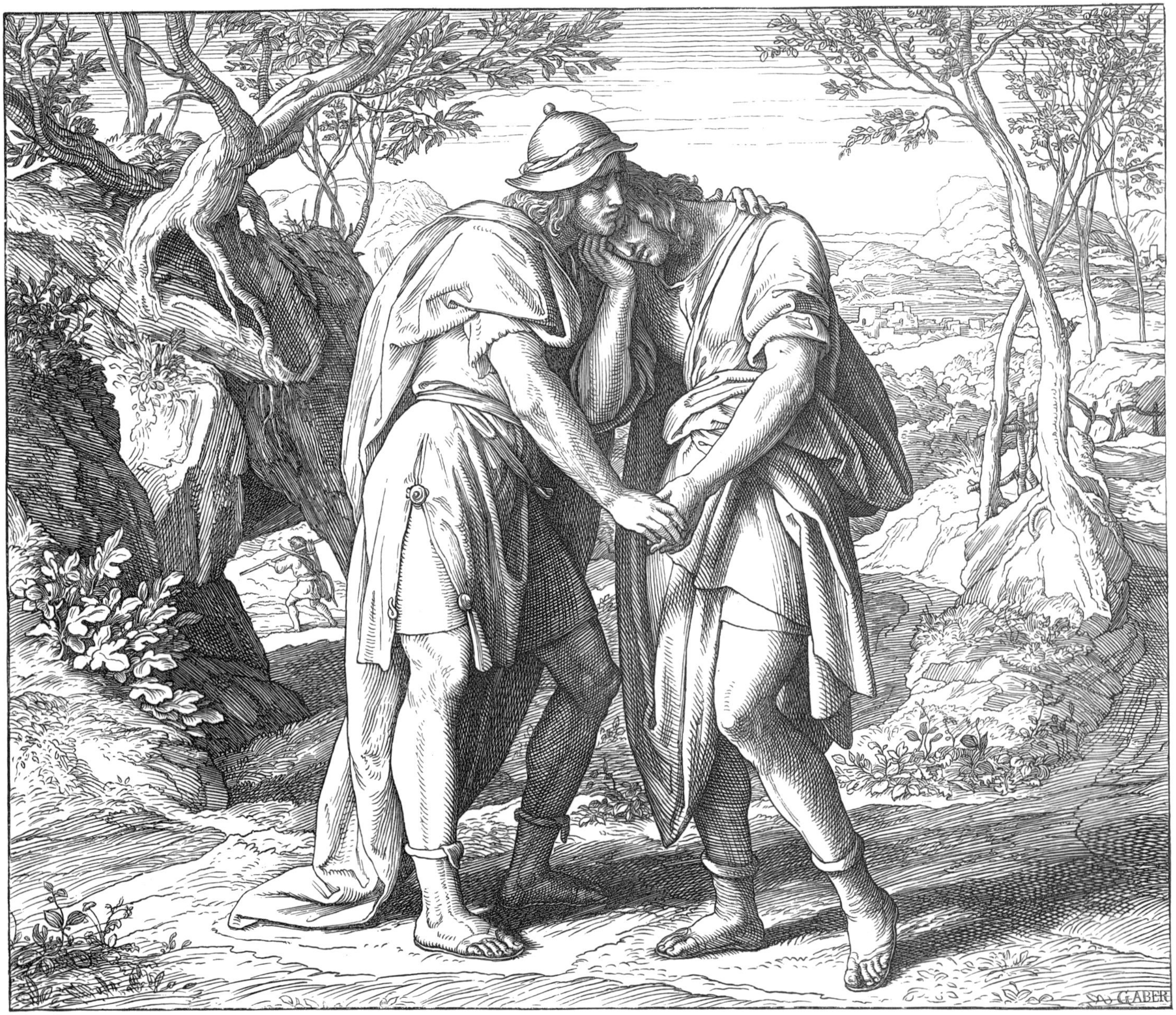

THE FRIENDSHIP OF DAVID AND JONATHAN

The First Book of Samuel. Chapter 20.

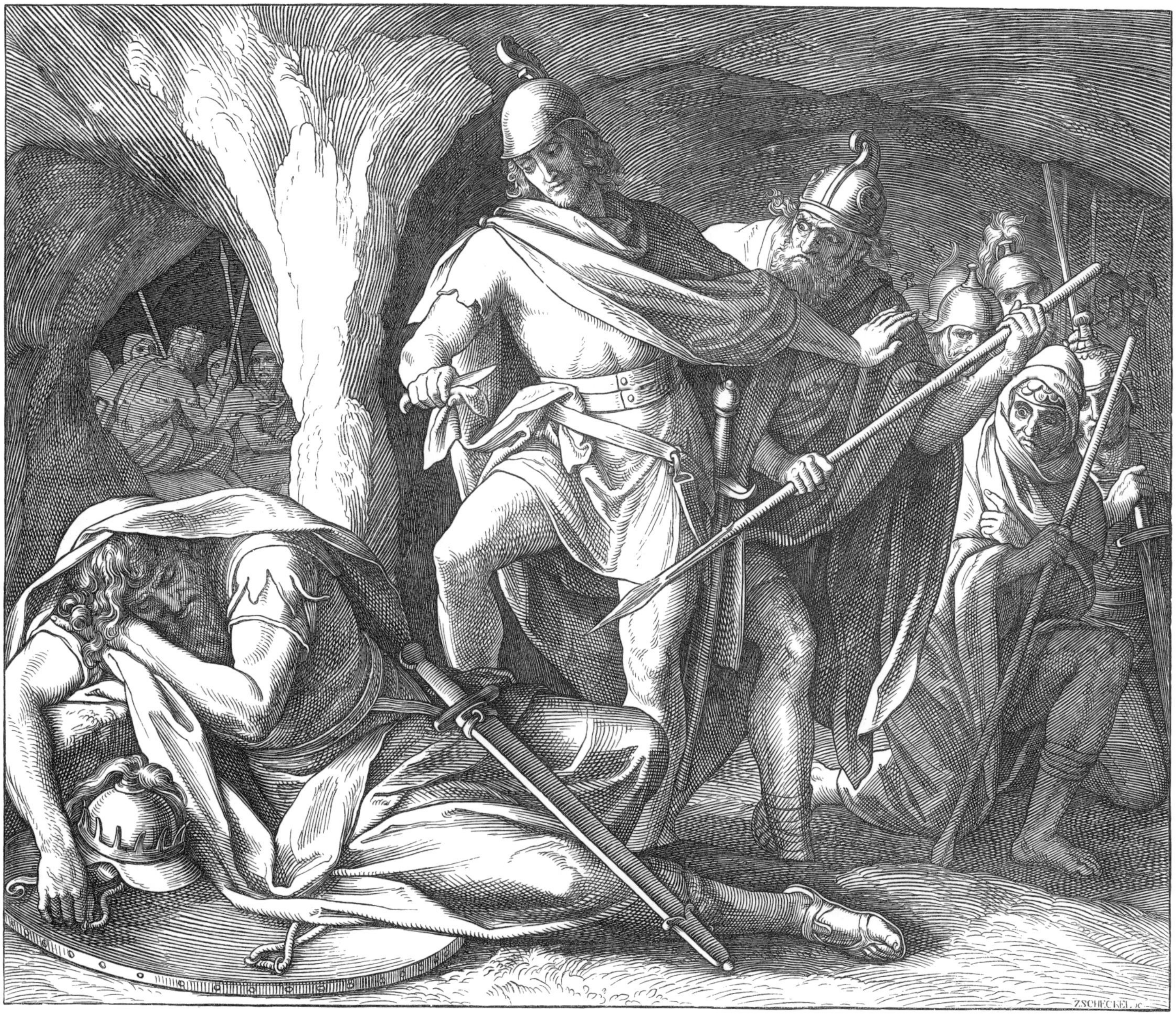

David Spares Saul's Life

The First Book of Samuel. Chapter 24.

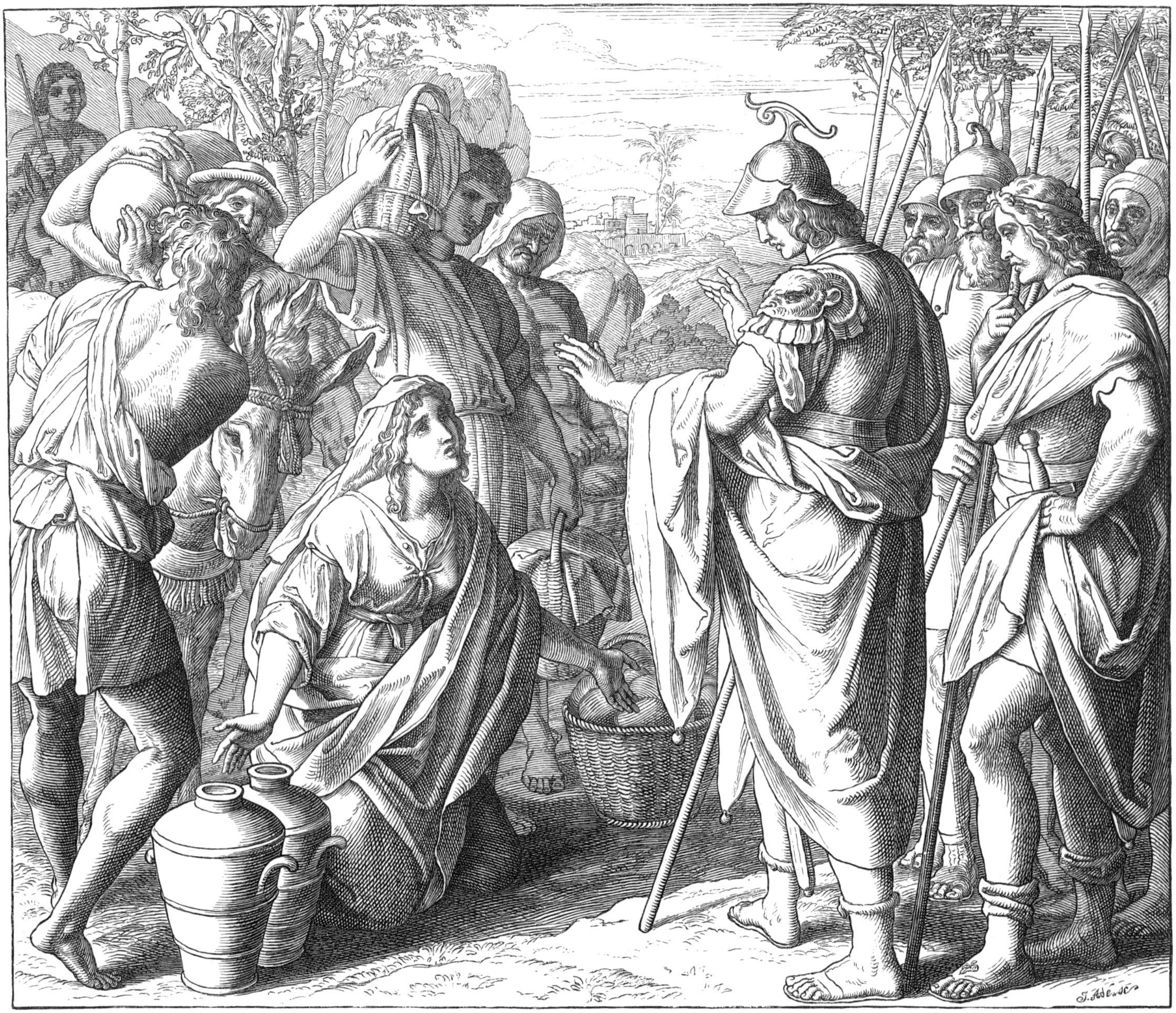

David and Abigail

The First Book of Samuel. Chapter 25.

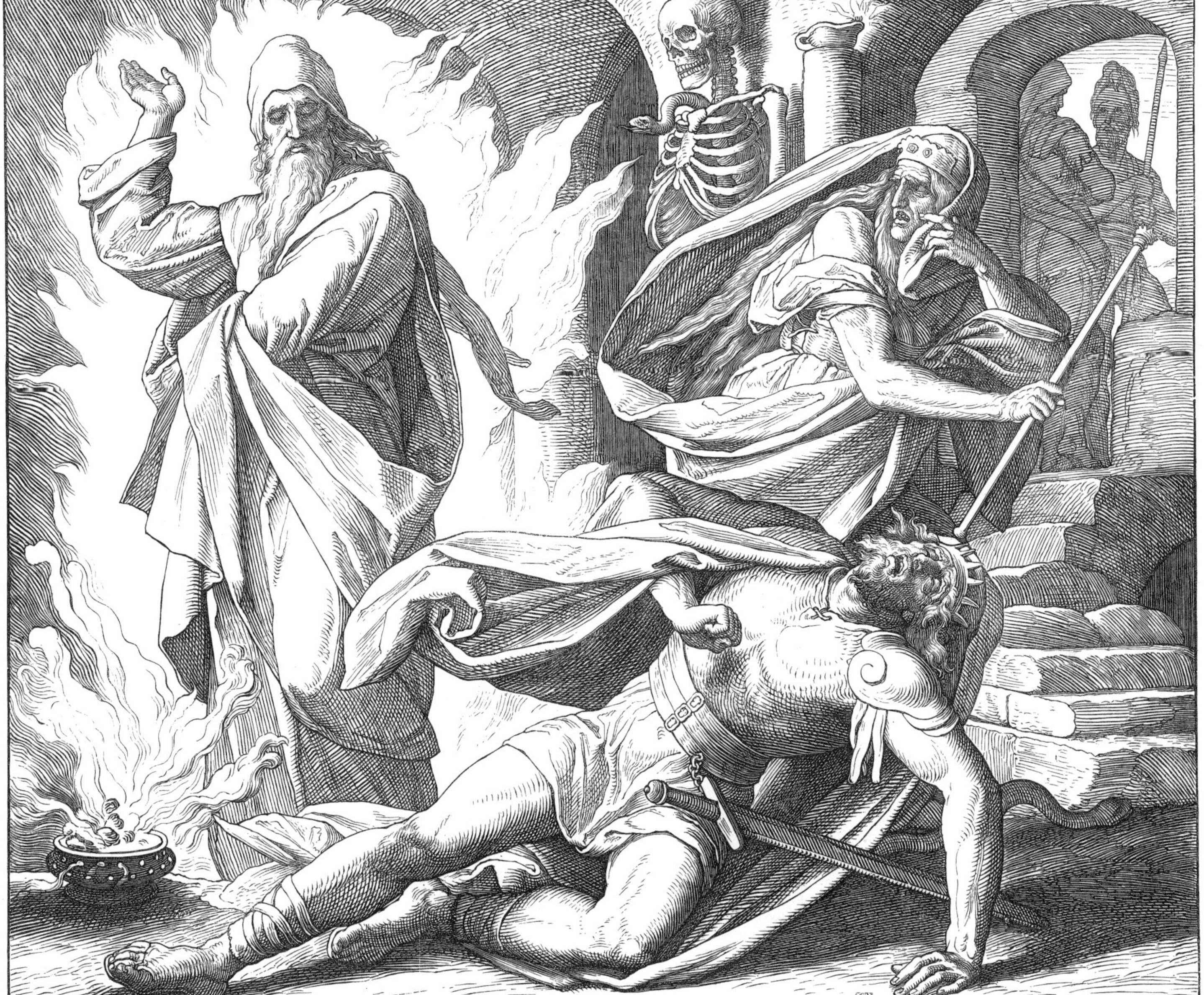

SAUL AND SAMUEL AT ENDOR
The First Book of Samuel. Chapter 28.

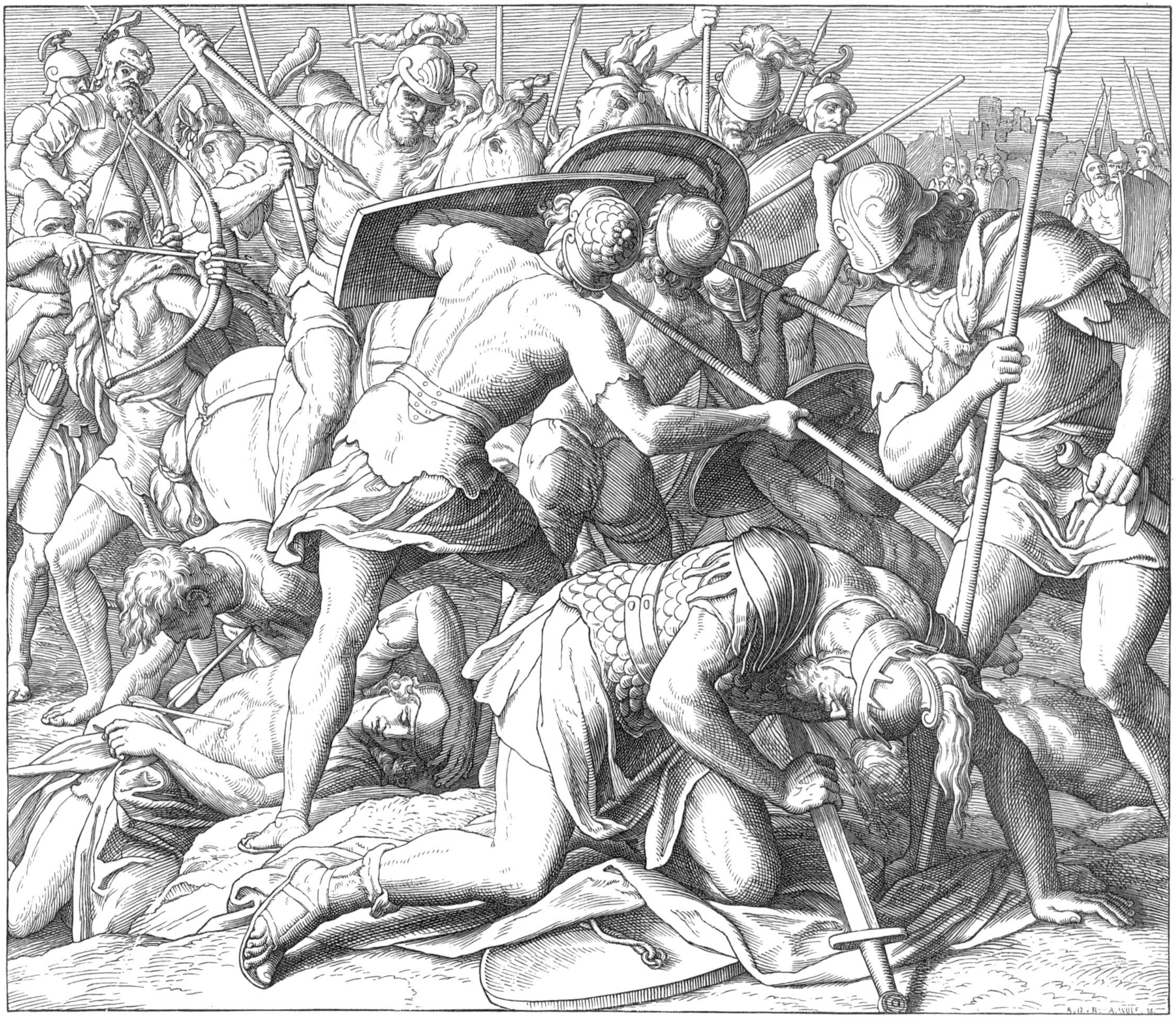

SAUL'S DEATH

The First Book of Samuel. Chapter 31.

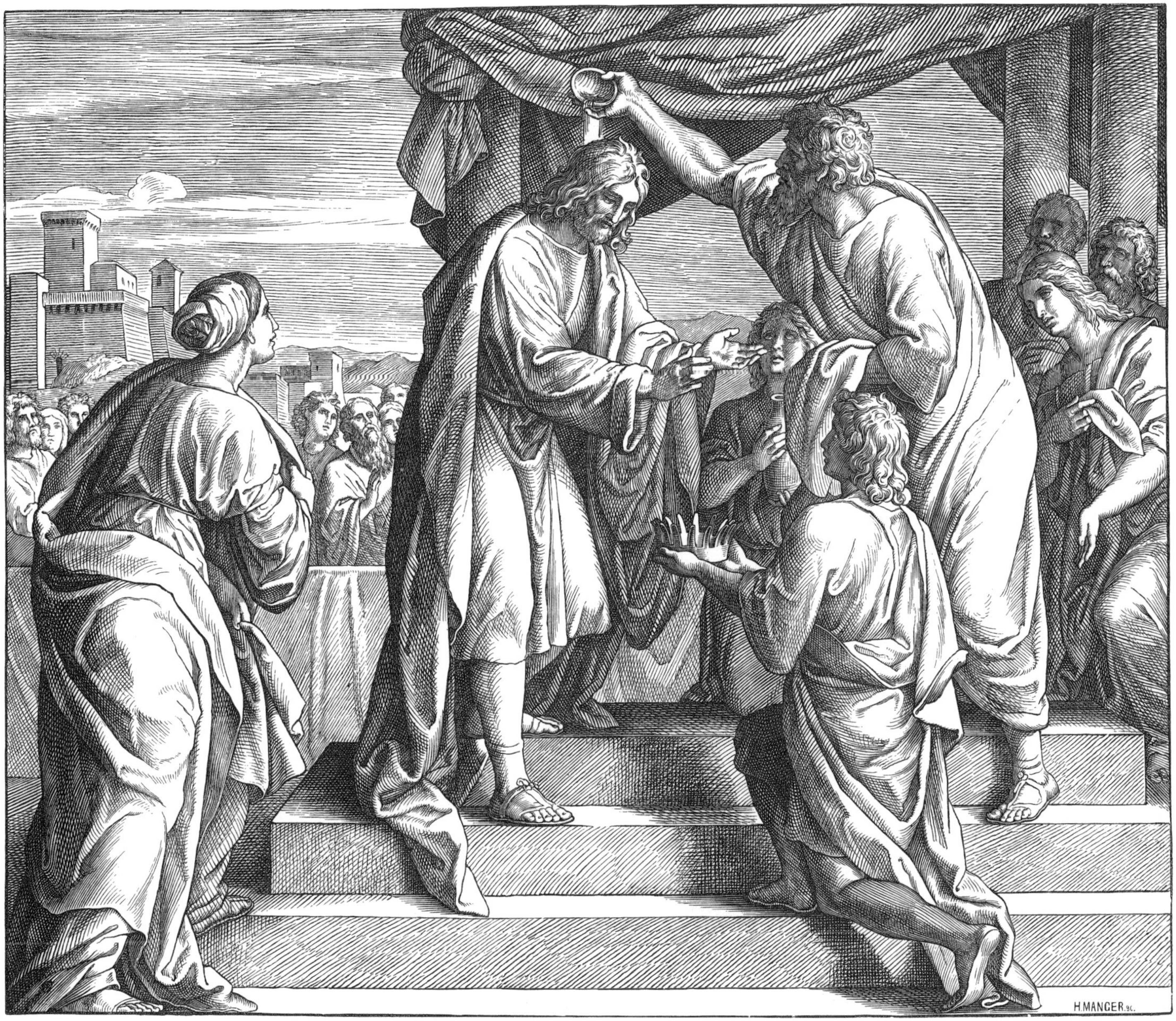

DAVID IS MADE KING OF JUDAH

The Second Book of Samuel. Chapter 2.

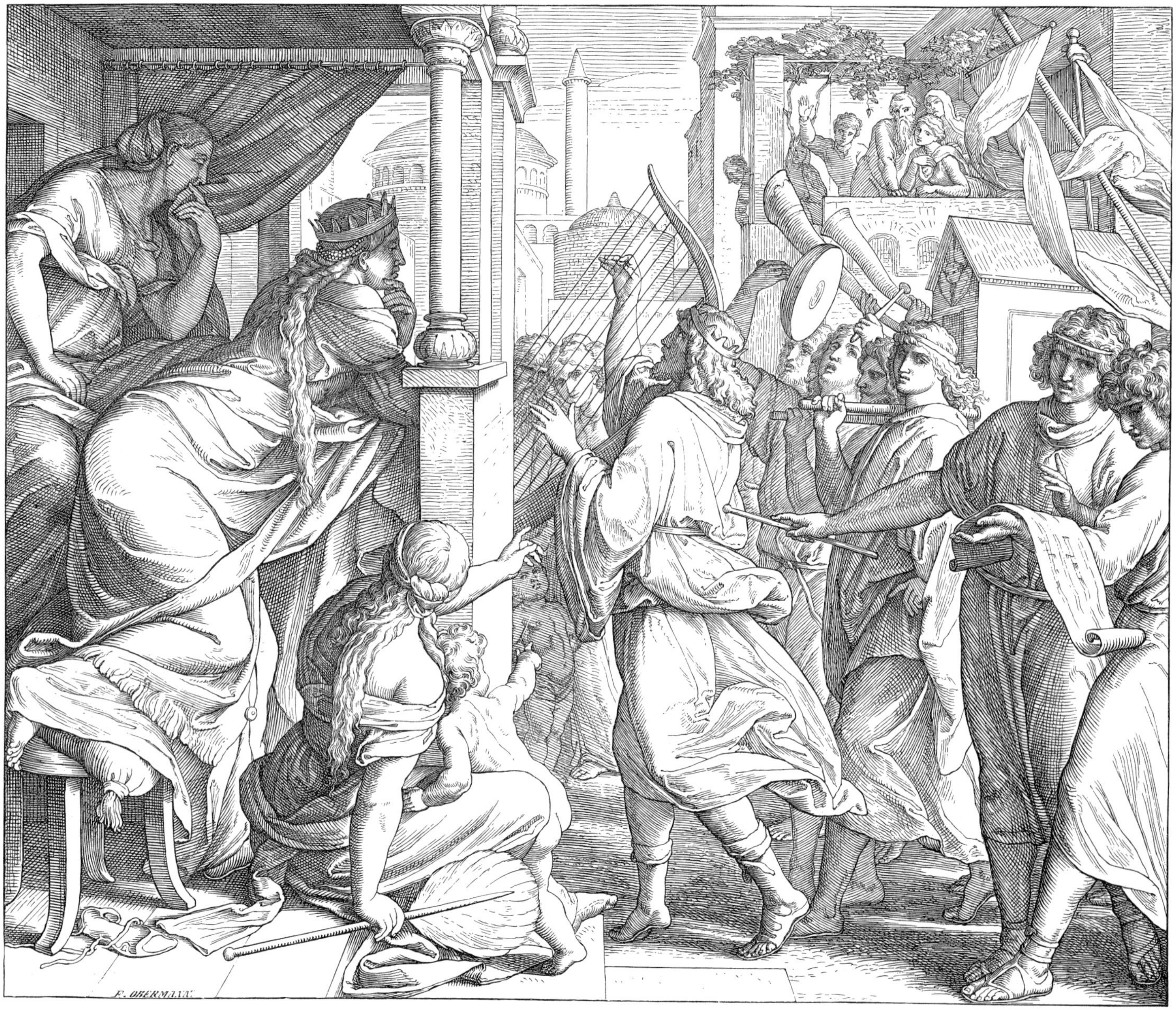

DAVID IS DESPISED BY HIS WIFE MICHAL
The Second Book of Samuel. Chapter 6.

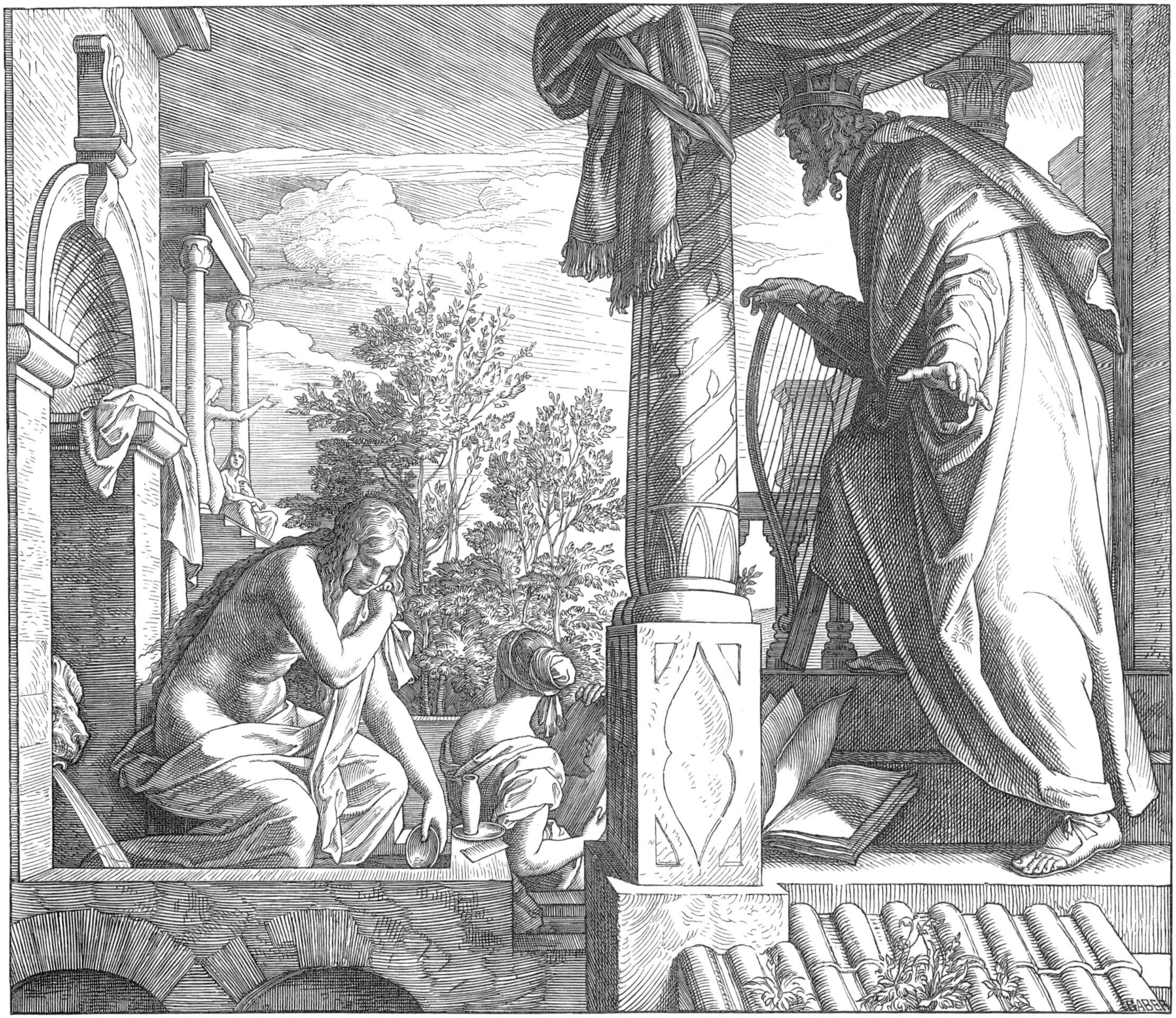

DAVID AND BATHSHEBA

The Second Book of Samuel. Chapter 11.

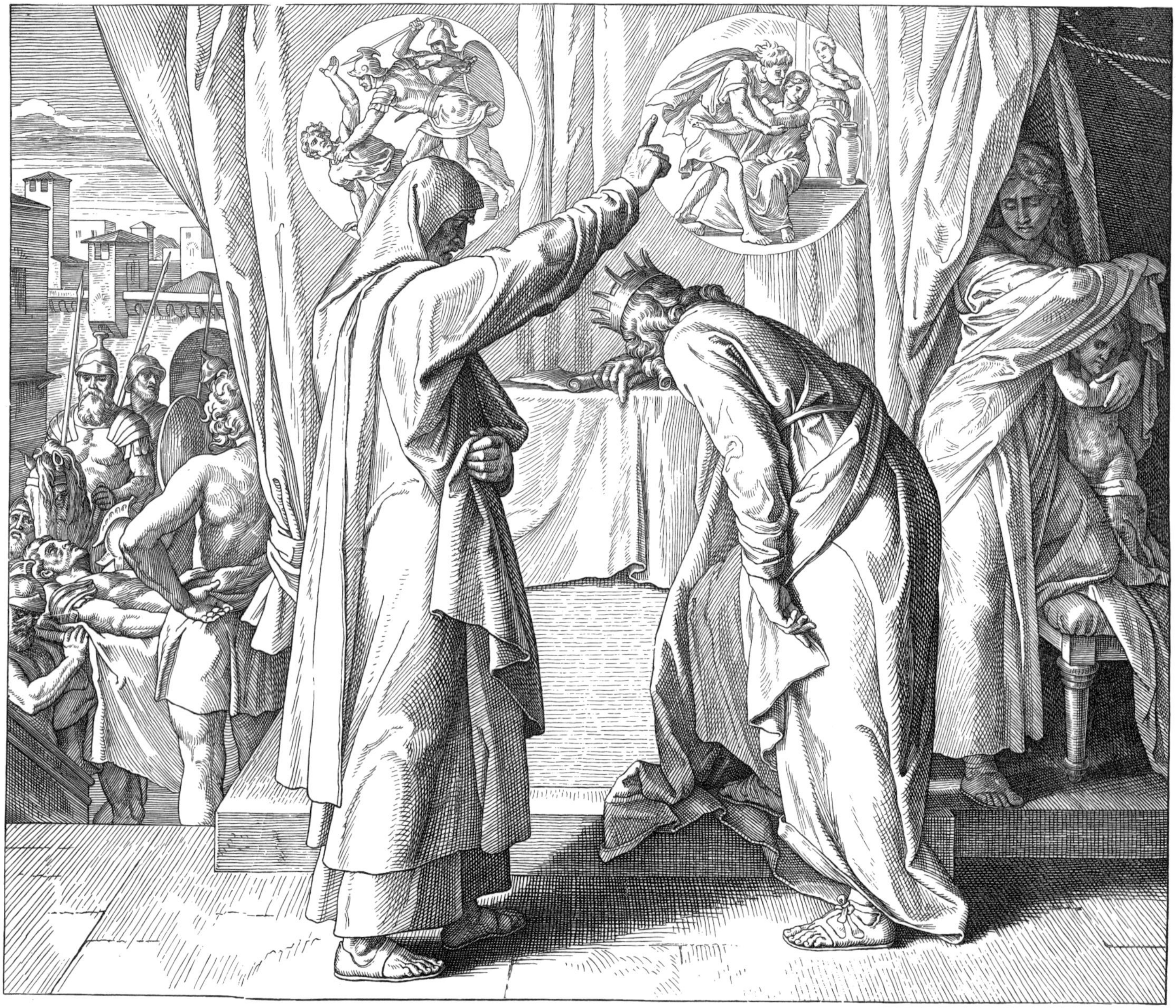

Nathan's Reproof of David

The Second Book of Samuel. Chapter 12.

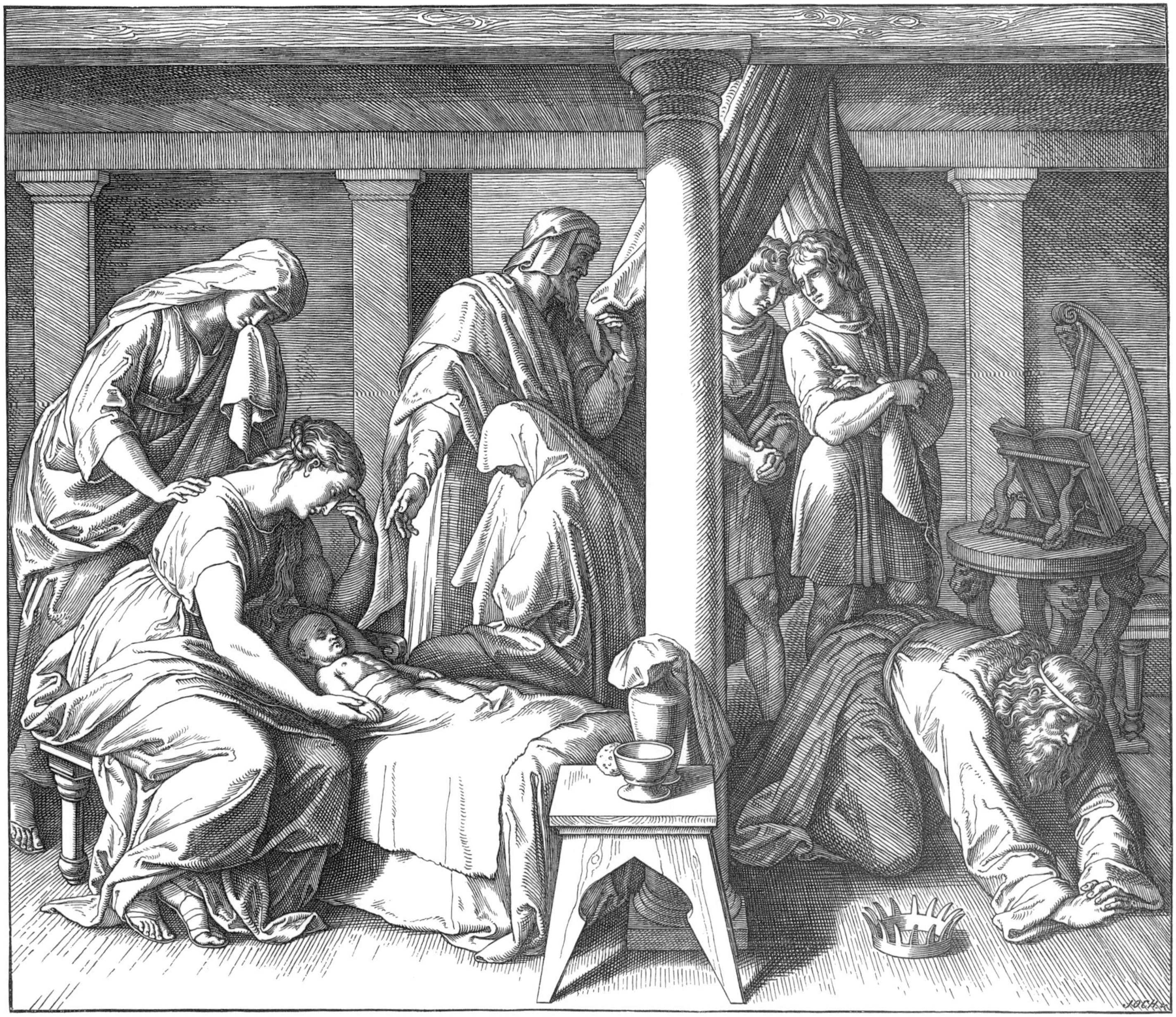

David and Bathsheba's Child Dies

The Second Book of Samuel. Chapter 12.

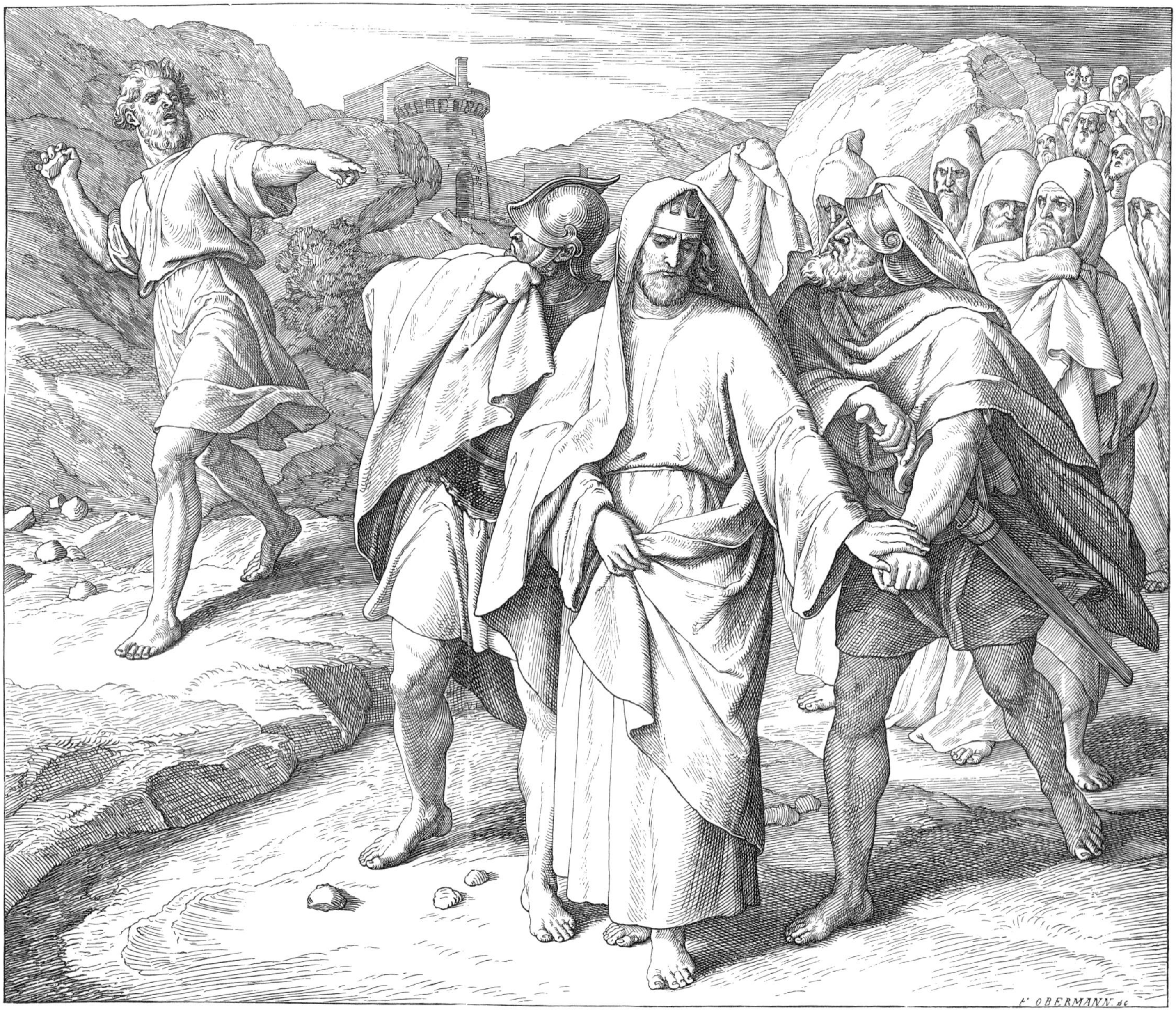

SHIMEI'S BLASPHEMY

The Second Book of Samuel. Chapter 16.

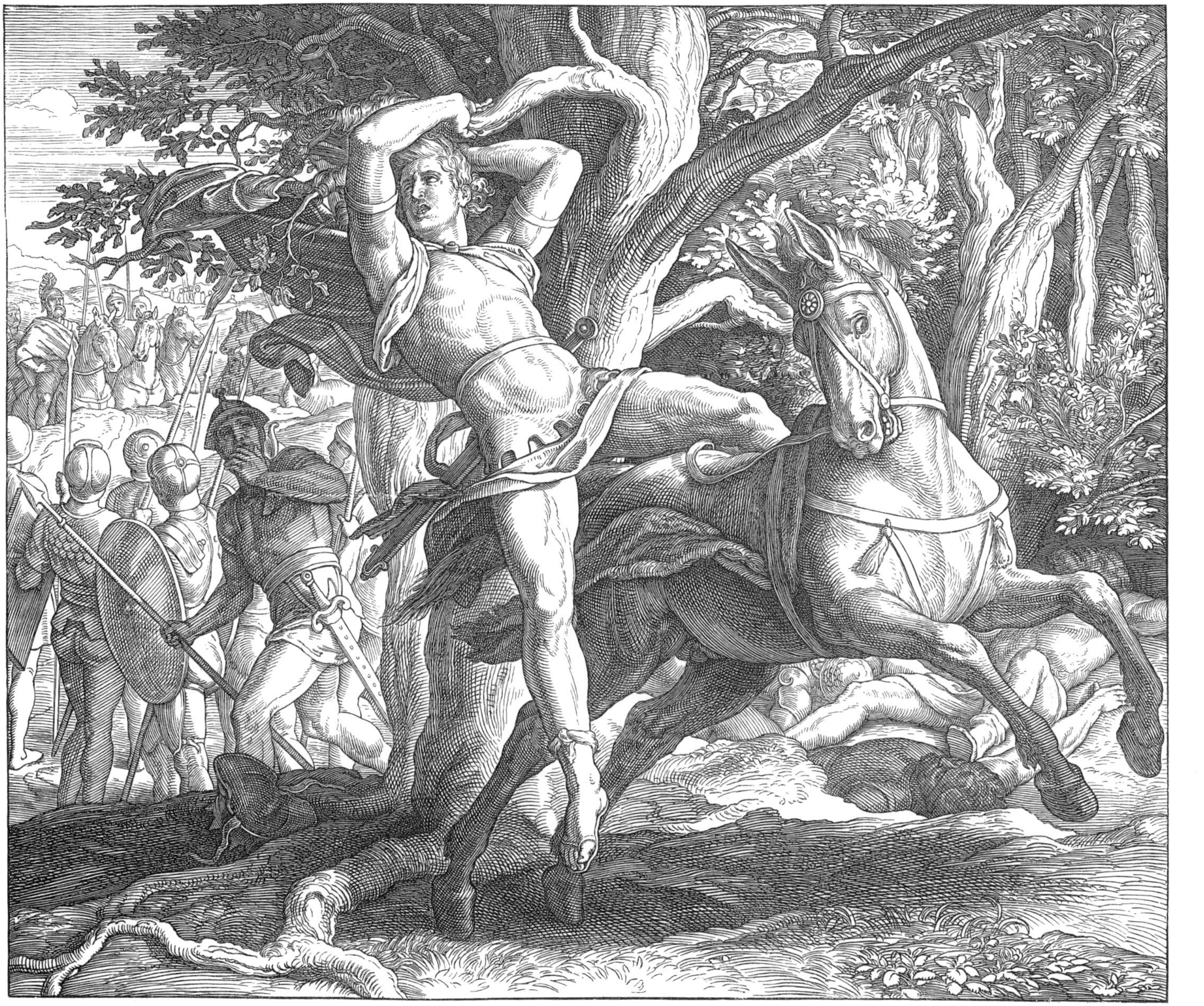

ABSALOM'S DEATH
The Second Book of Samuel. Chapter 18.

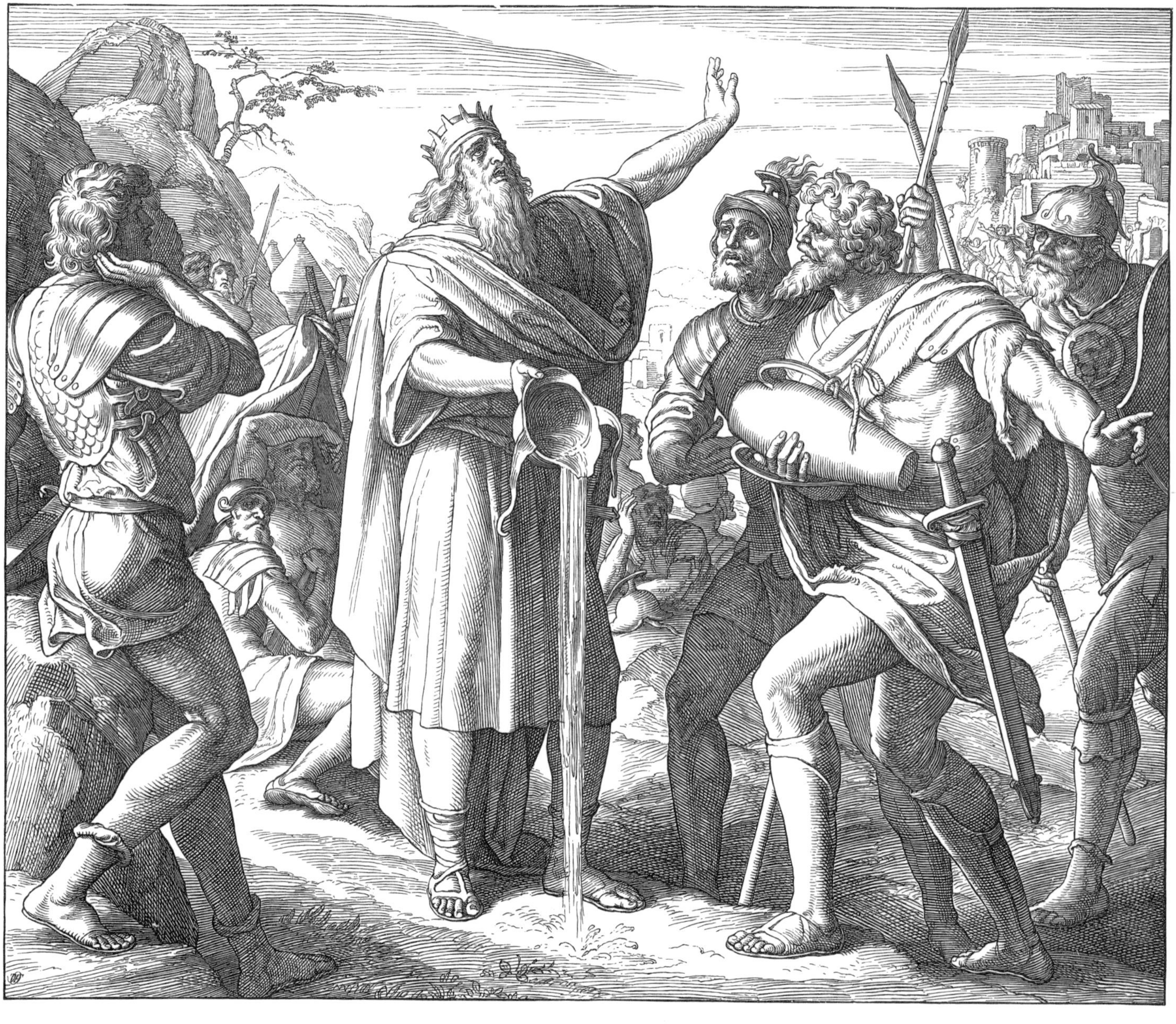

David and His Heroes

The Second Book of Samuel. Chapter 23.

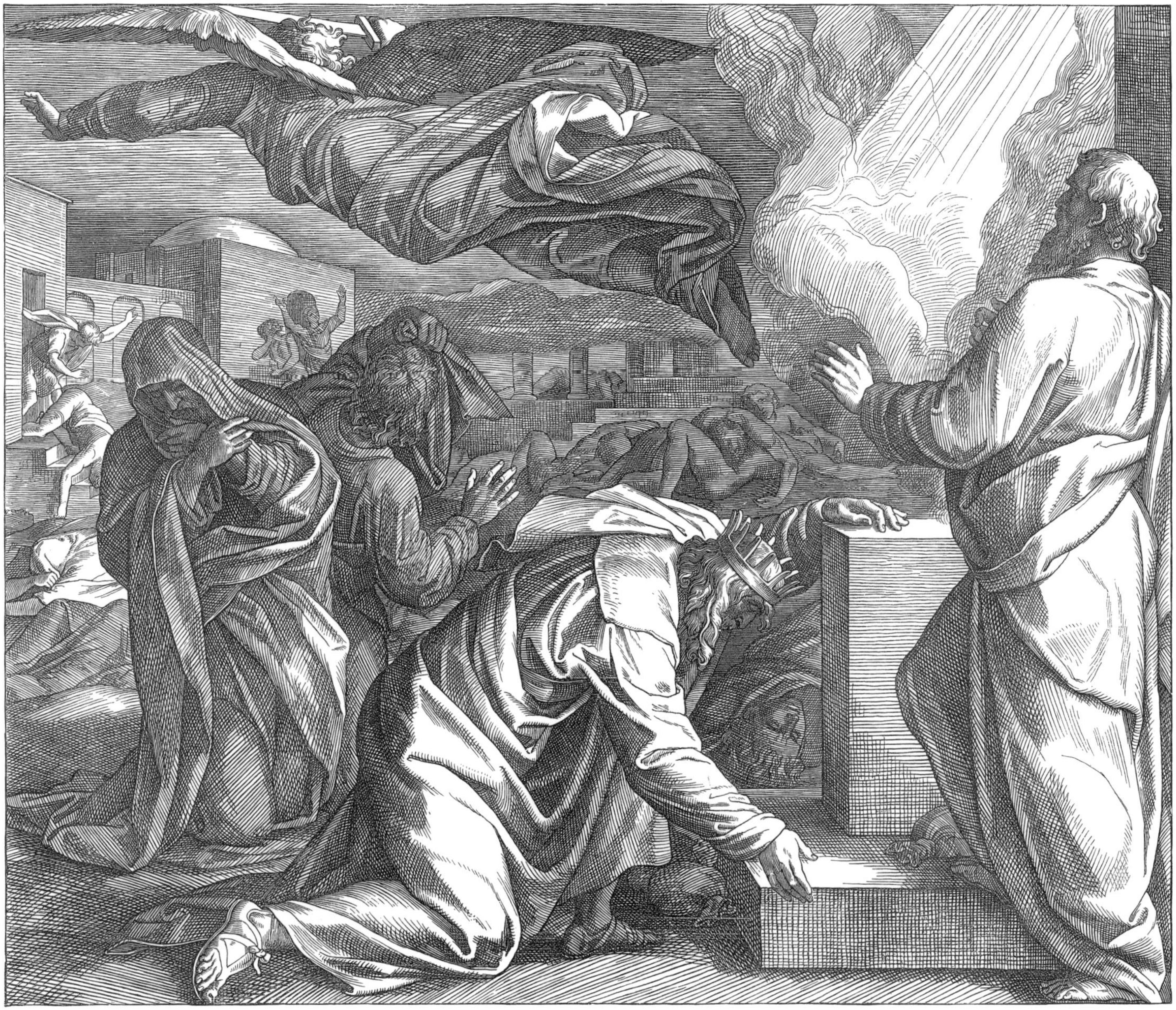

DAVID'S CENSUS IS PUNISHED WITH PESTILENCE

The Second Book of Samuel. Chapter 24.

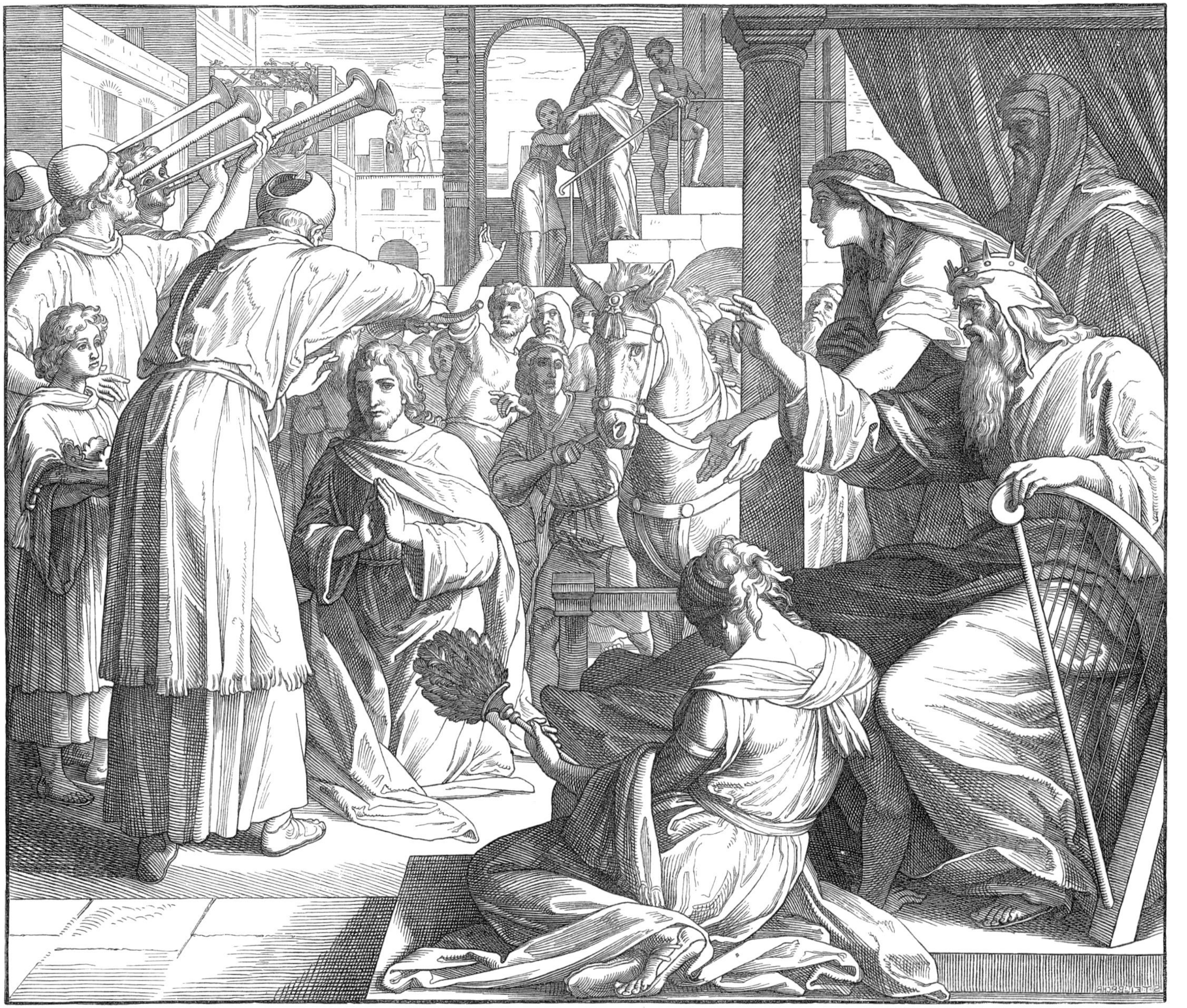

Solomon Is Anointed King

The First Book of Kings. Chapter 1.

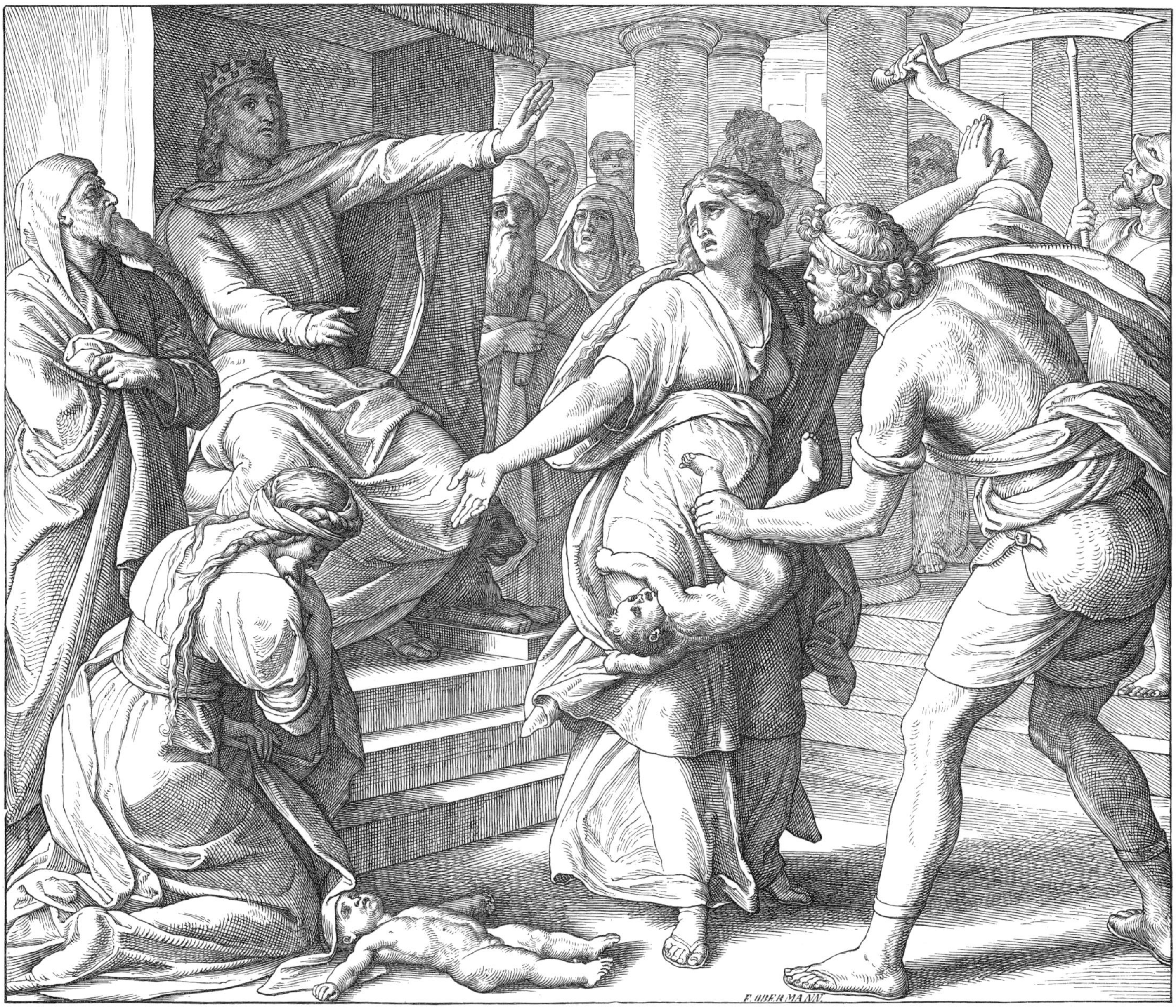

SOLOMON'S JUDGMENT

The First Book of Kings. Chapter 3.

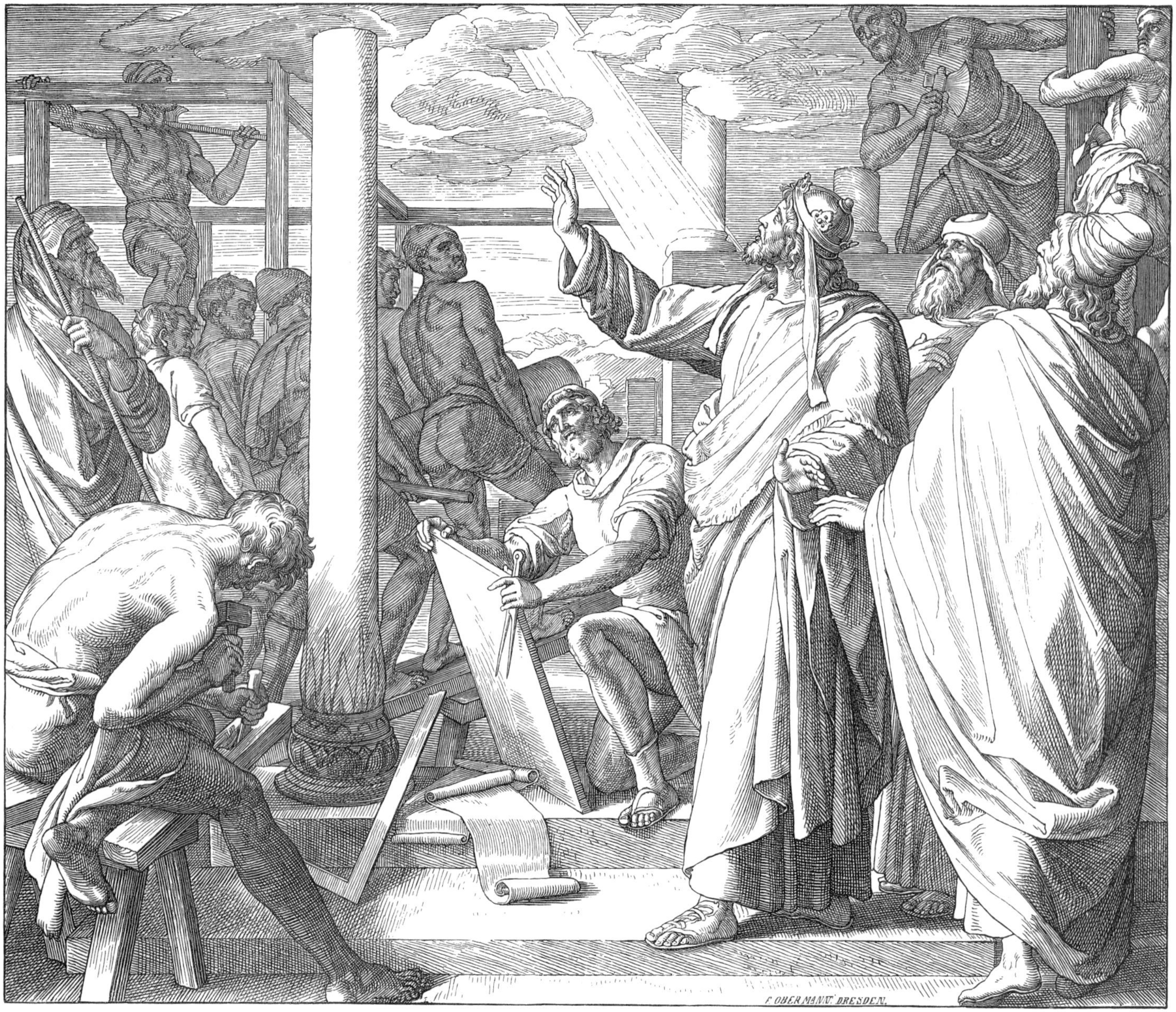

SOLOMON BUILDS THE TEMPLE

The First Book of Kings. Chapter 6.

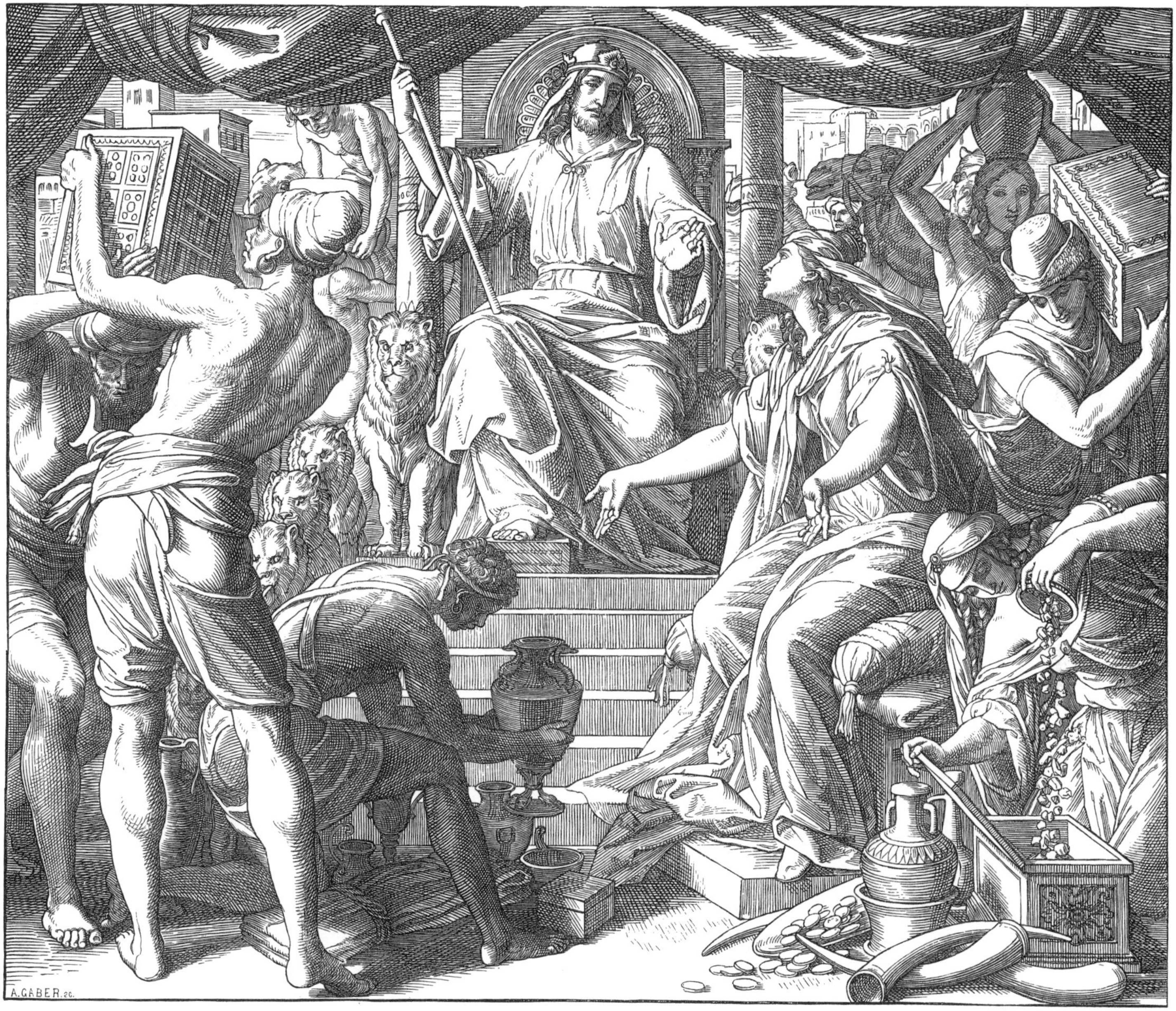

The Queen of Sheba Pays Homage to Solomon
The First Book of Kings. Chapter 10.

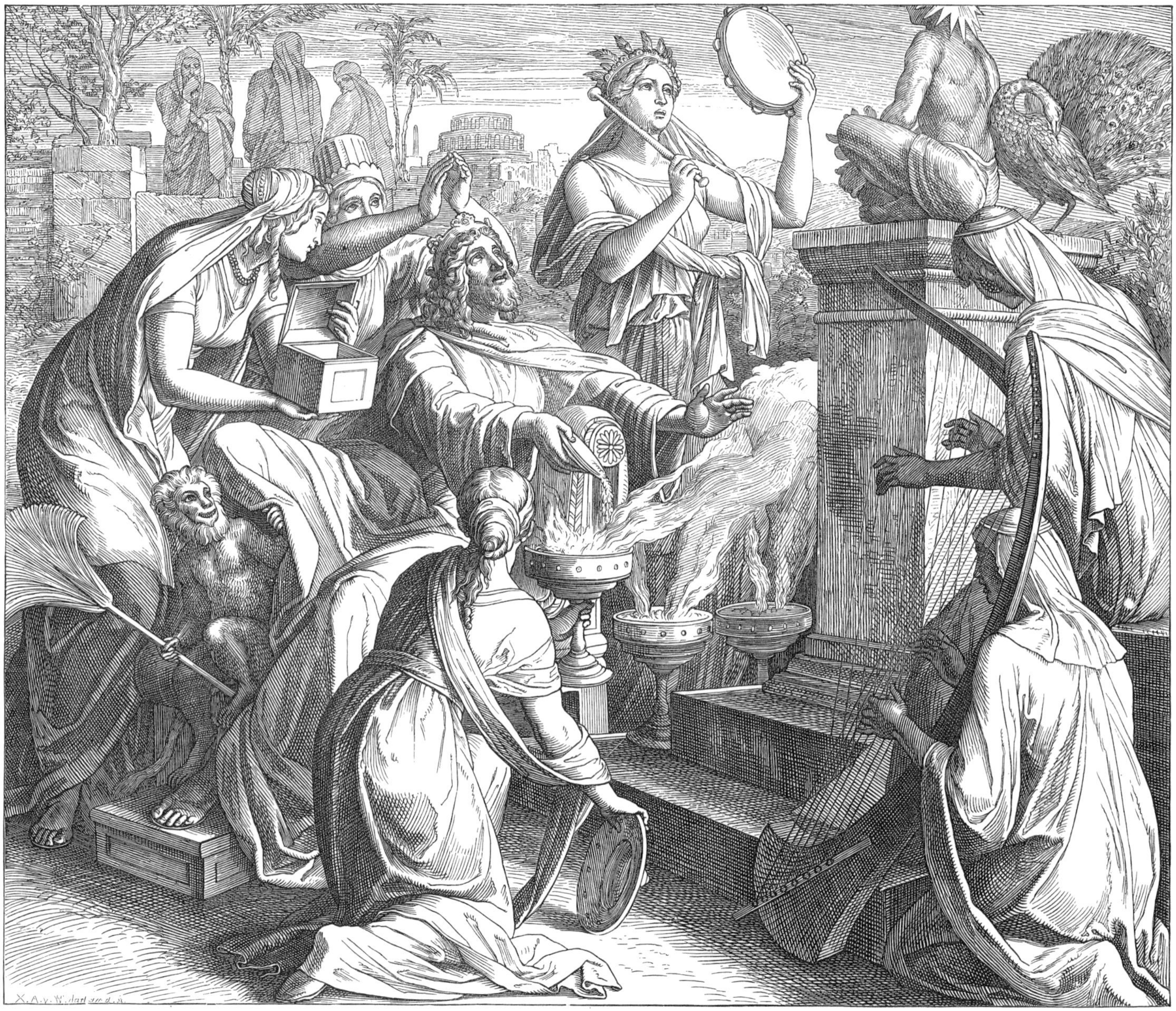

Solomon Falls Into Idolatry

The First Book of Kings. Chapter 11.

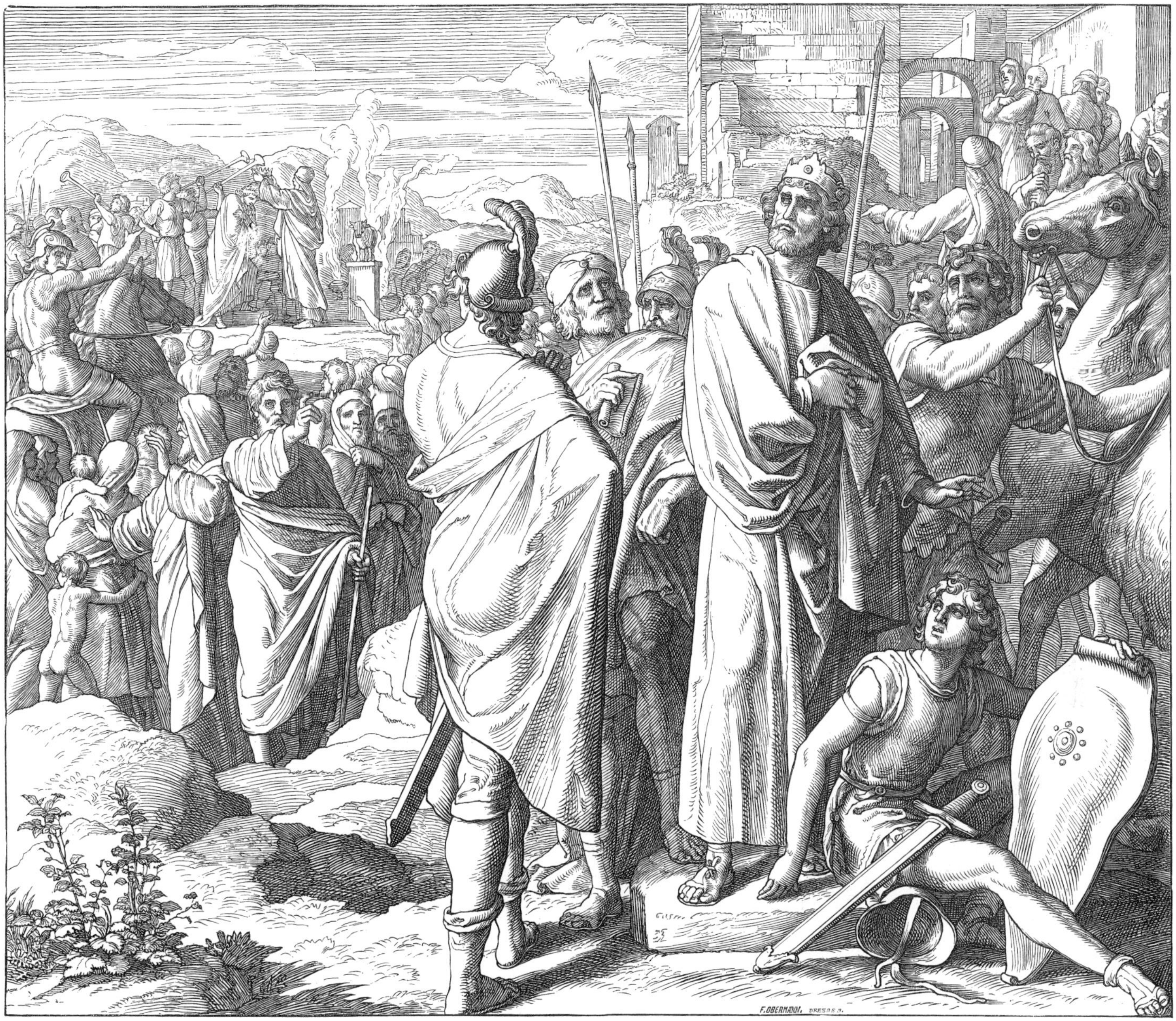

Rehoboam Succeeds Solomon

The First Book of Kings. Chapter 12.

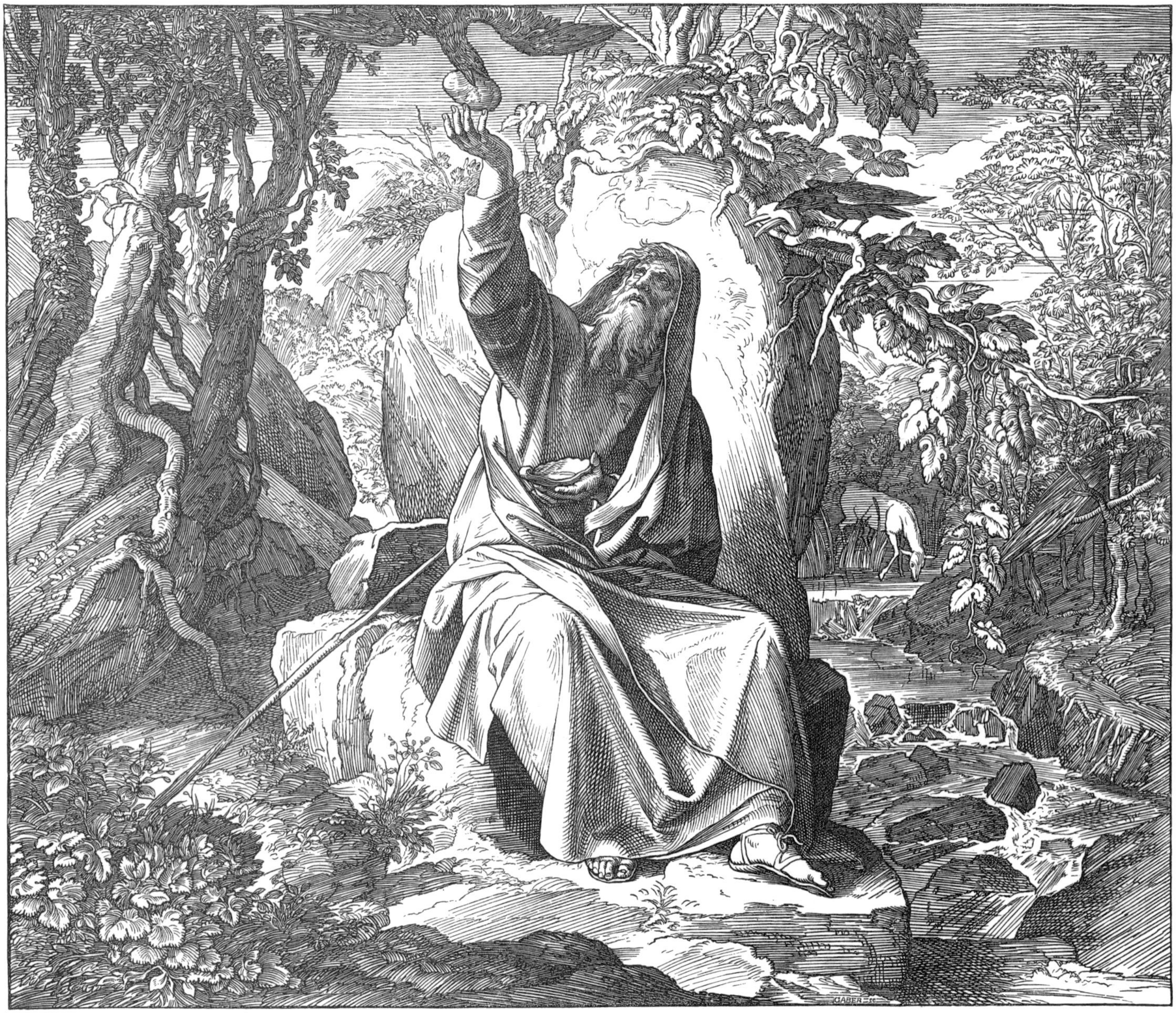

ELIJAH RECEIVES FOOD FROM THE RAVENS
The First Book of Kings. Chapter 17.

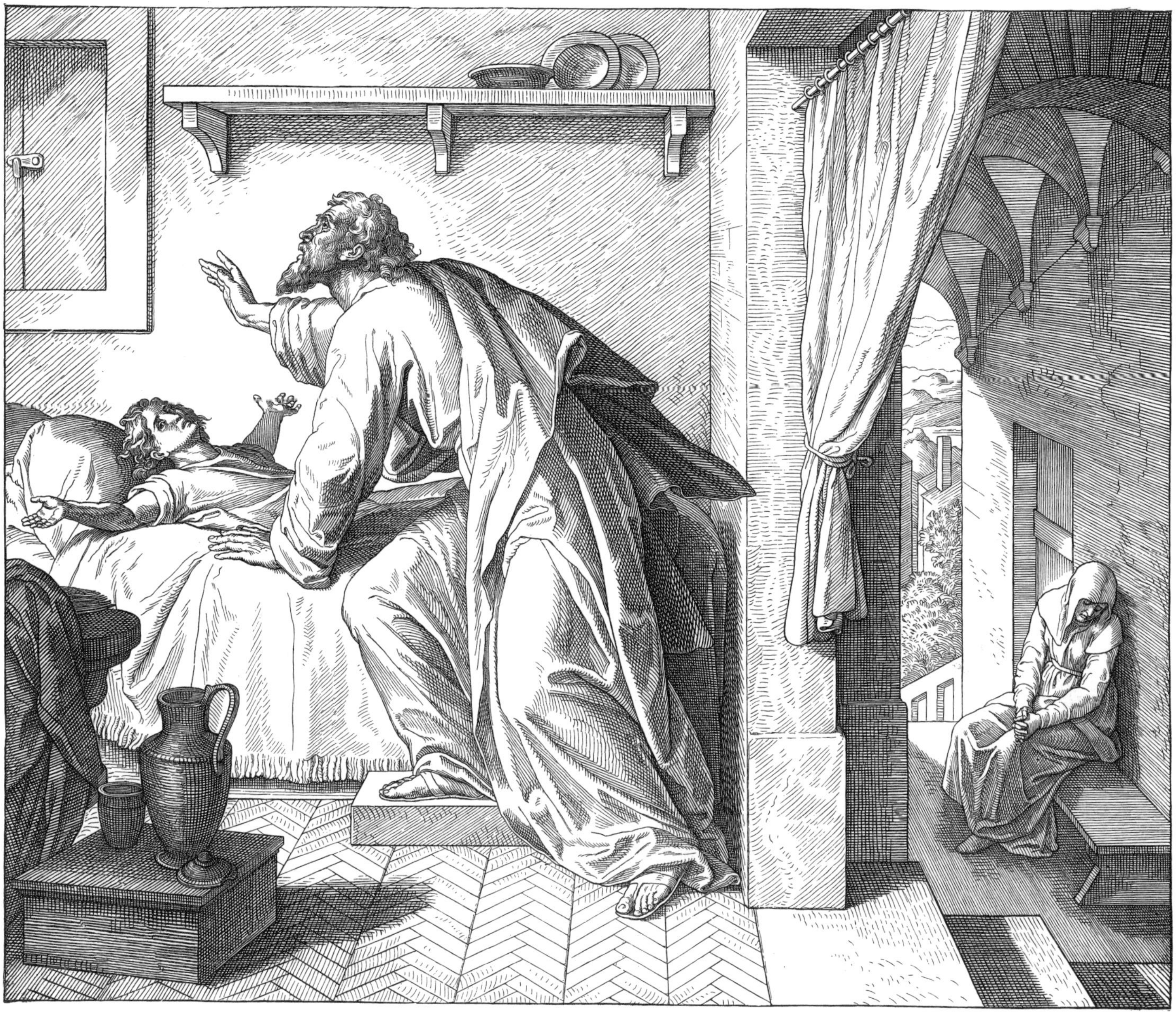

Elijah Revives the Widow's Son
The First Book of Kings. Chapter 17.

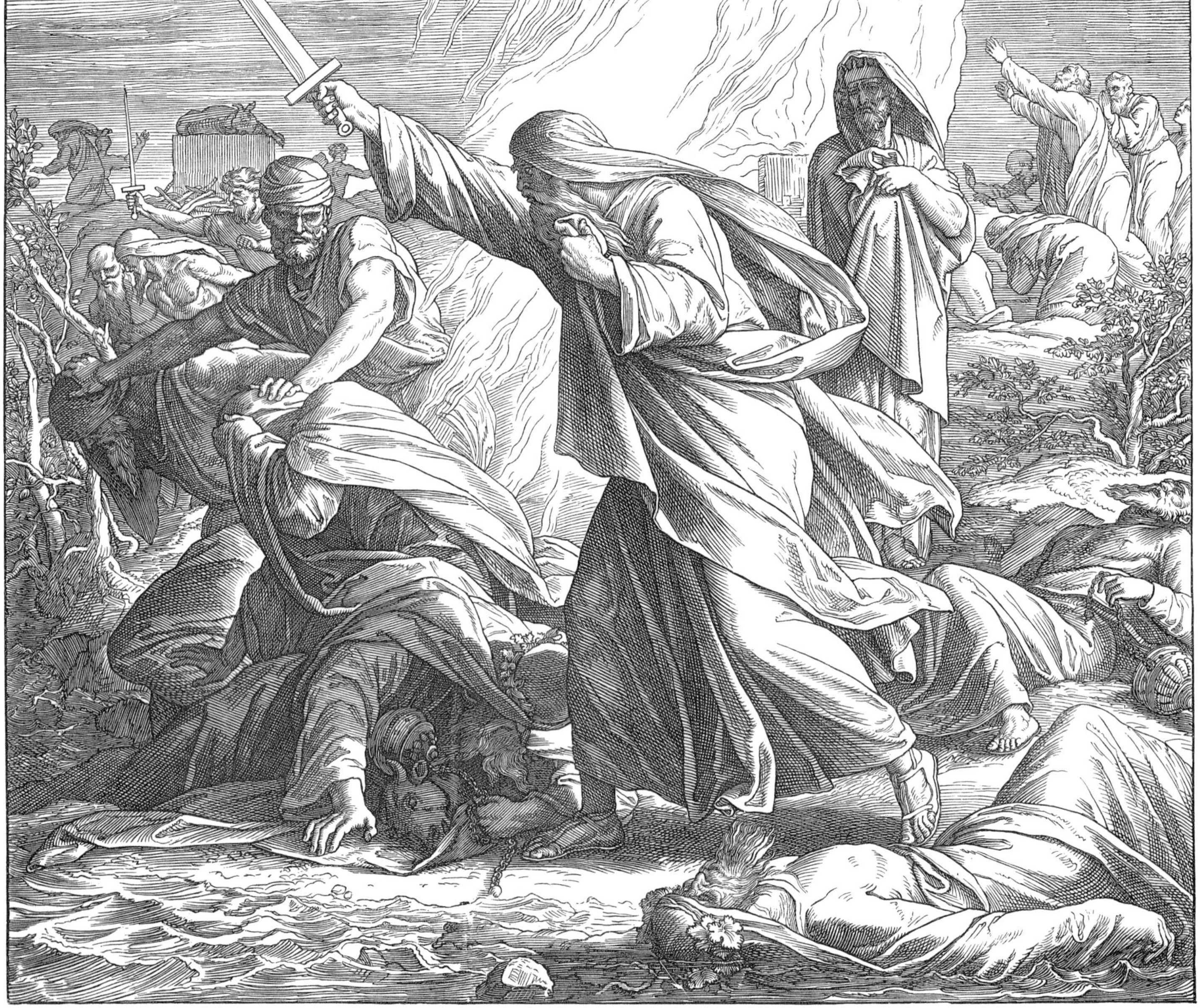

The Test of Baal's Prophets

The First Book of Kings. Chapter 18.

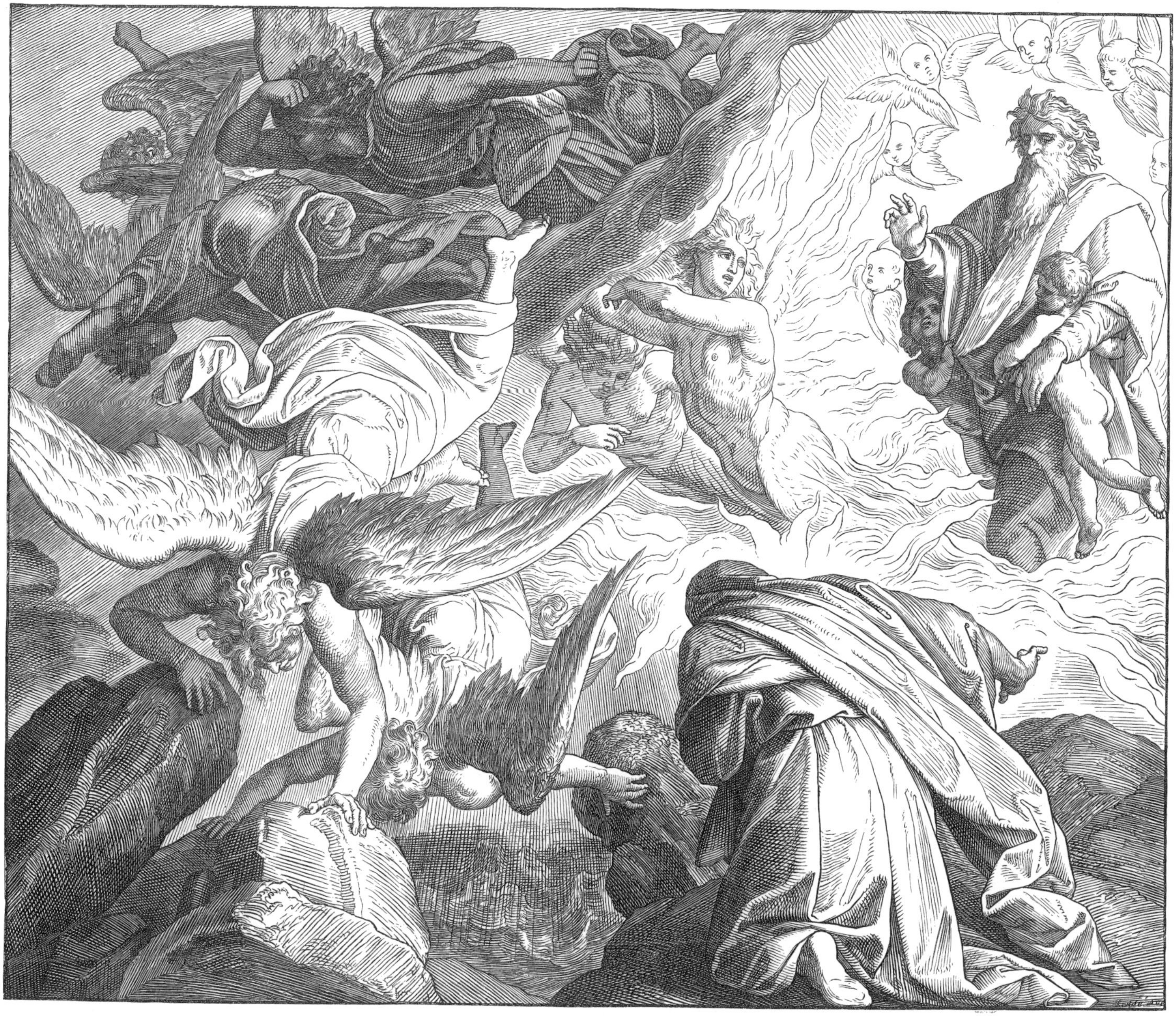

The Lord Appears to Elijah on the Mount
The First Book of Kings. Chapter 19.

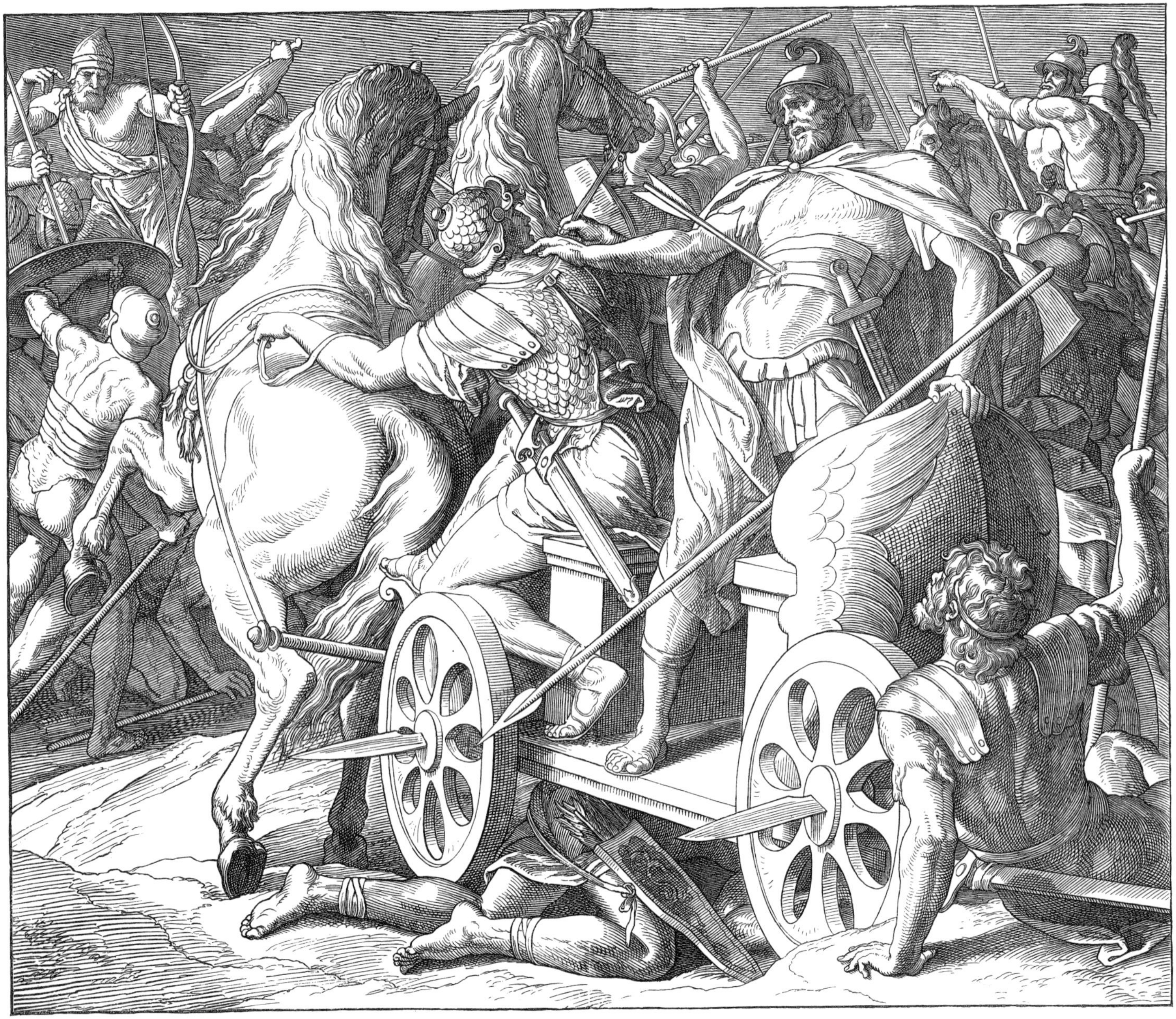

AHAB IS SLAIN IN BATTLE

The First Book of Kings. Chapter 22.

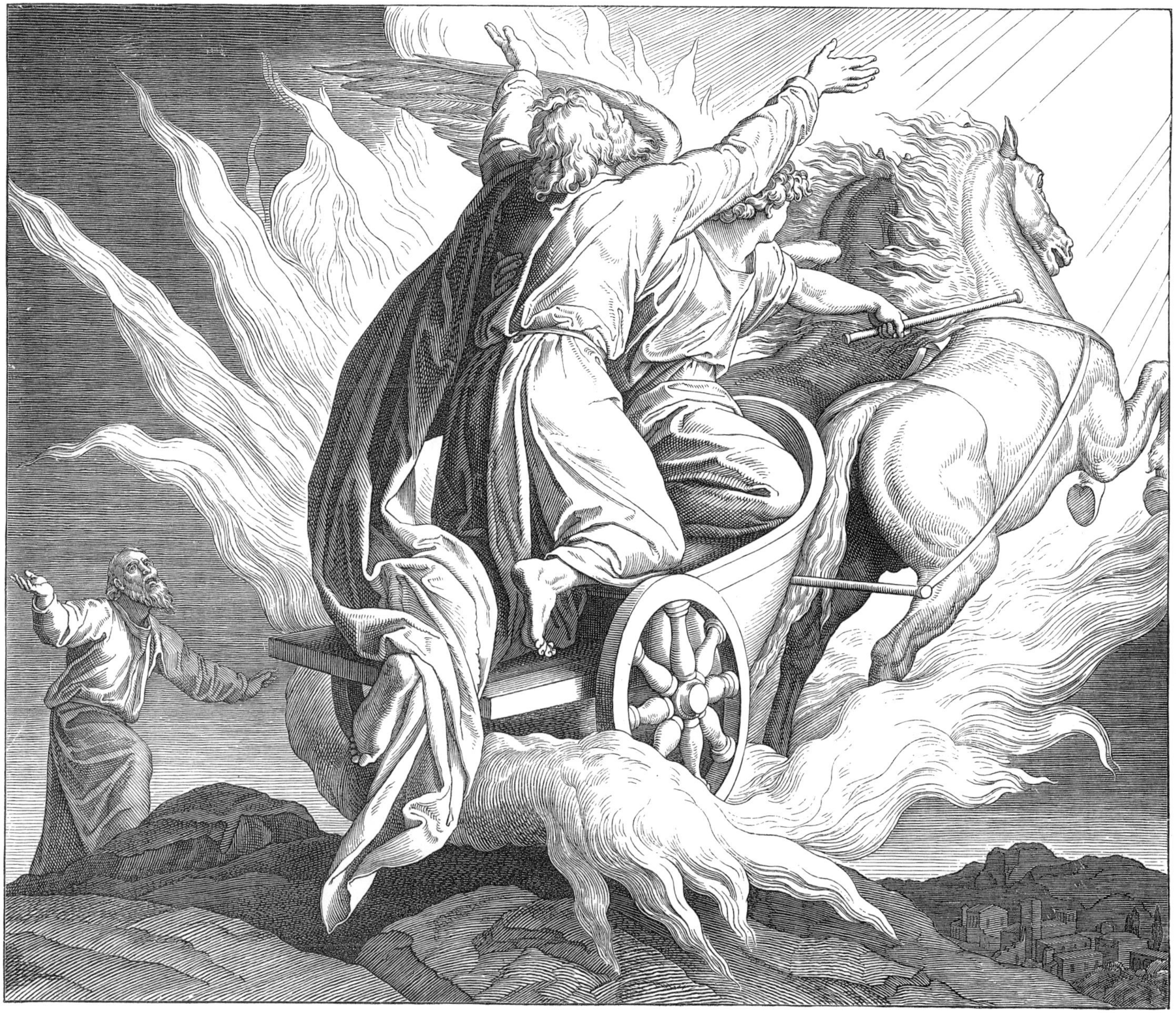

Elijah Ascends to Heaven

The Second Book of Kings. Chapter 2.

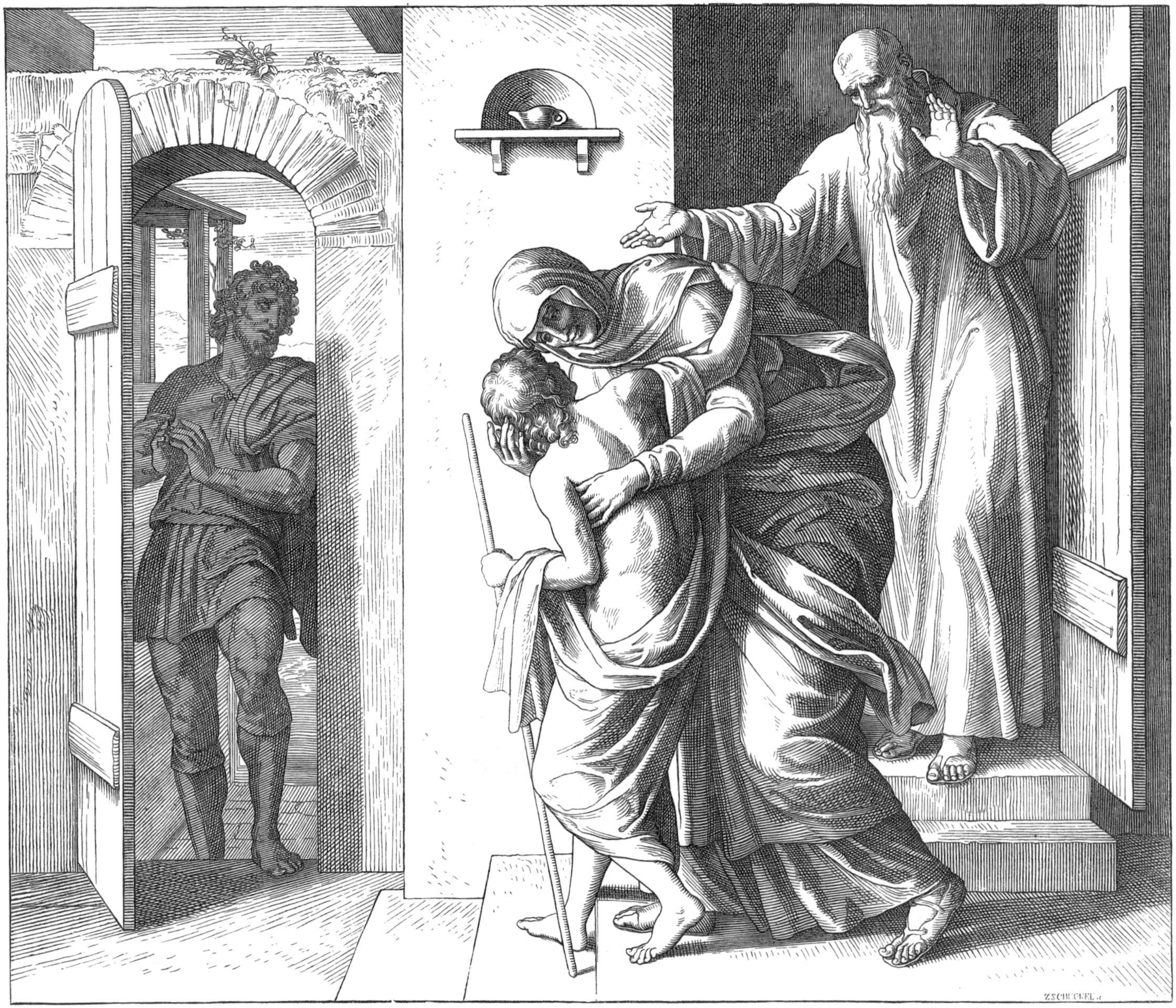

Elisha Raises the Shunammite's Son from the Dead
The Second Book of Kings. Chapter 4.

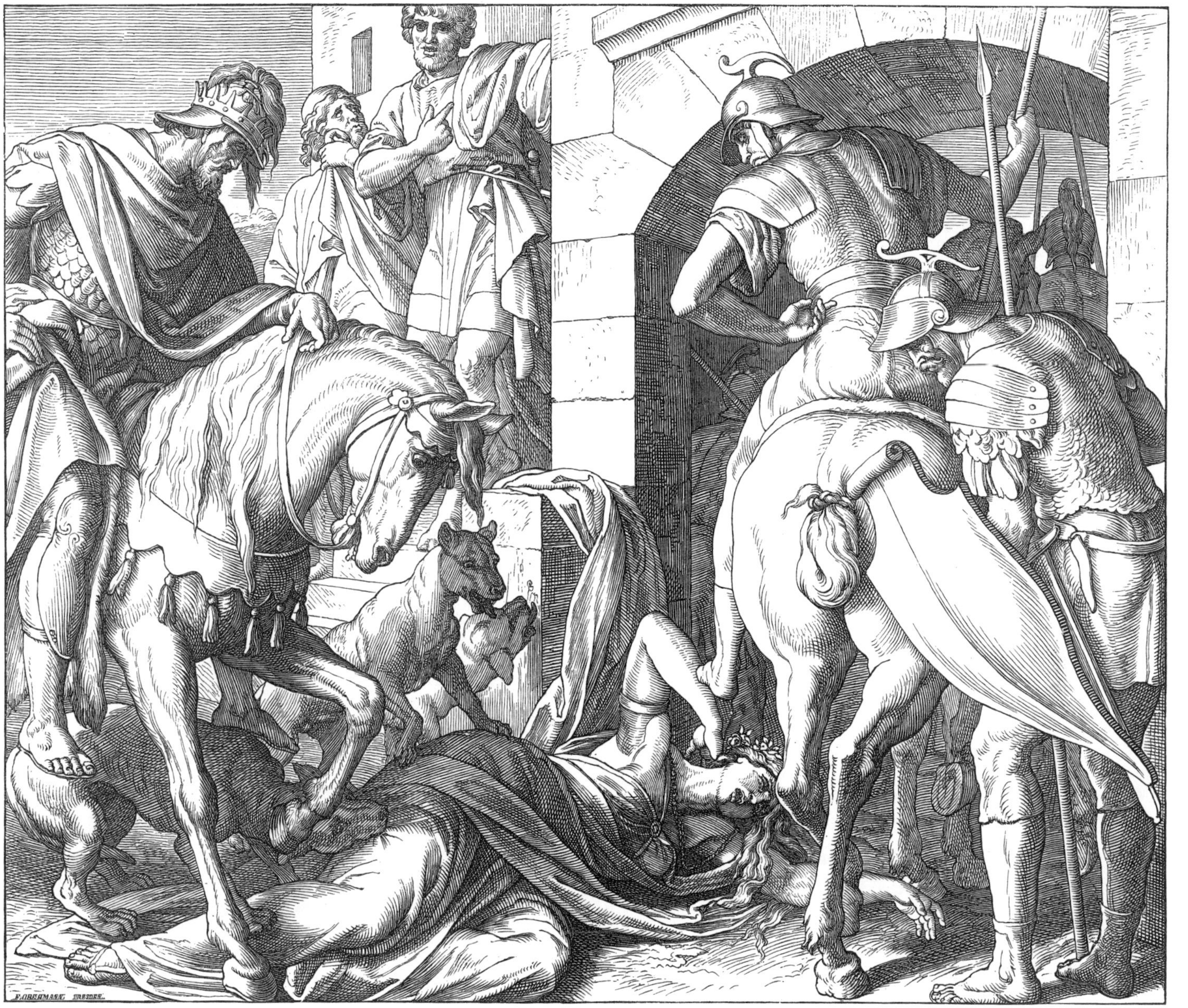

JEZEBEL'S END

The Second Book of Kings. Chapter 9.

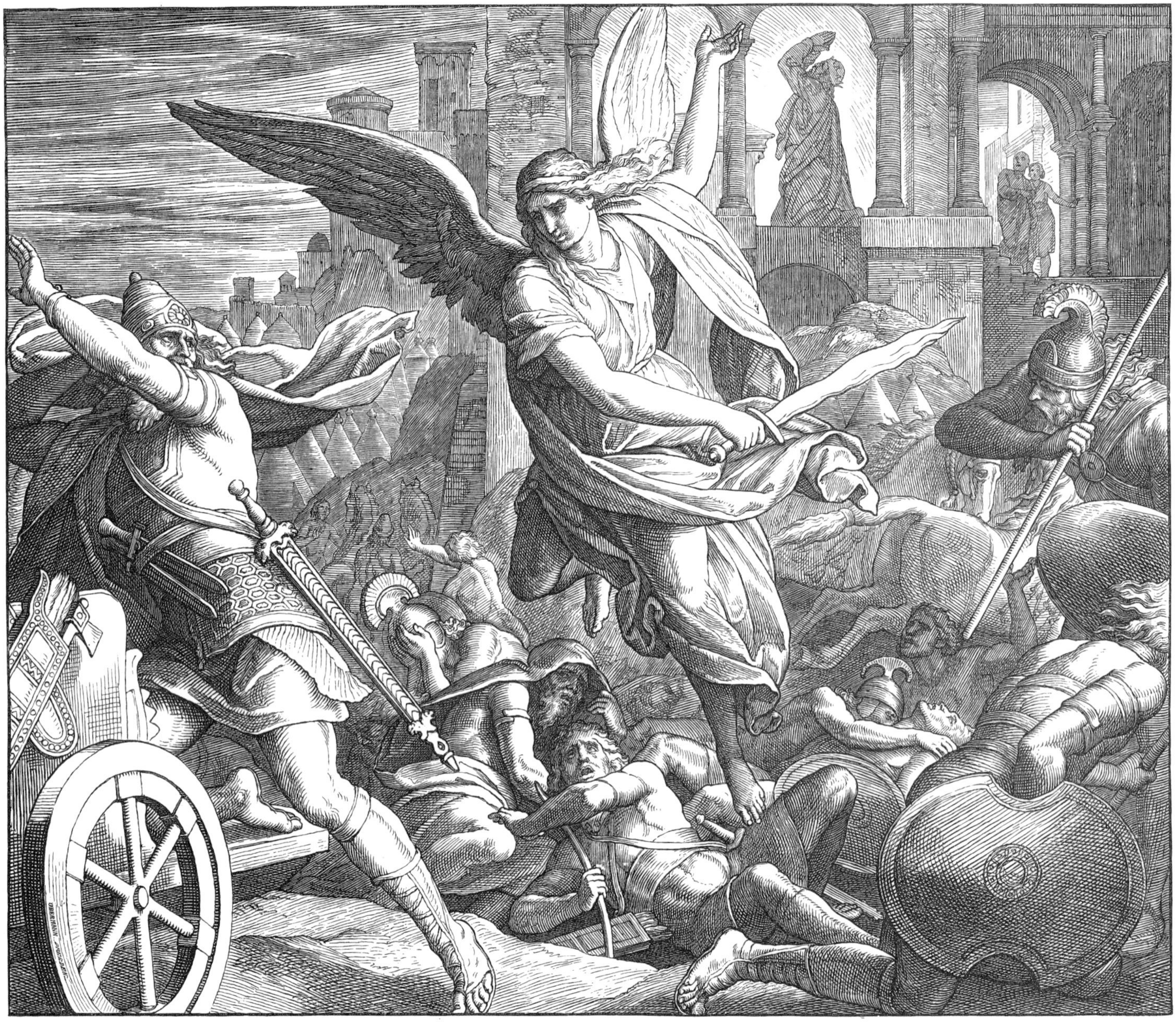

The Angel of the Lord Smites the Assyrians
The Second Book of Kings. Chapter 19.

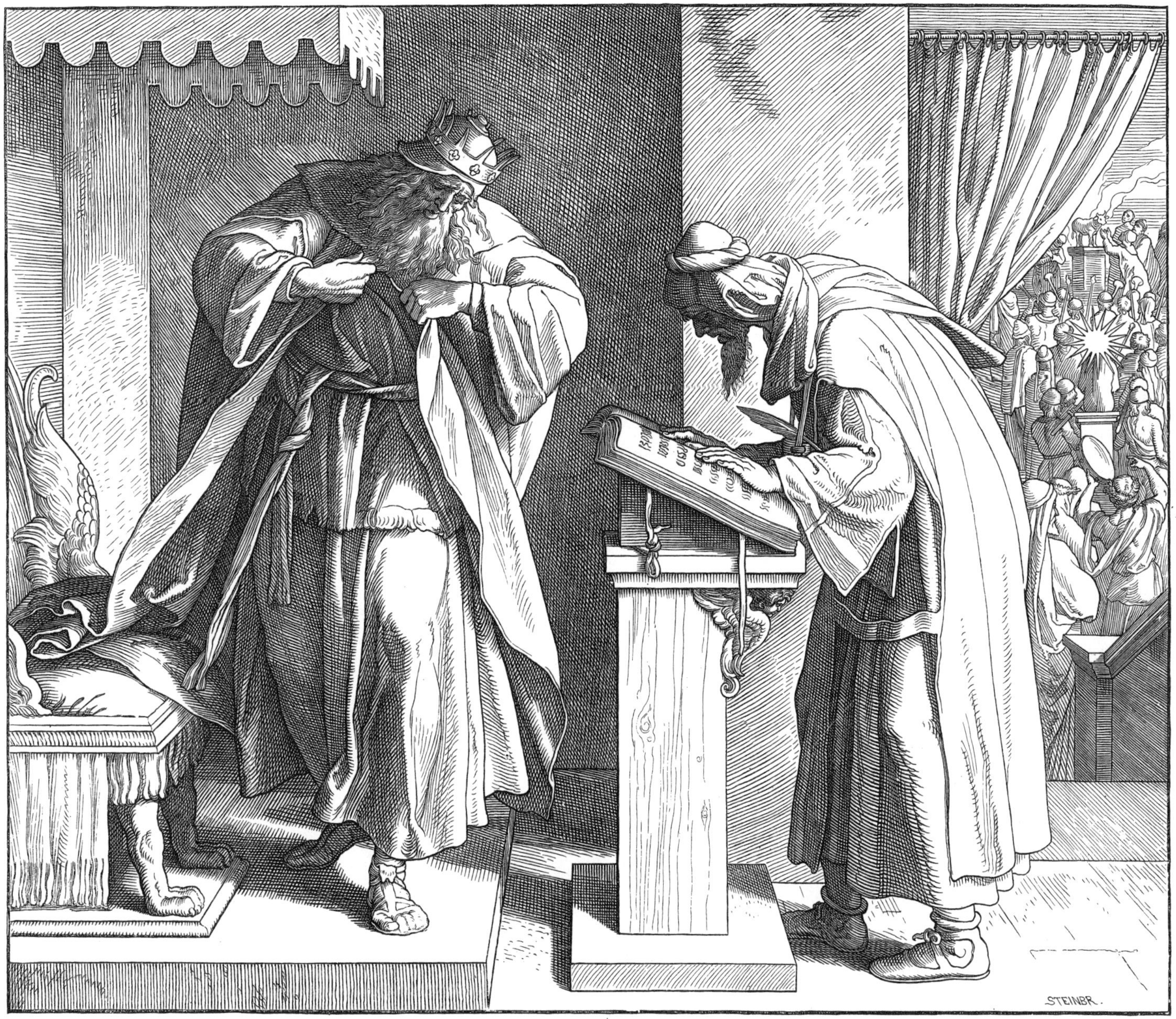

Josiah Learns the Word of the Lord from a Book of Law
The Second Book of Kings. Chapter 22.

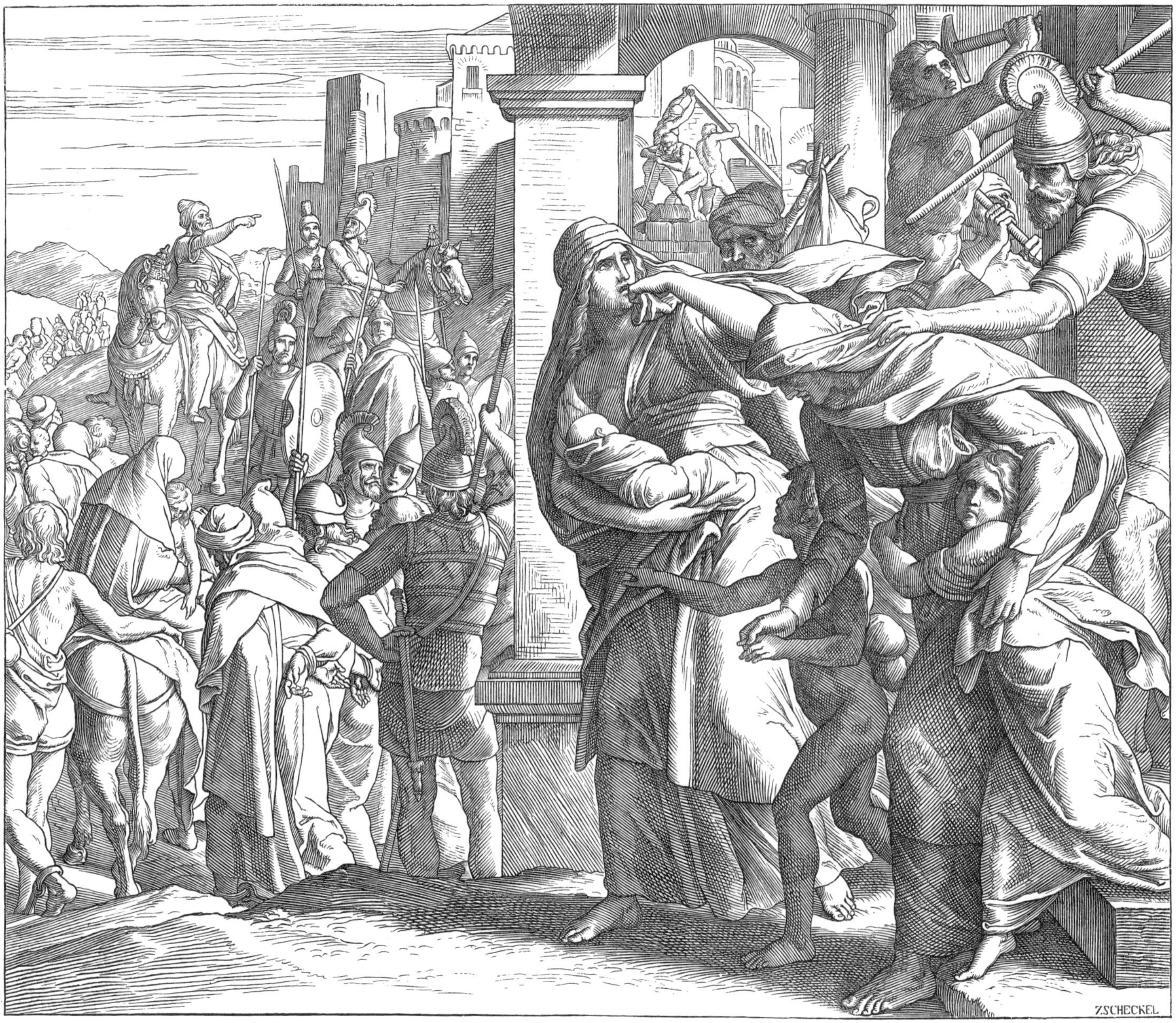

Jerusalem Is Despoiled

The Second Book of Kings. Chapter 25.

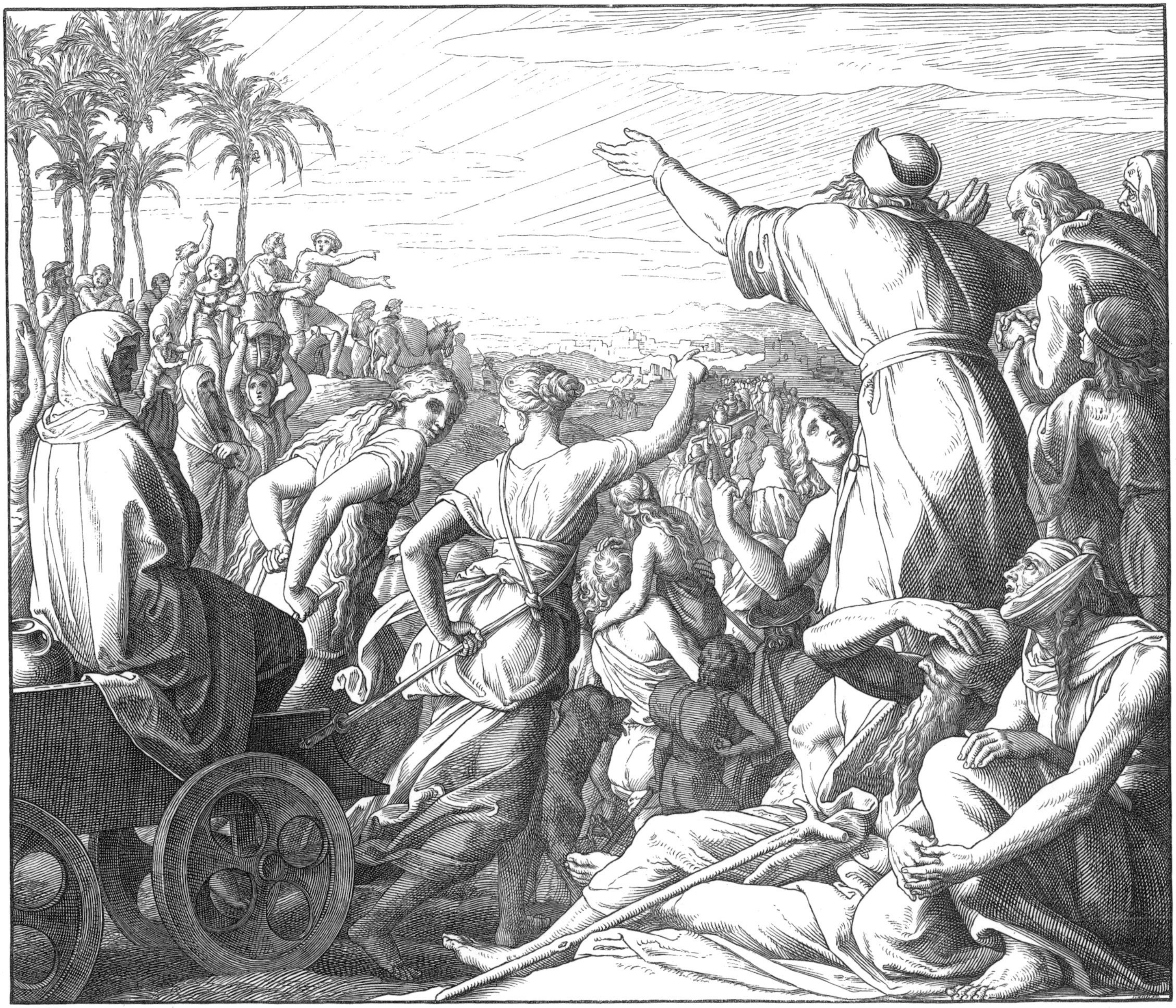

The Return of the Exiles to Jerusalem
The Book of Ezra. Chapter 1.

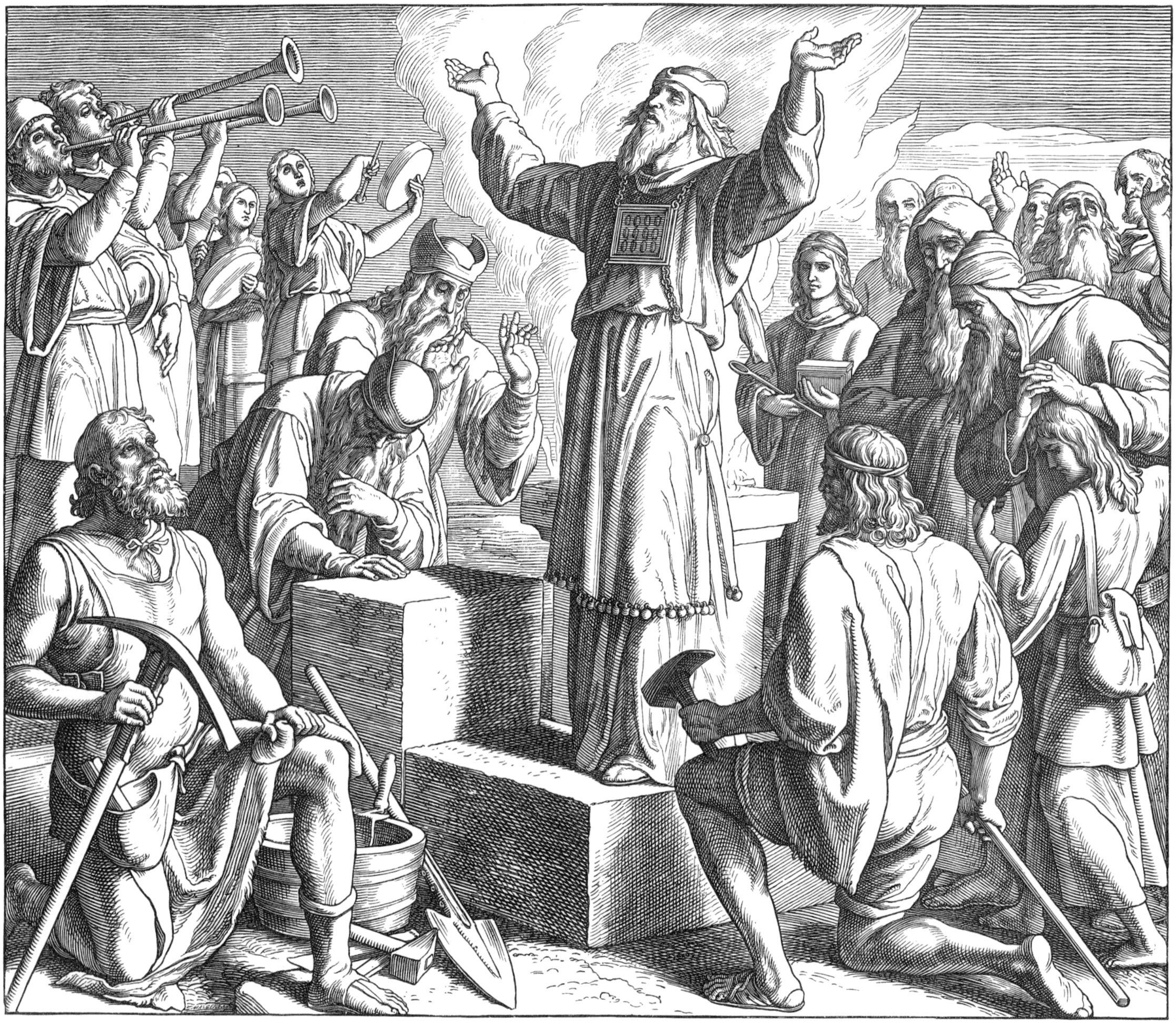

THE FOUNDATION OF THE TEMPLE IS LAID

The Book of Ezra. Chapter 3.

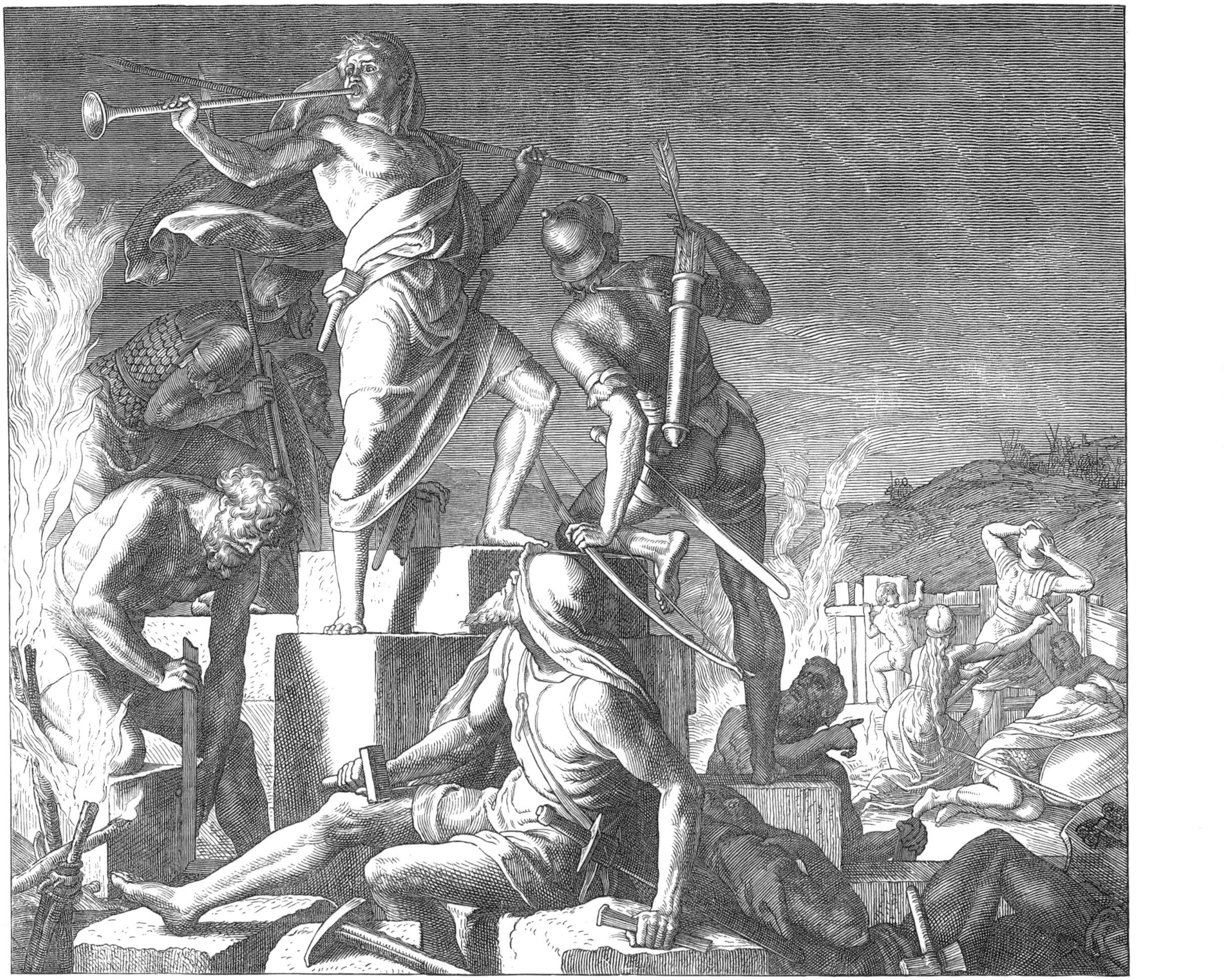

Defending the Temple Walls
The Book of Nehemiah. Chapter 4.

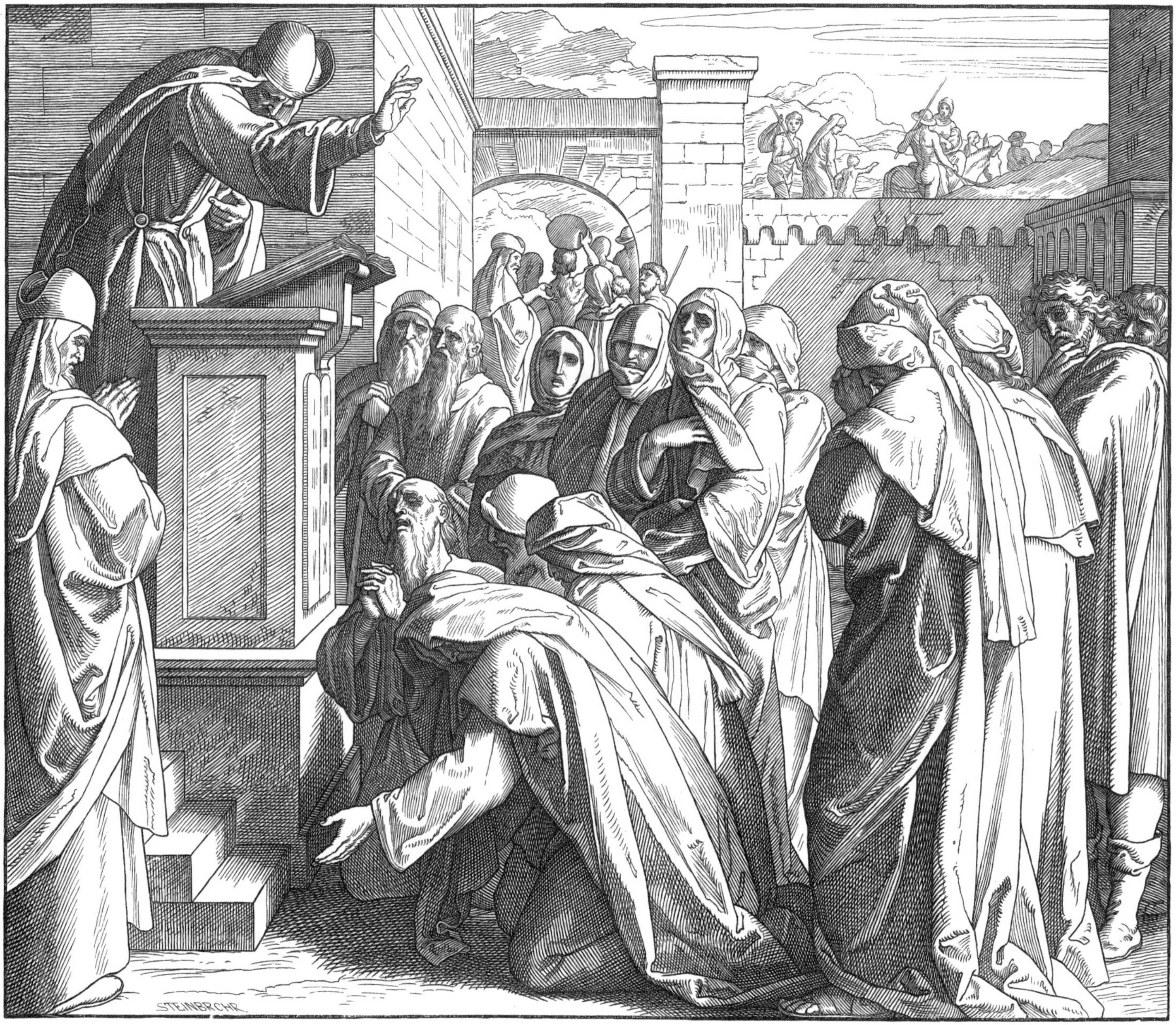

The People Repent

The Book of Nehemiah. Chapter 9.

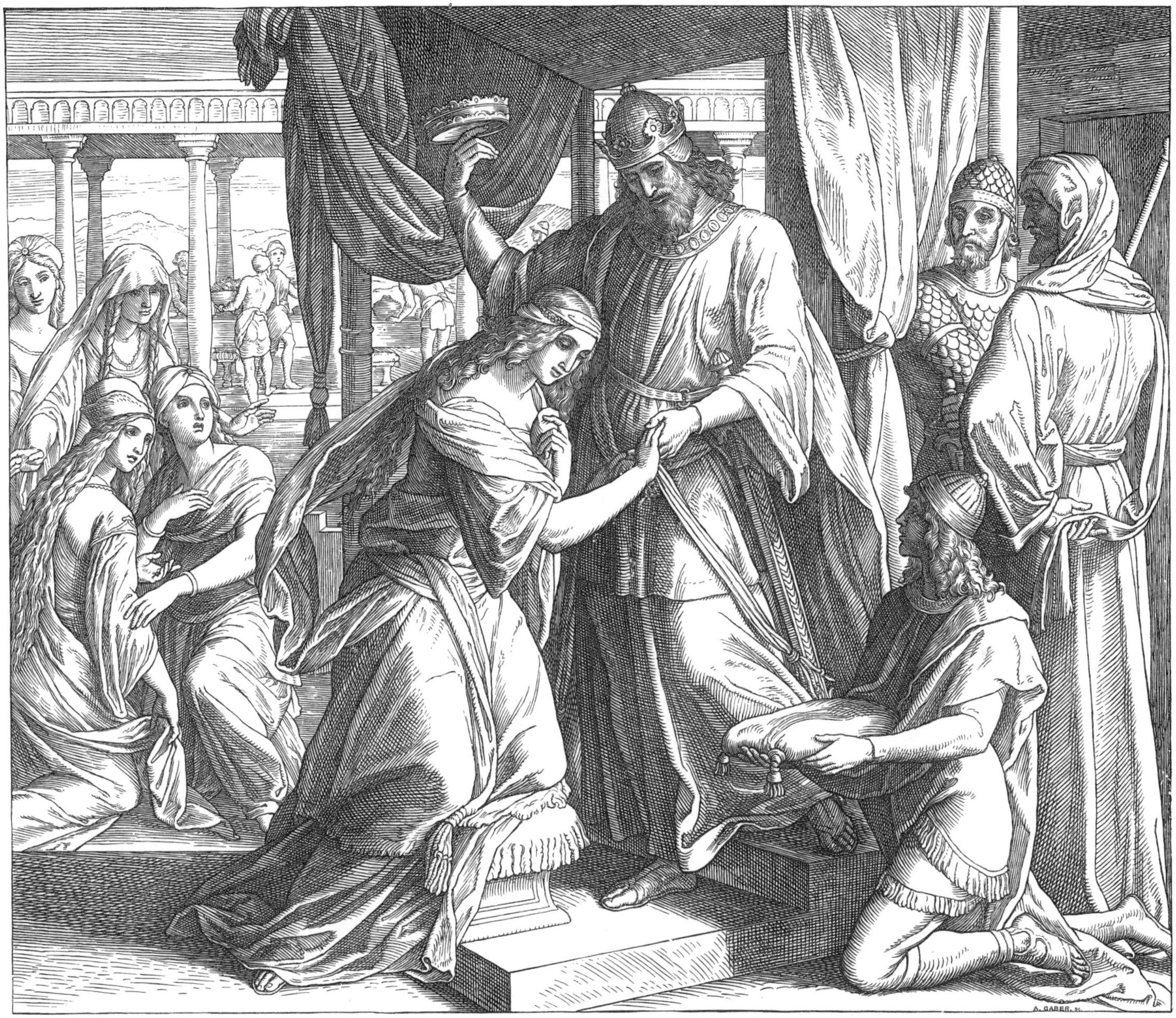

Esther Is Made Queen by King Ahasuerus

The Book of Esther. Chapter 2.

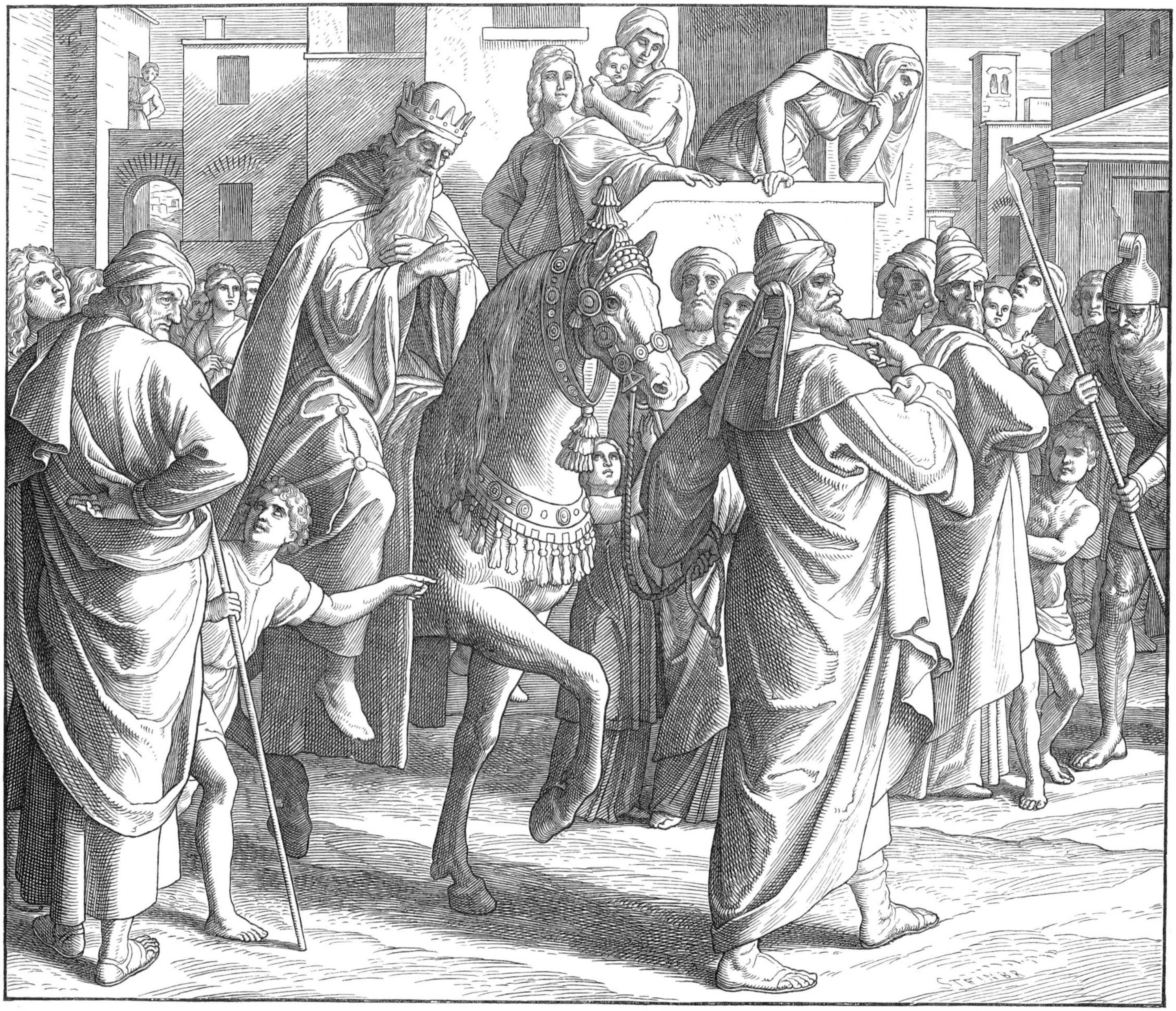

Mordecai Is Honored

The Book of Esther. Chapter 6.

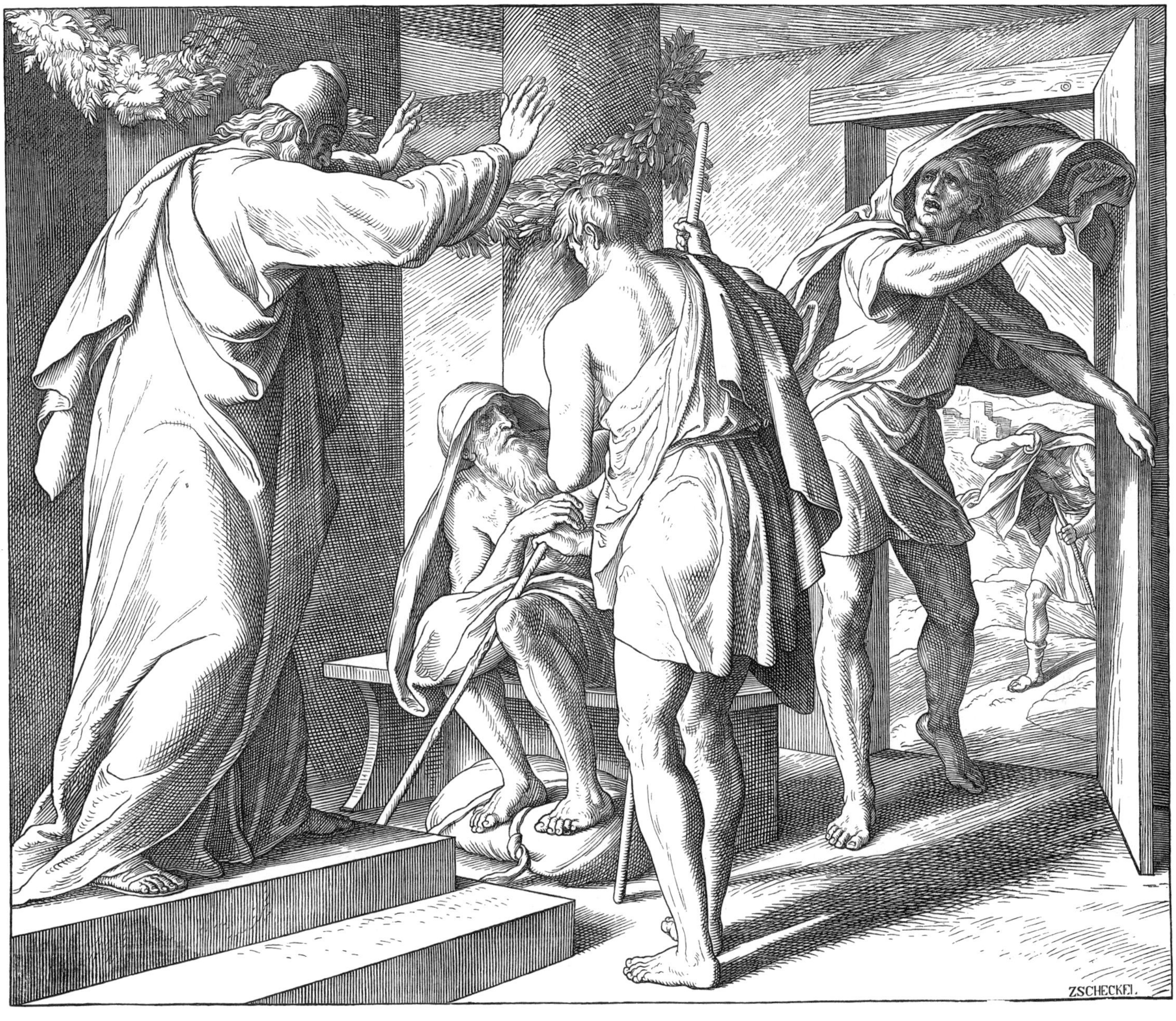

Job's Adversity and Forbearance

The Book of Job. Chapter 1.

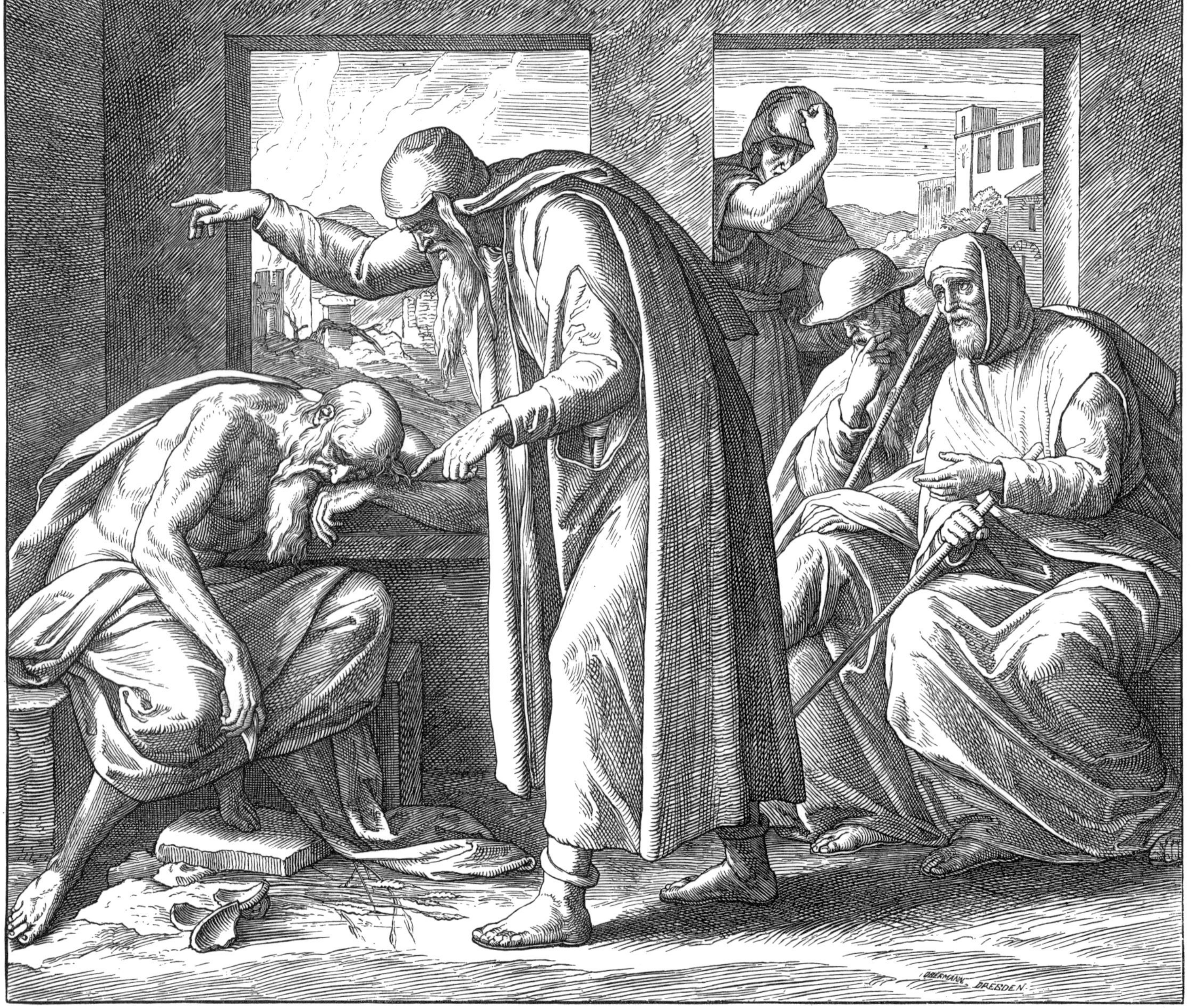

Job Laments His State

The Book of Job. Chapter 2.

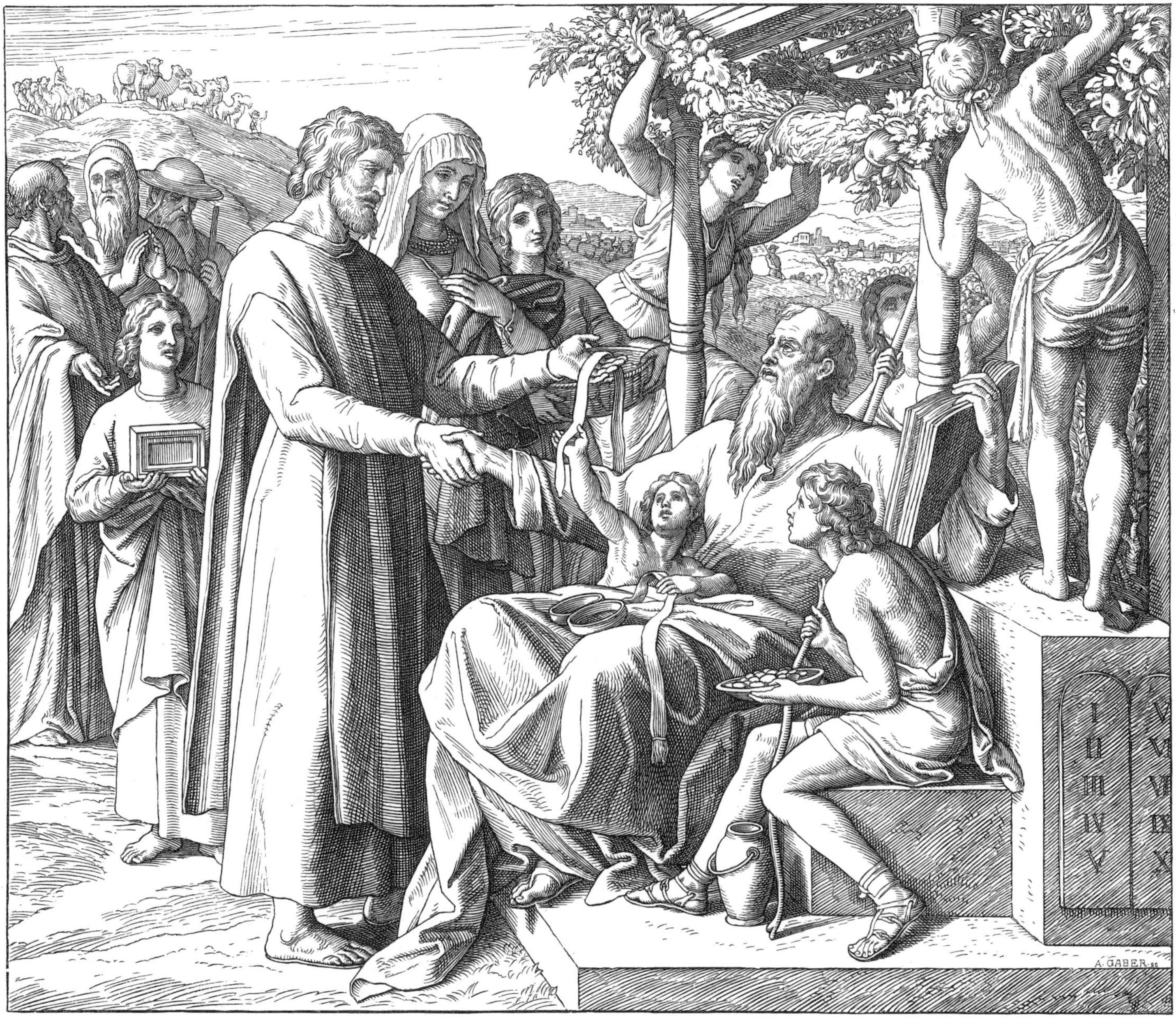

JOB RECEIVES GOD'S BLESSING

The Book of Job. Chapter 42.

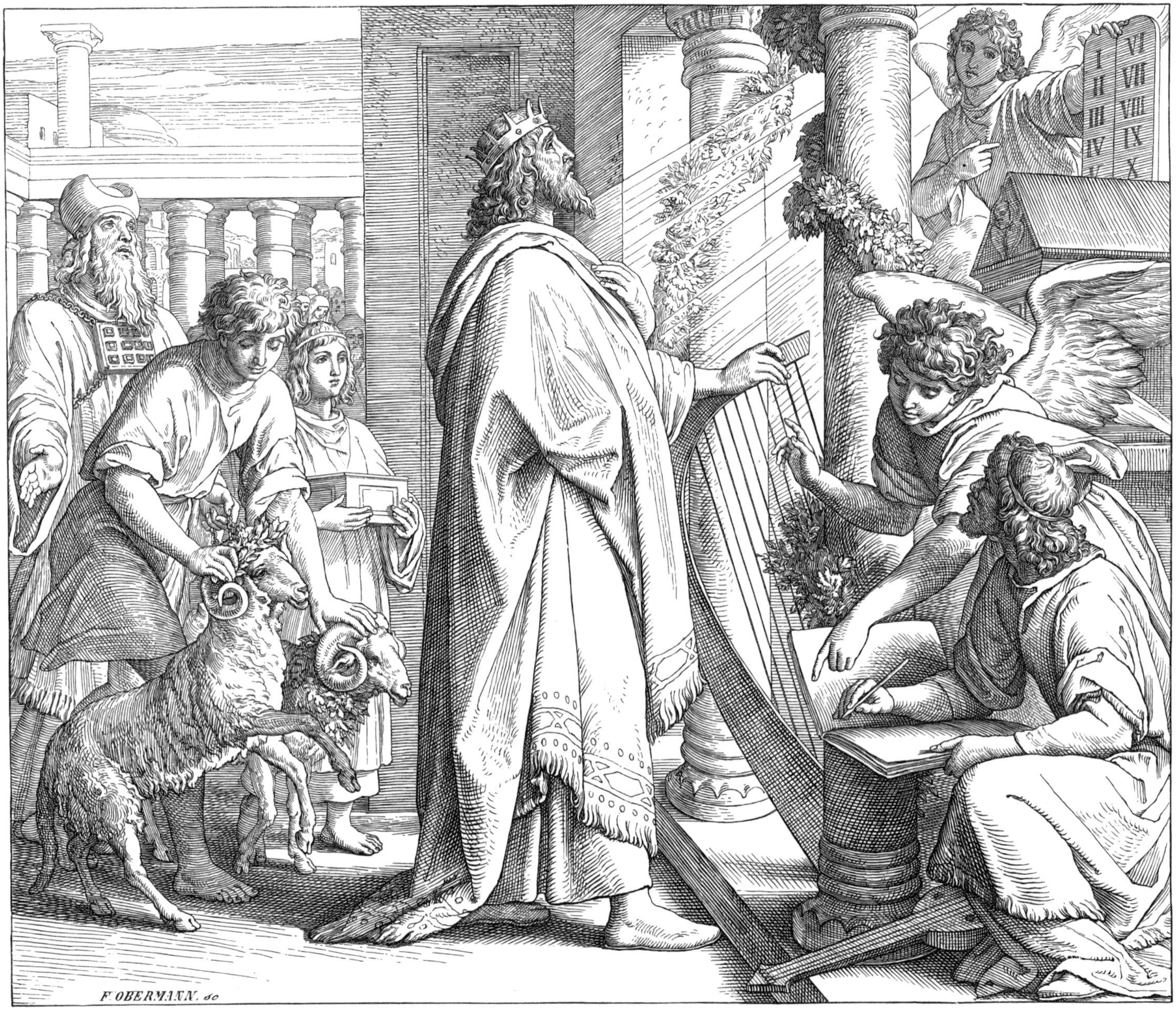

David, the Psalmist—Giving Thanks

Psalms 43 and 106.

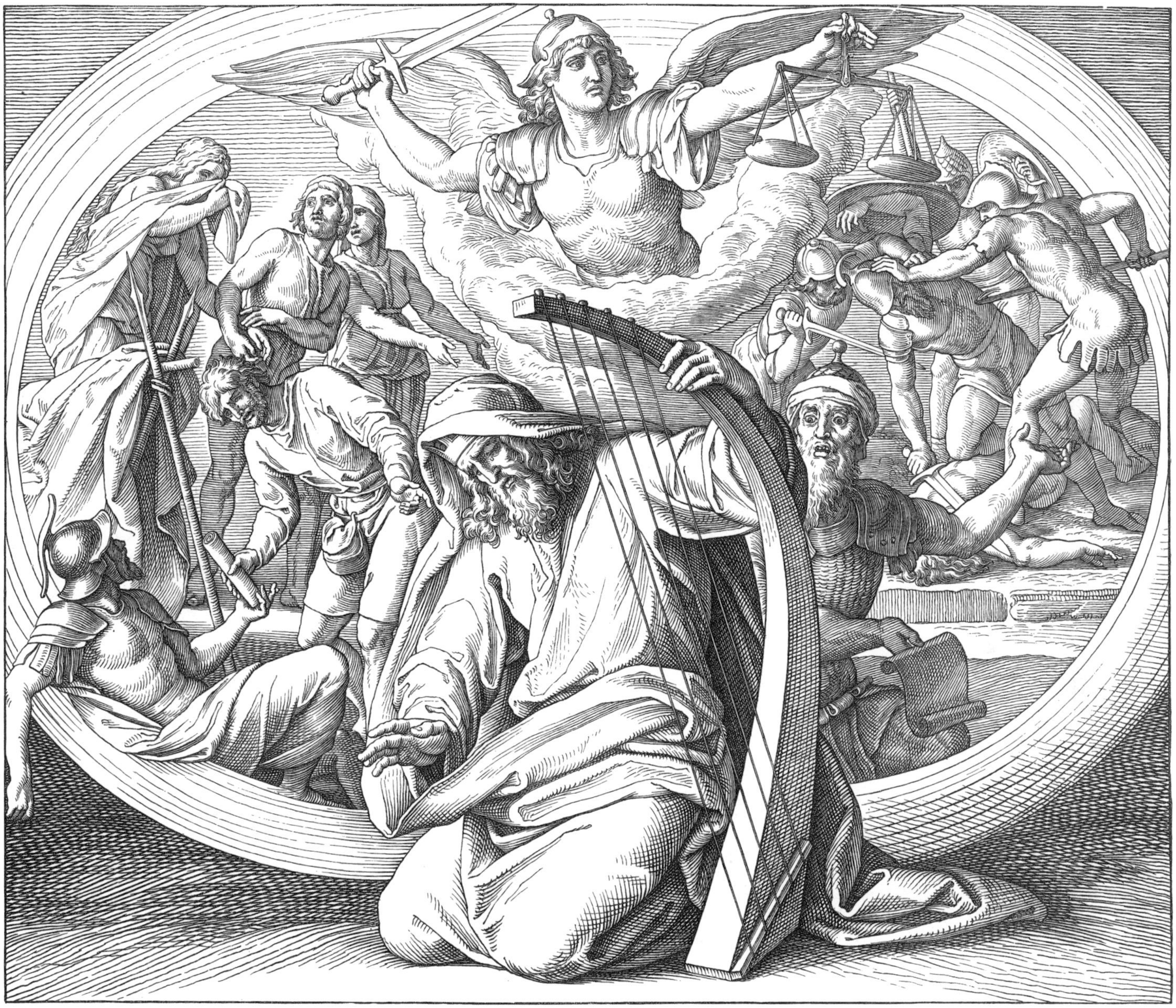

David, the Psalmist—Repentant

Psalm 51.

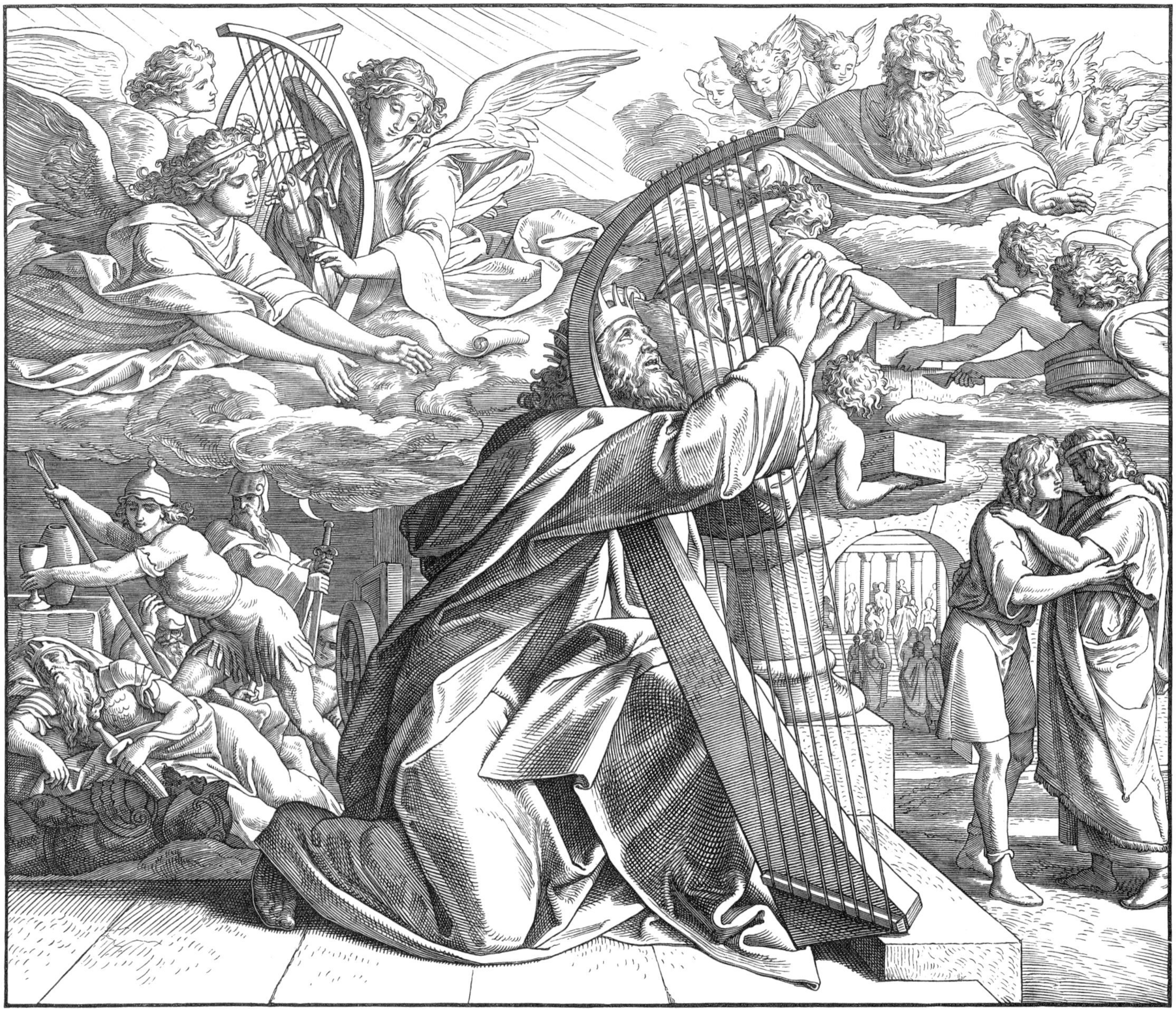

David, the Psalmist—Asking Forgiveness
Psalm 51.

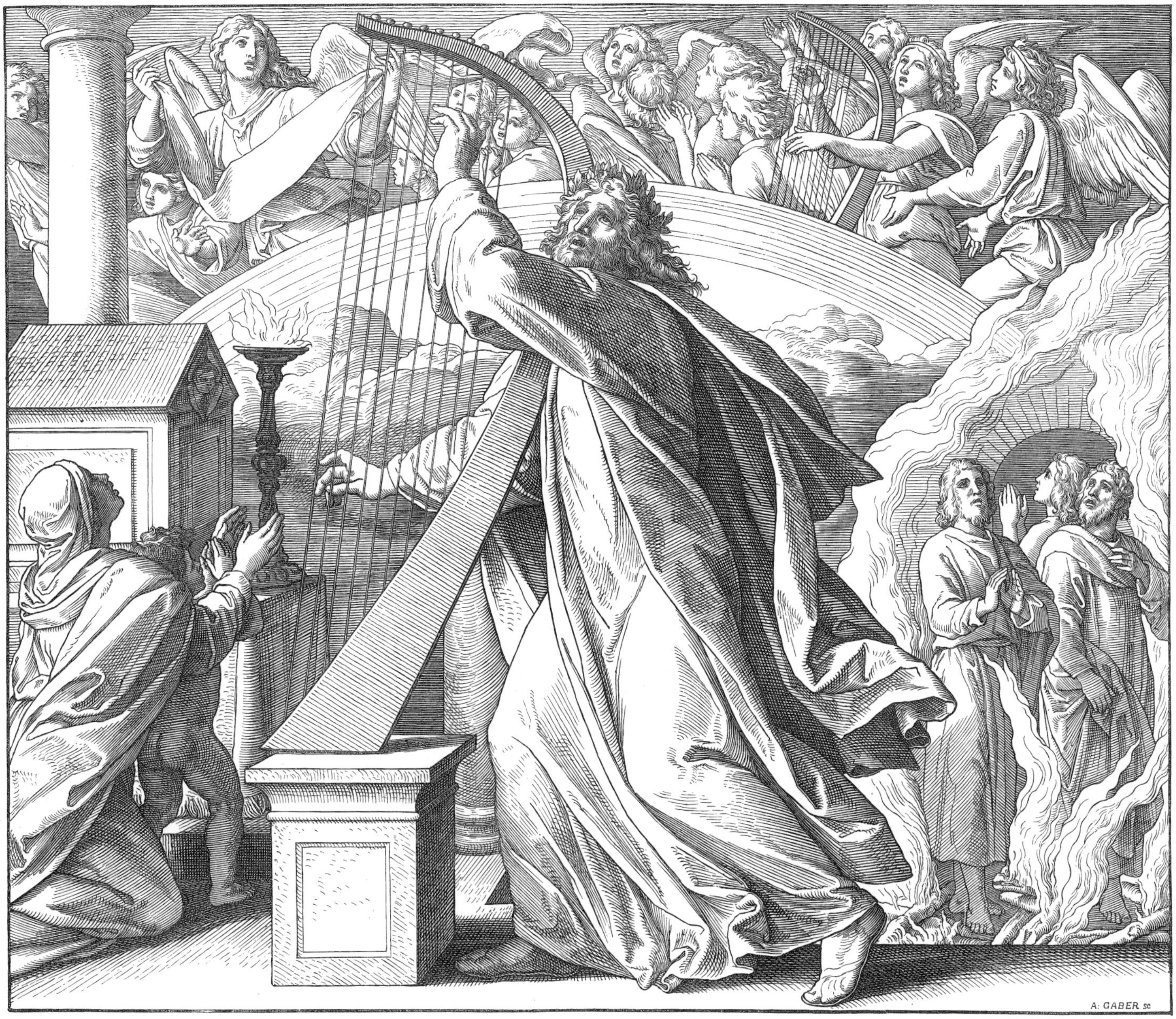

David, the Psalmist—Praising the Lord

Psalms 103 and 106.

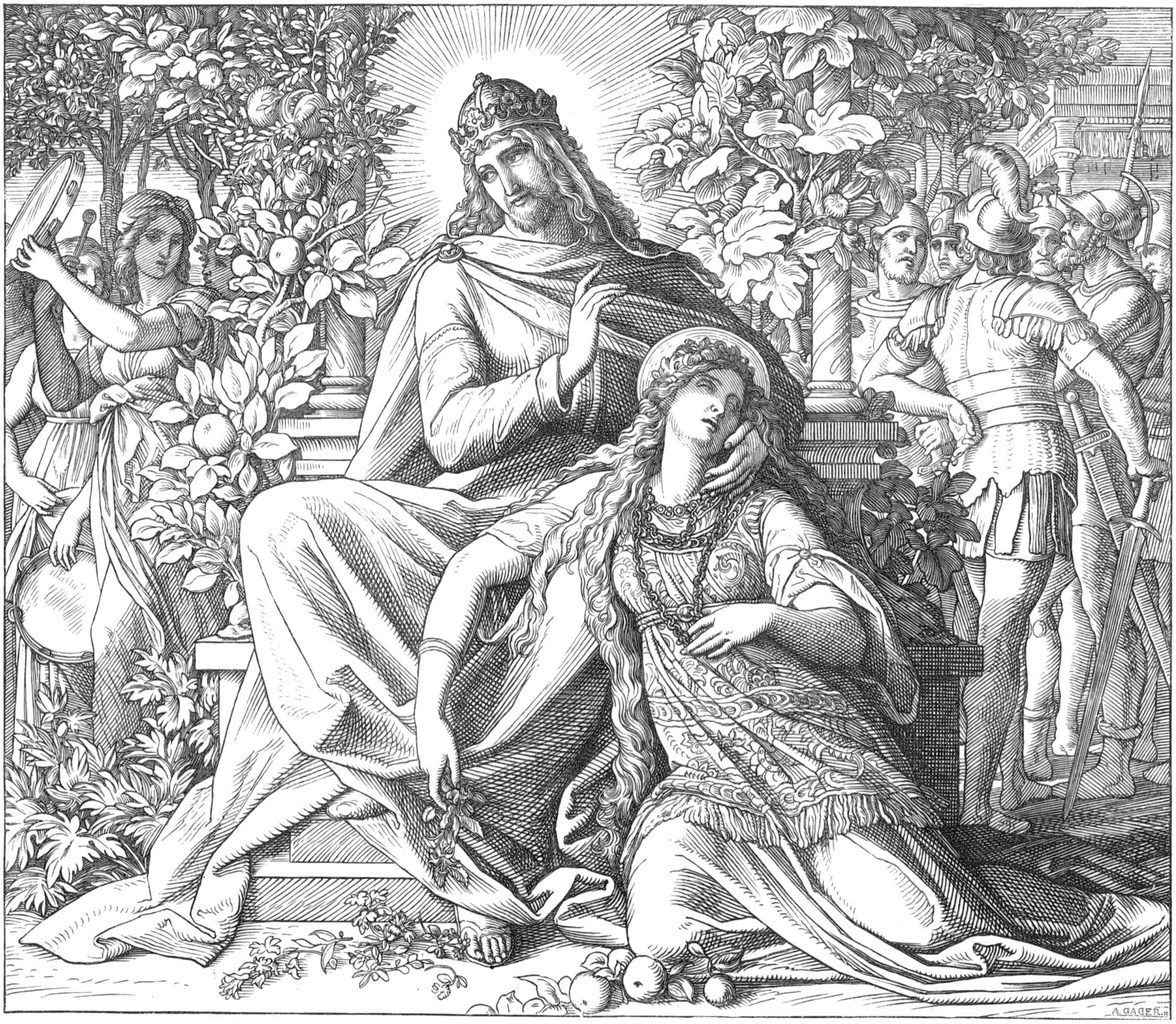

THE BELOVED RESTS, PROTECTED BY HER LOVER

The Song of Solomon. Chapter 2.

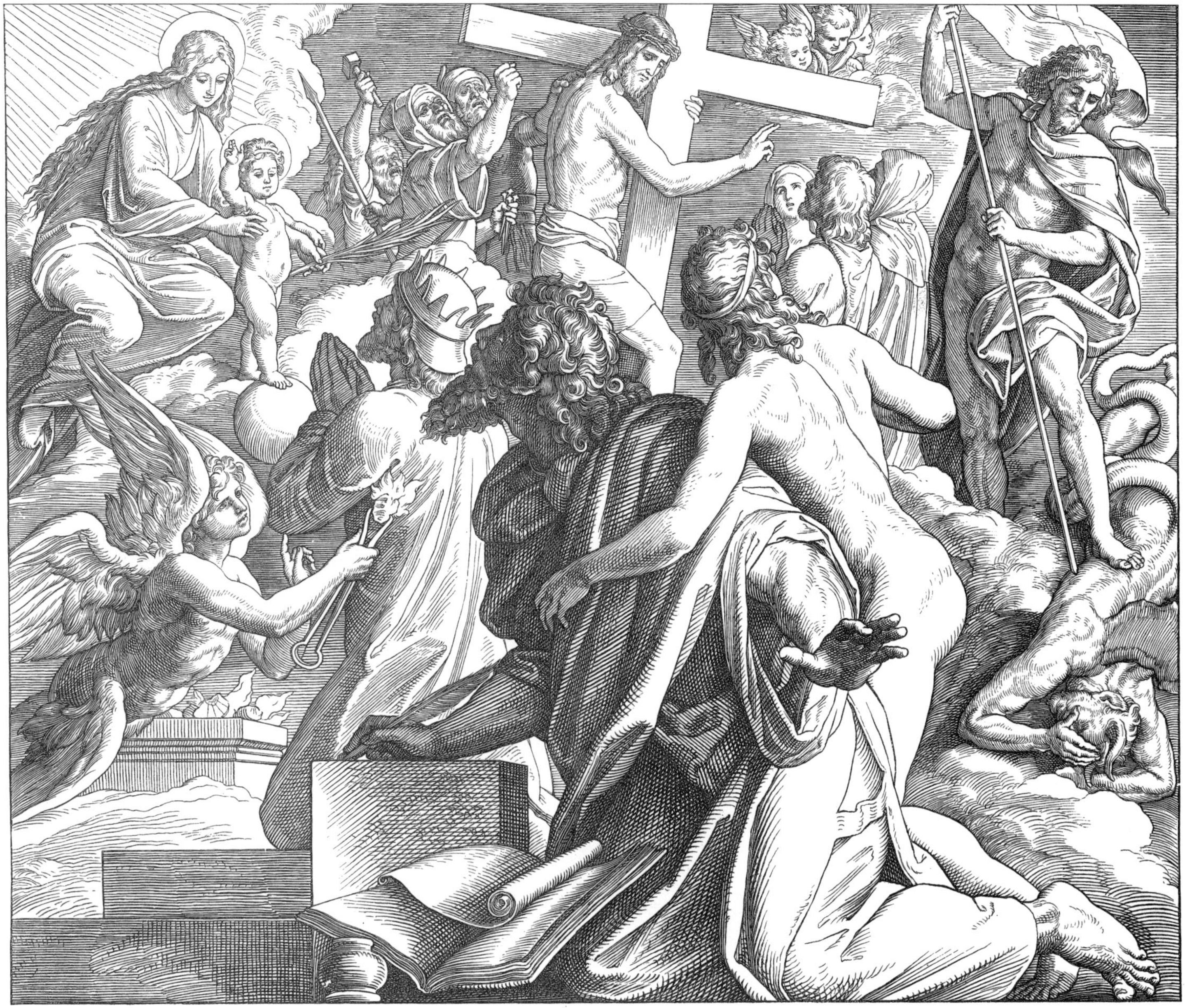

The Prophet Isaiah

The Book of the Prophet Isaiah. Chapters 9 and 53.

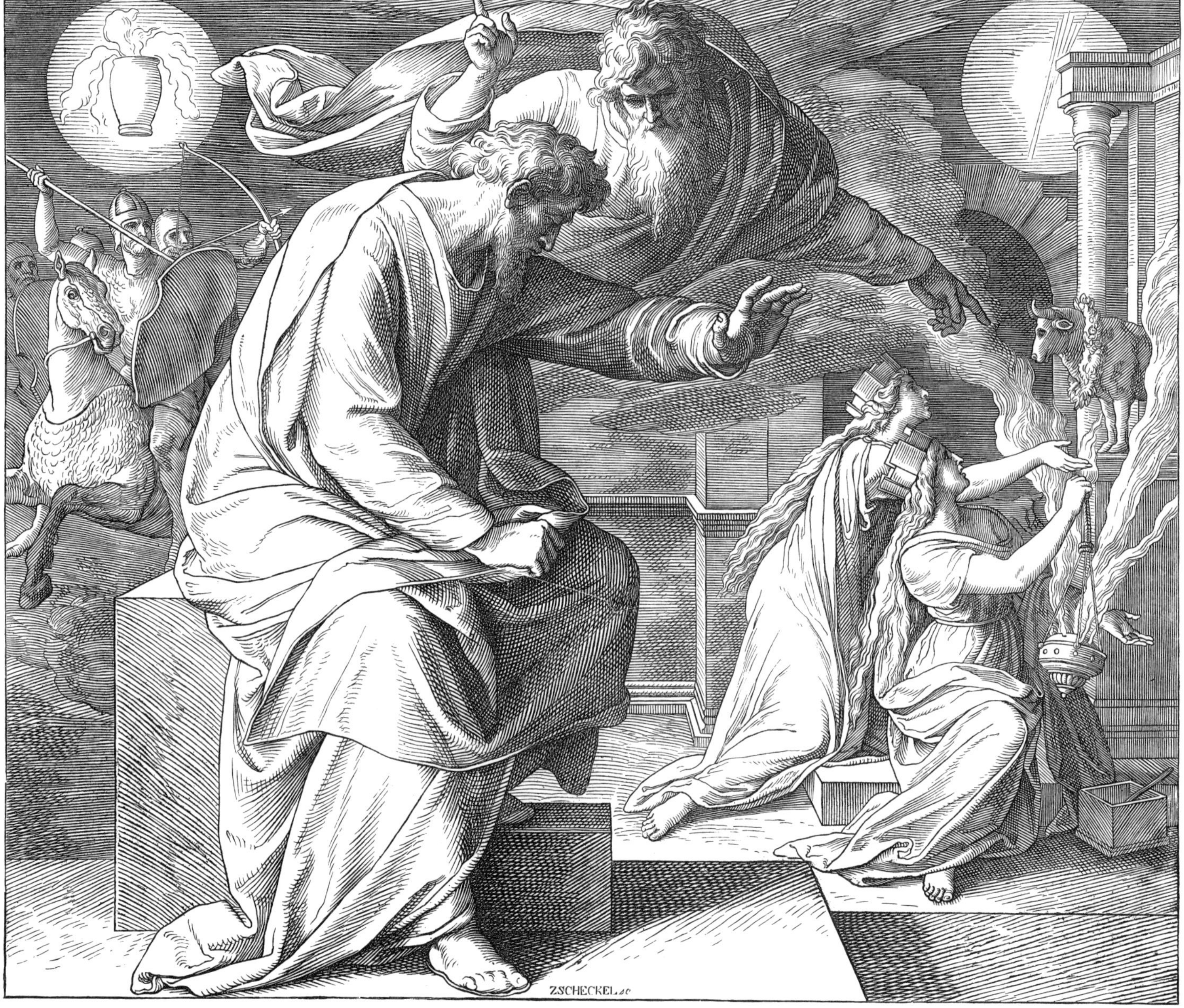

THE PROPHET JEREMIAH
The Book of the Prophet Jeremiah. Chapter 1.

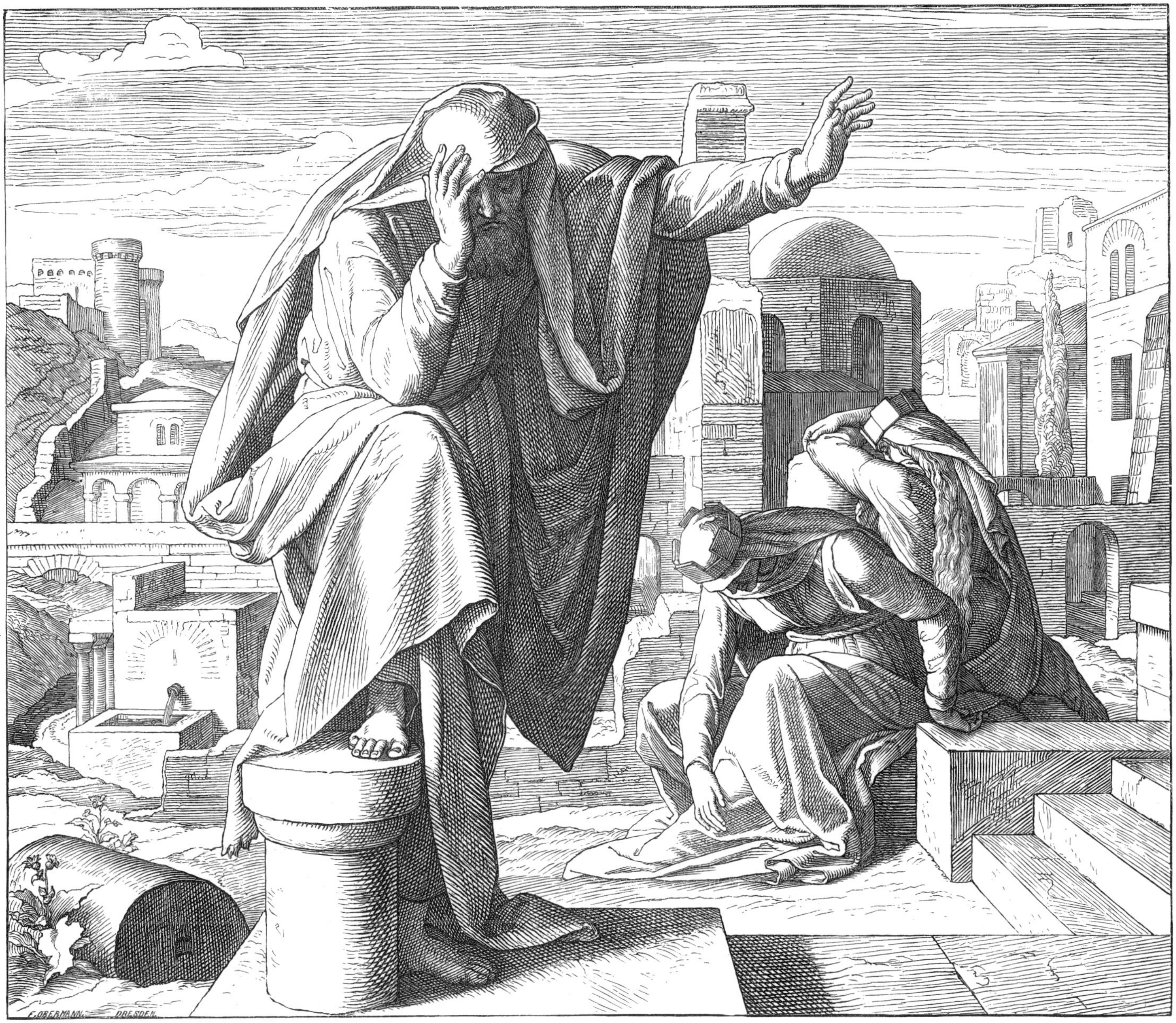

JEREMIAH'S LAMENT

The Book of the Prophet Jeremiah. Chapter 1.

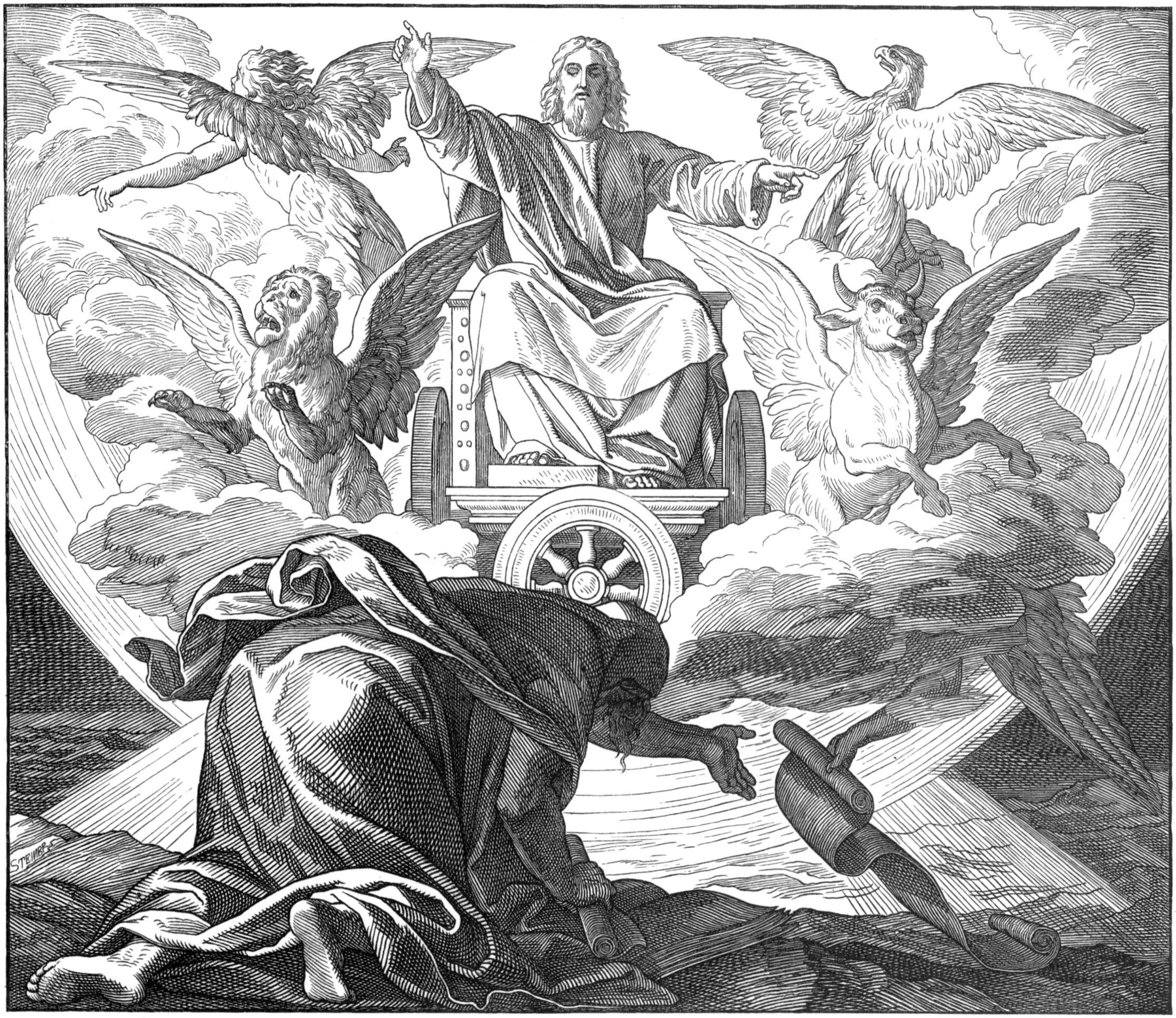

The Prophet Ezekiel

The Book of the Prophet Ezekiel. Chapter 1.

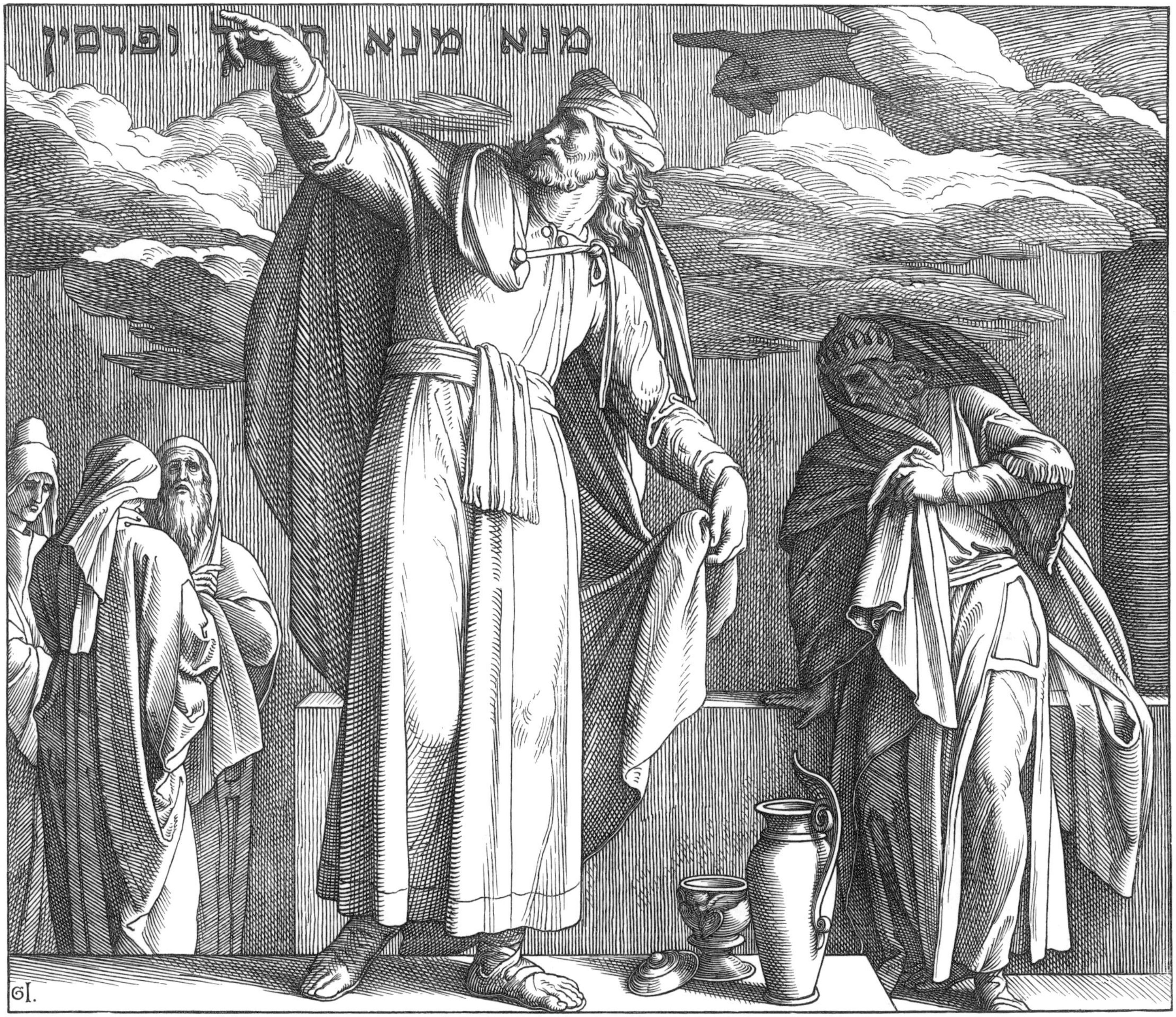

The Prophet Daniel

The Book of Daniel. Chapter 5.

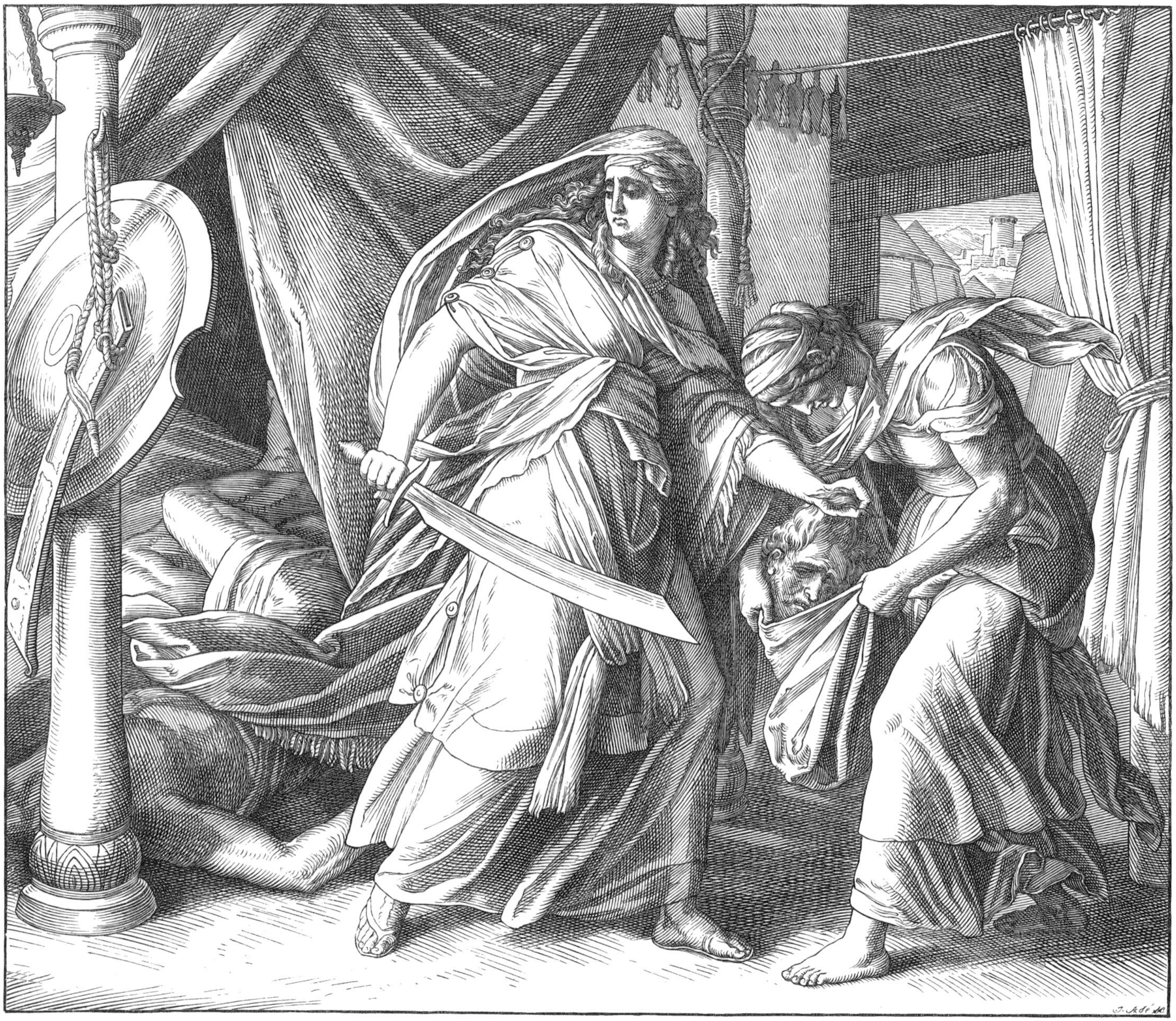

Judith Beheads Holofernes
Judith. Chapter 13.

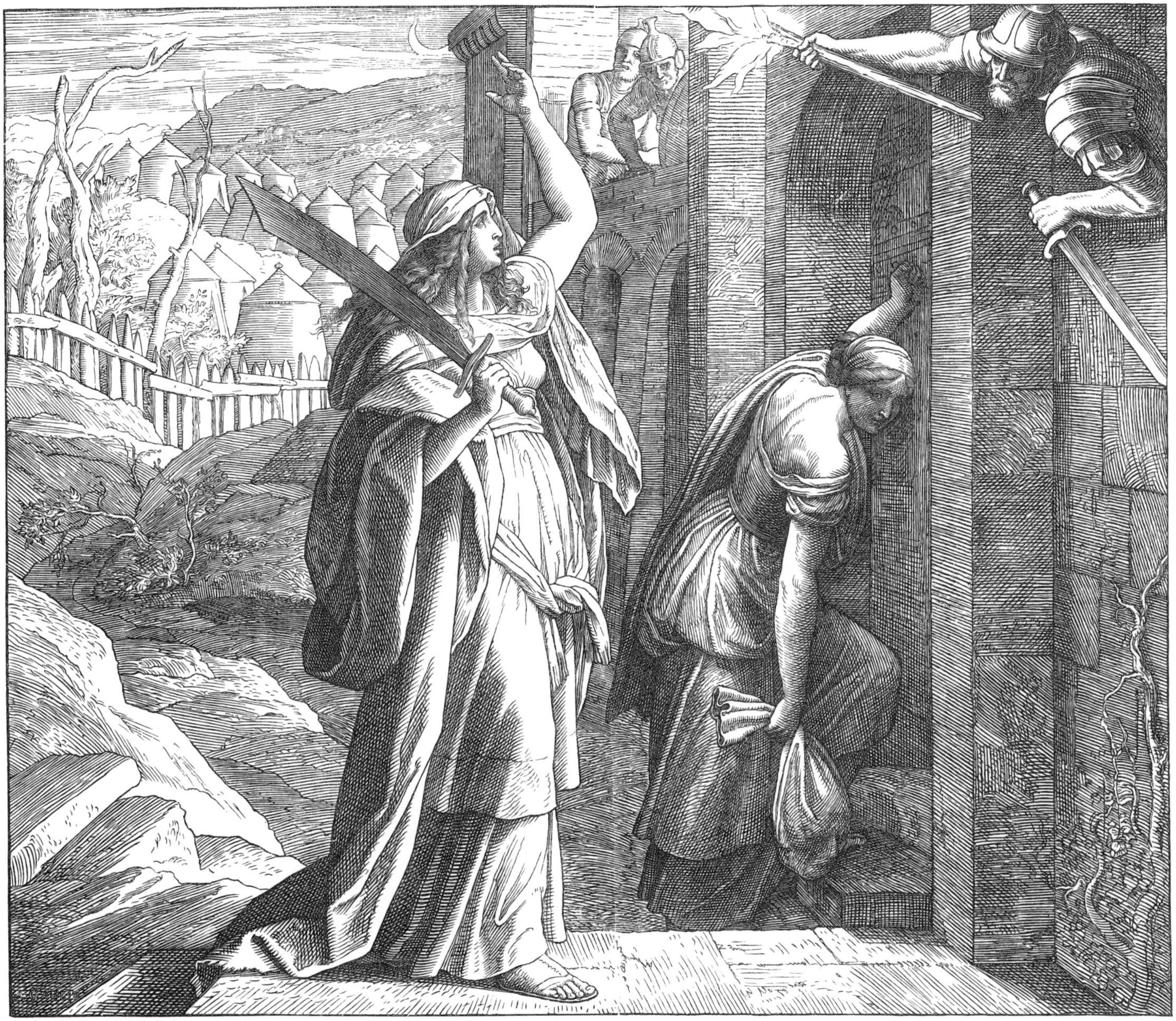

JUDITH RETURNS UNSCATHED TO HER PEOPLE
Judith. Chapter 13.

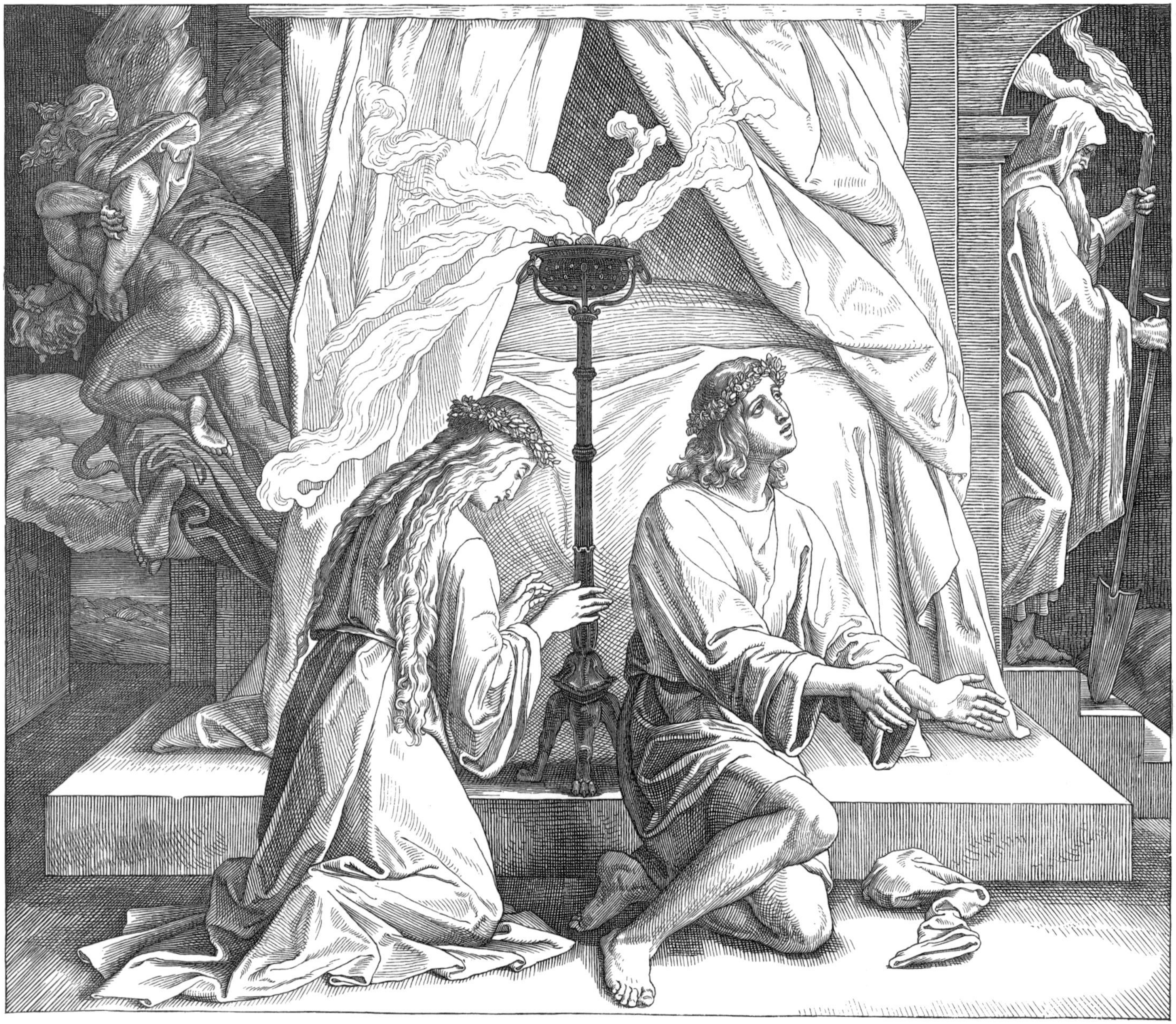

THE PRAYER OF TOBIAS AND SARA
Tobias. Chapter 8.

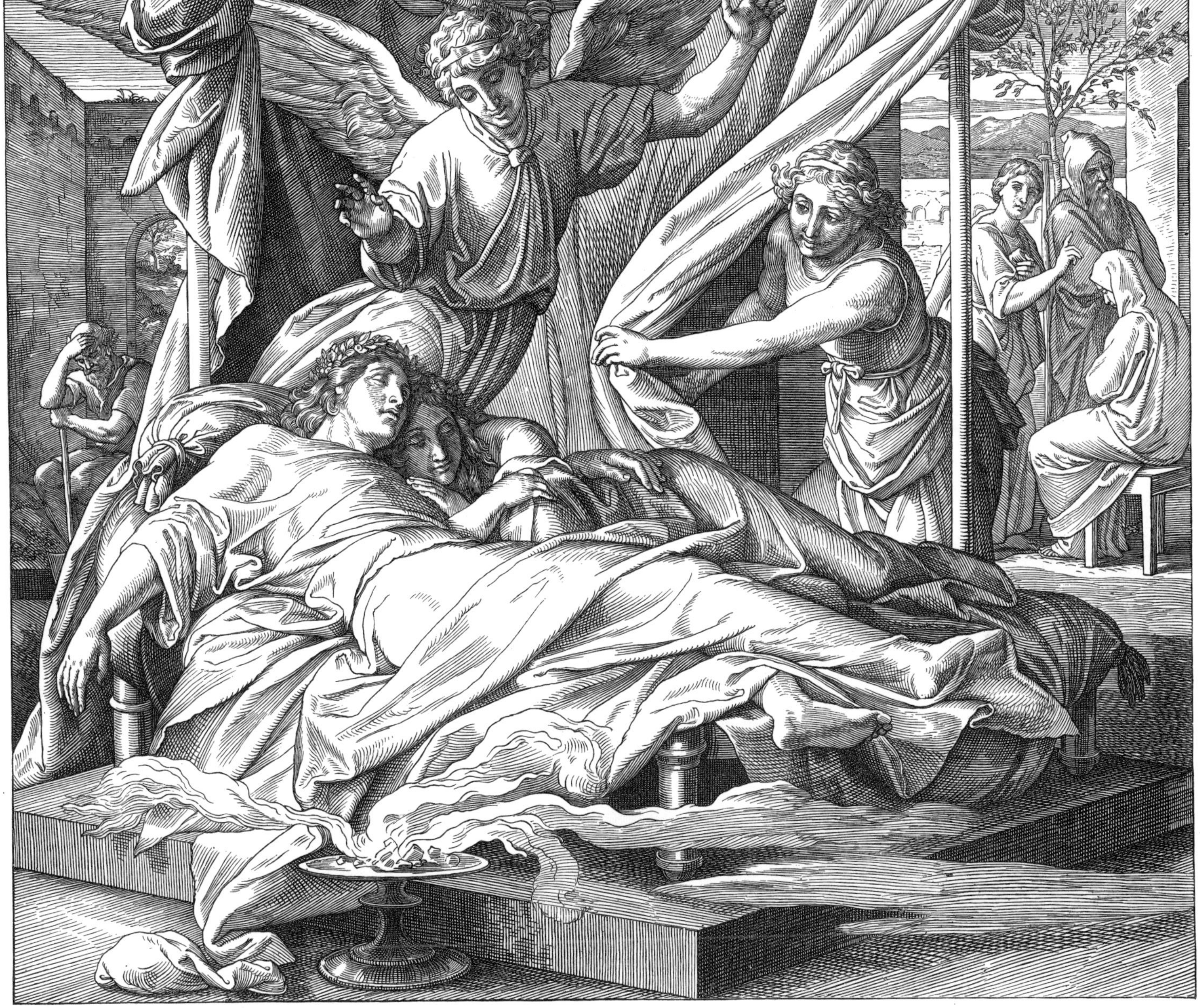

Tobias and Sara Found the Morning After Their Wedding Night

Tobias. Chapter 8.

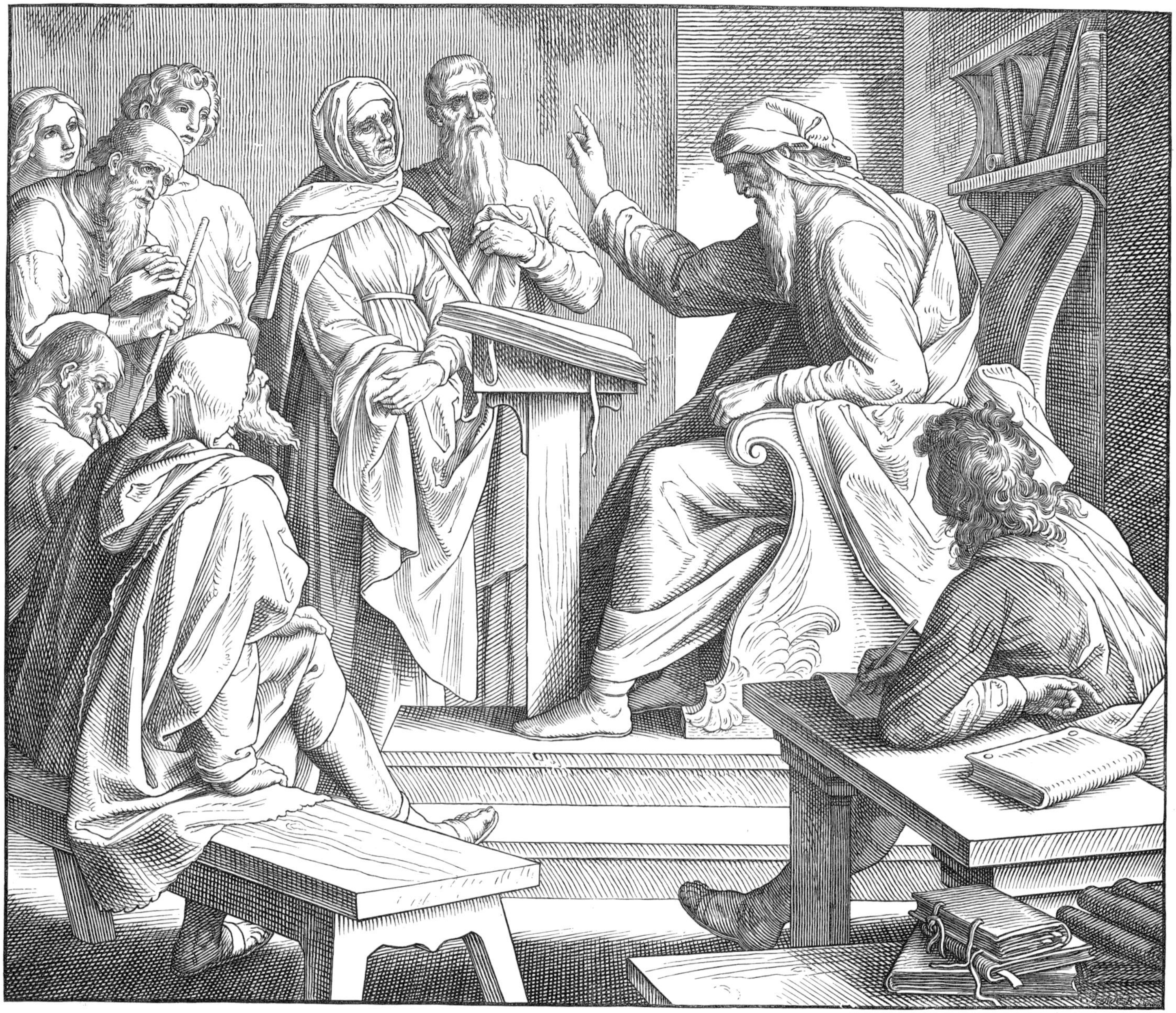

GLORY OF THE WISDOM AND MIGHT OF GOD

The Wisdom of Jesus the Son of Sirach, or, Ecclesiasticus. Chapter 1.

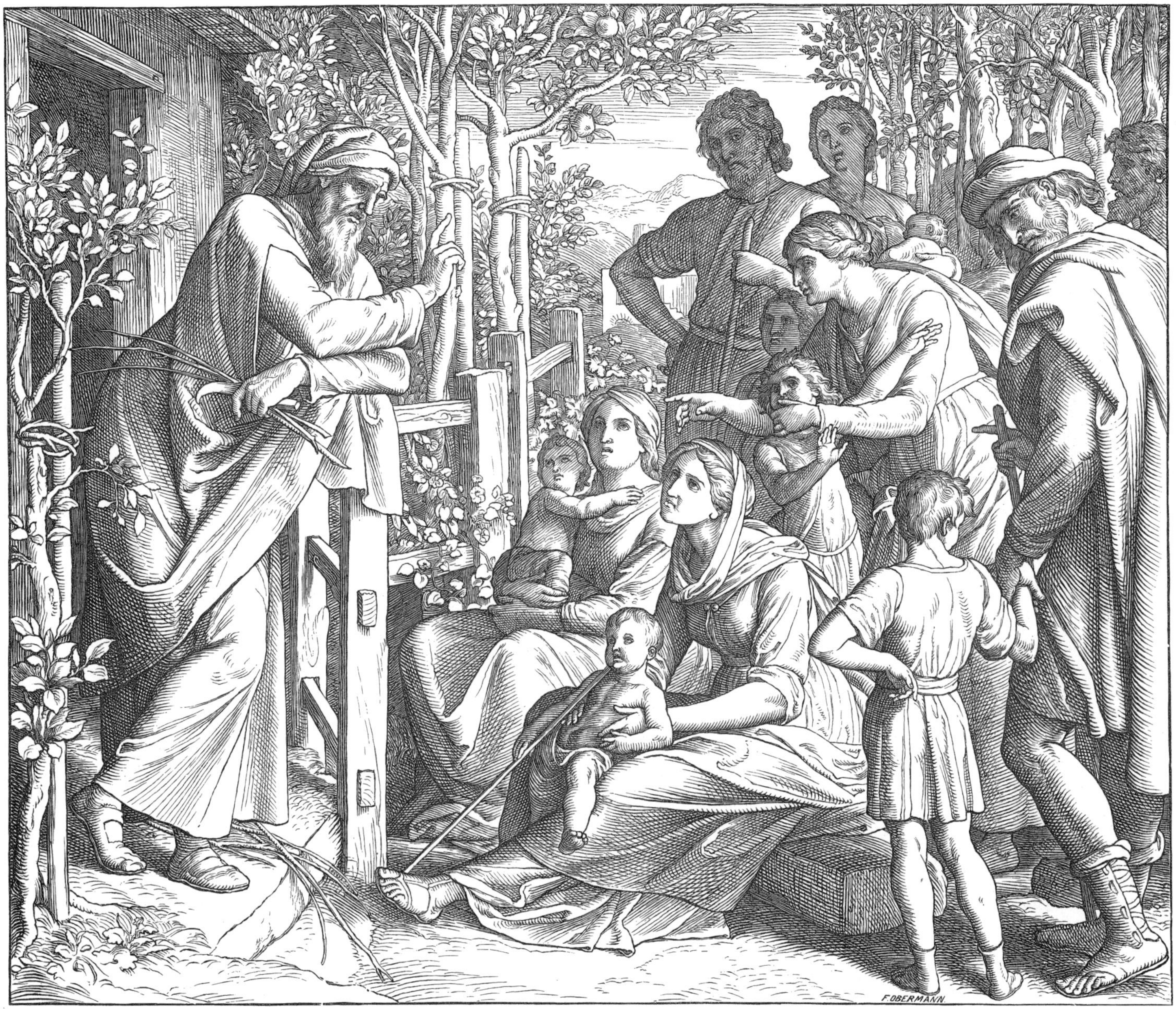

THE WAYS OF WISDOM

The Wisdom of Jesus the Son of Sirach, or, Ecclesiasticus. Chapter 30.

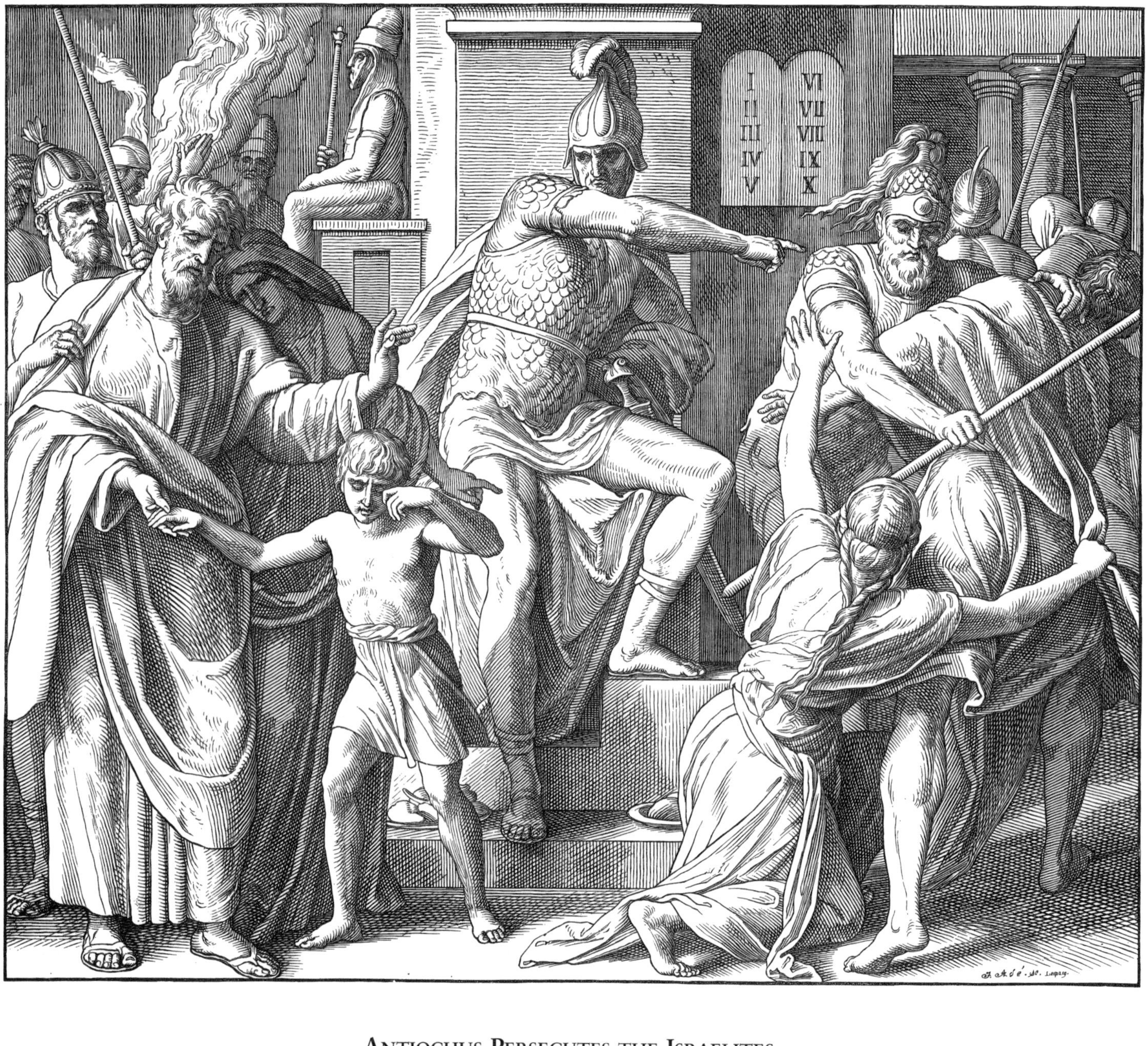

ANTIOCHUS PERSECUTES THE ISRAELITES

The First Book of the Maccabees. Chapter 1.

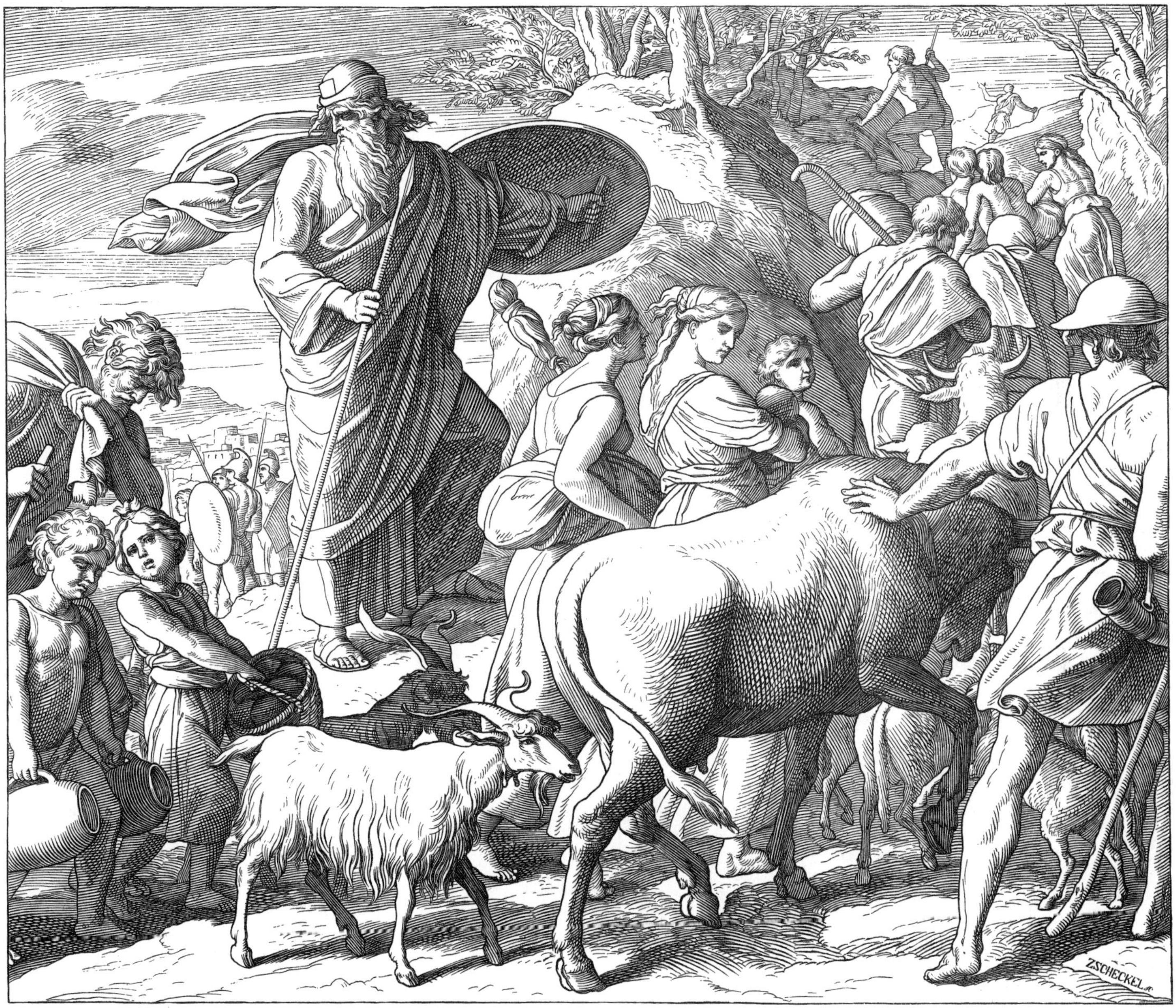

Mattathias Leads the Flight from the Oppressors

The First Book of the Maccabees. Chapter 2.

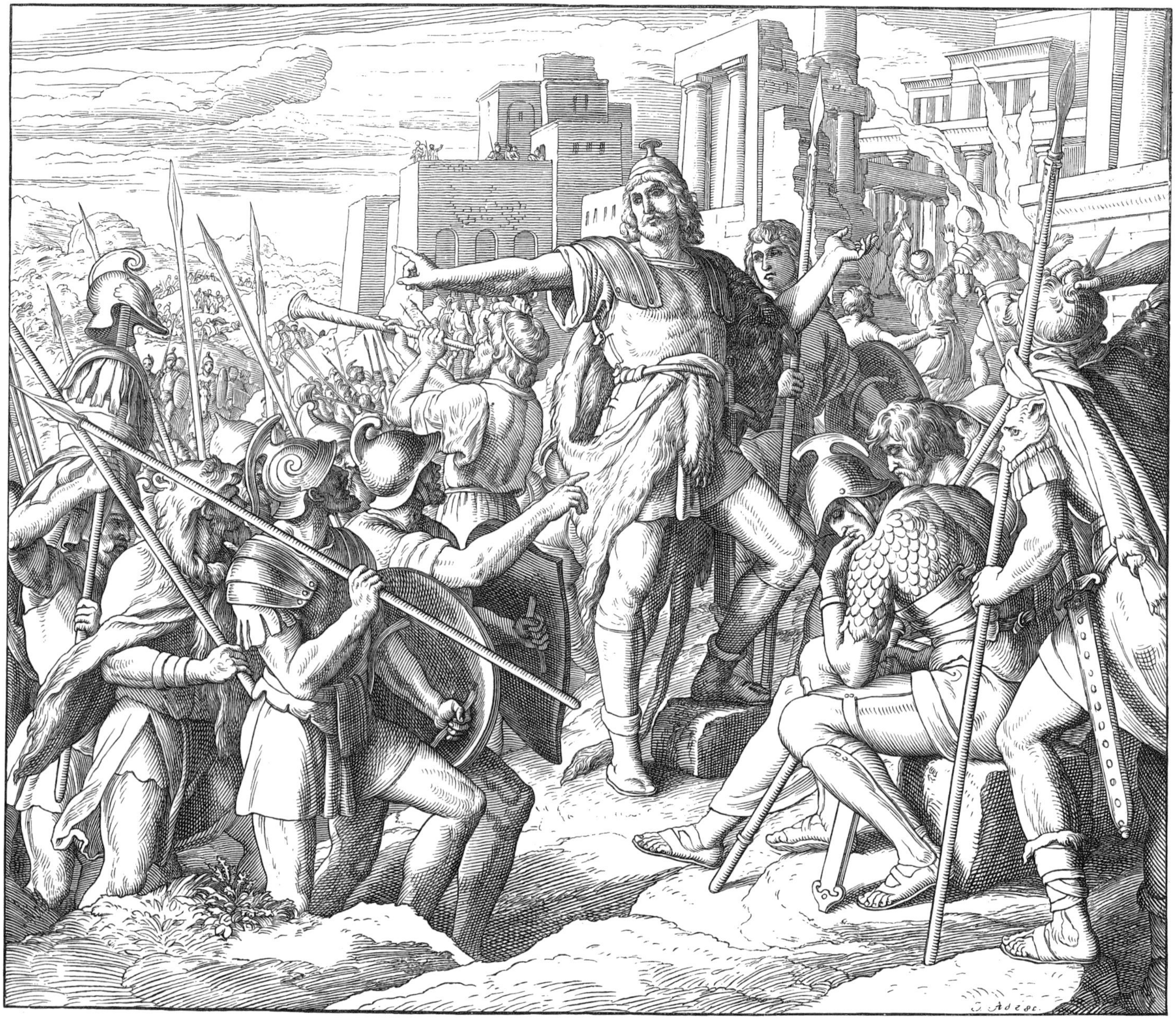

Judas Maccabeus Attacks His Enemies and Purifies the Temple

The First Book of the Maccabees. Chapter 4.

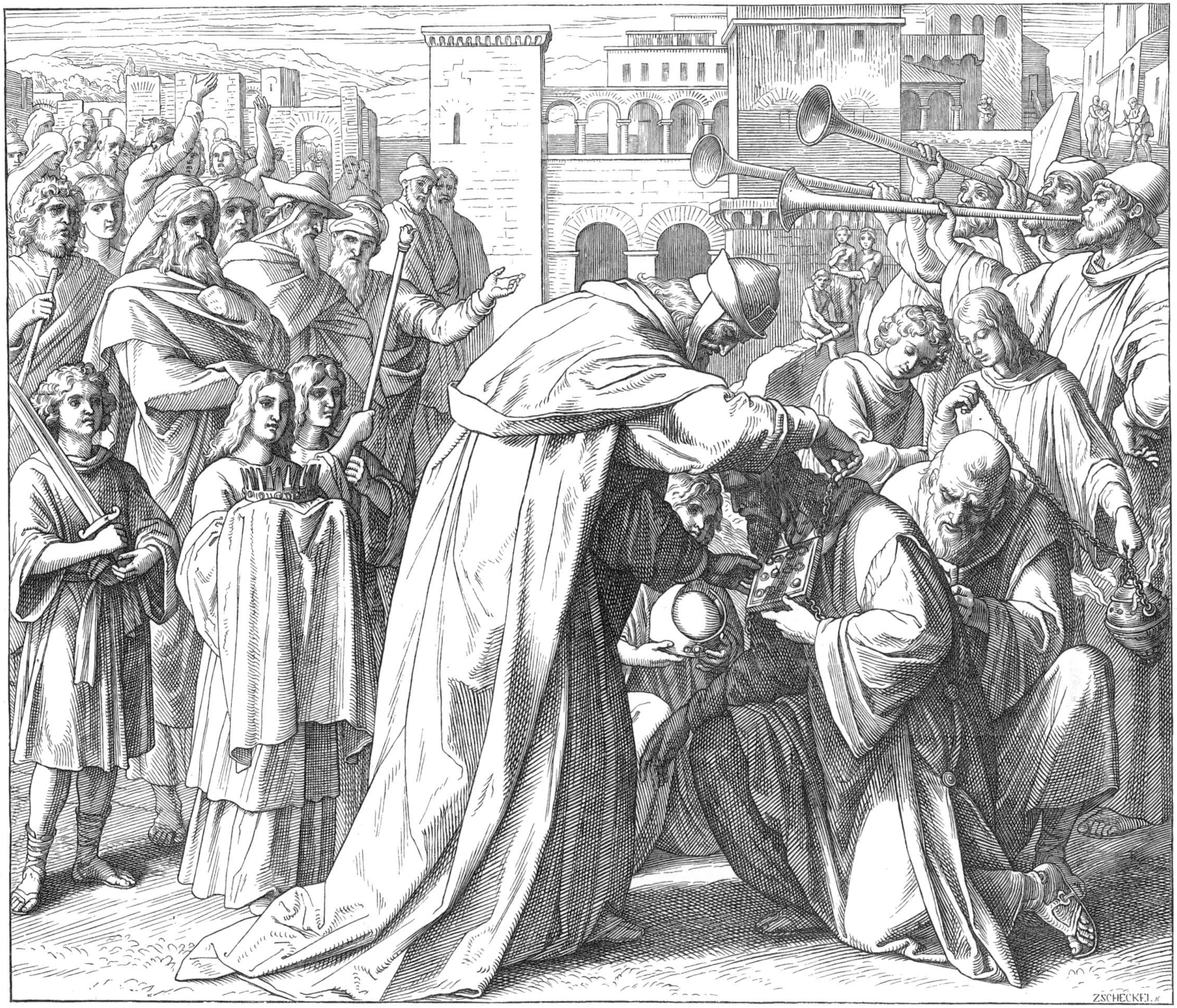

SIMON BECOMES GOVERNOR AND CHIEF PRIEST

The First Book of the Maccabees. Chapter 14.

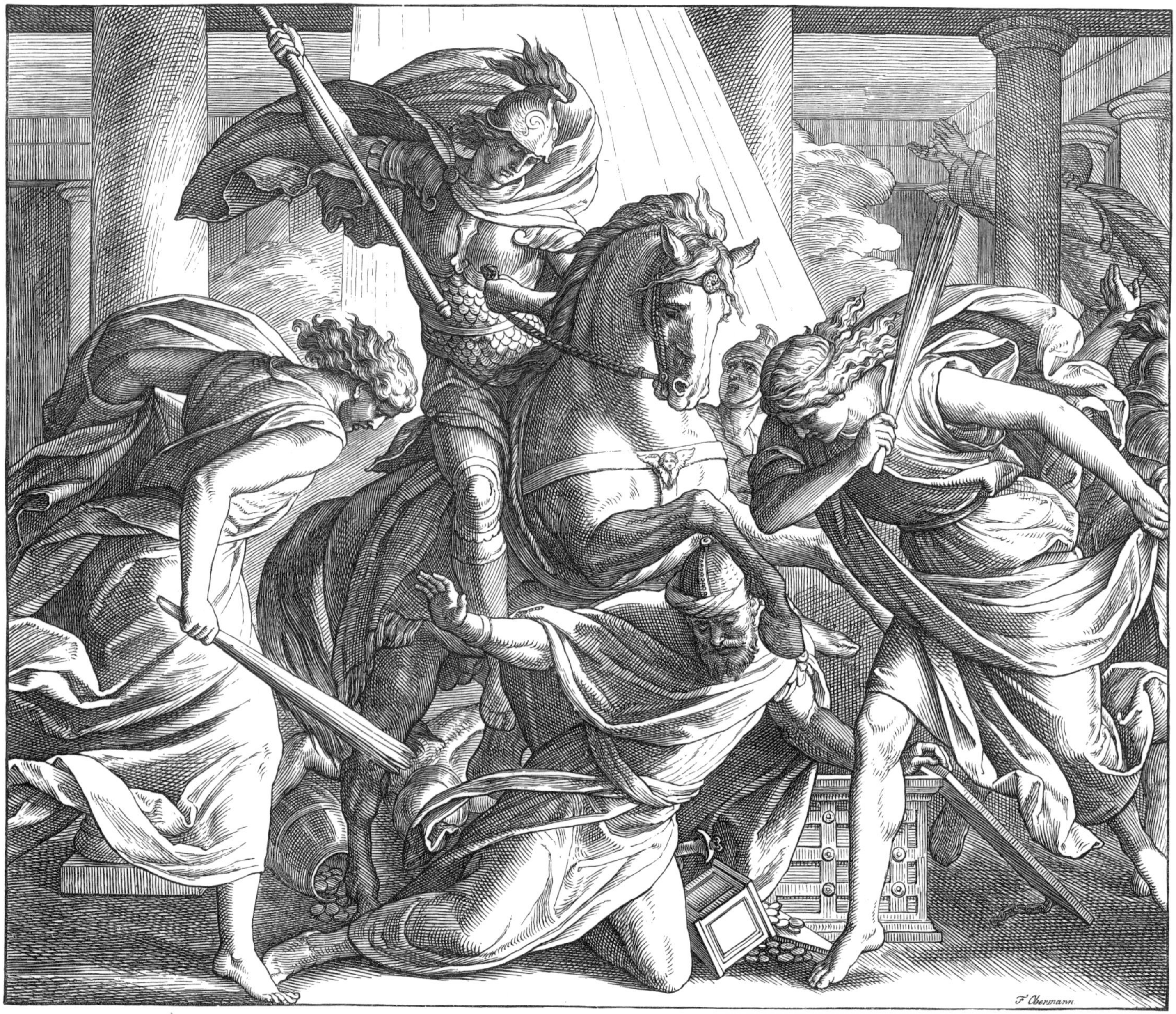

The Temple's Riches Protected from the Plundering of Heliodorus

The Second Book of the Maccabees. Chapter 3.

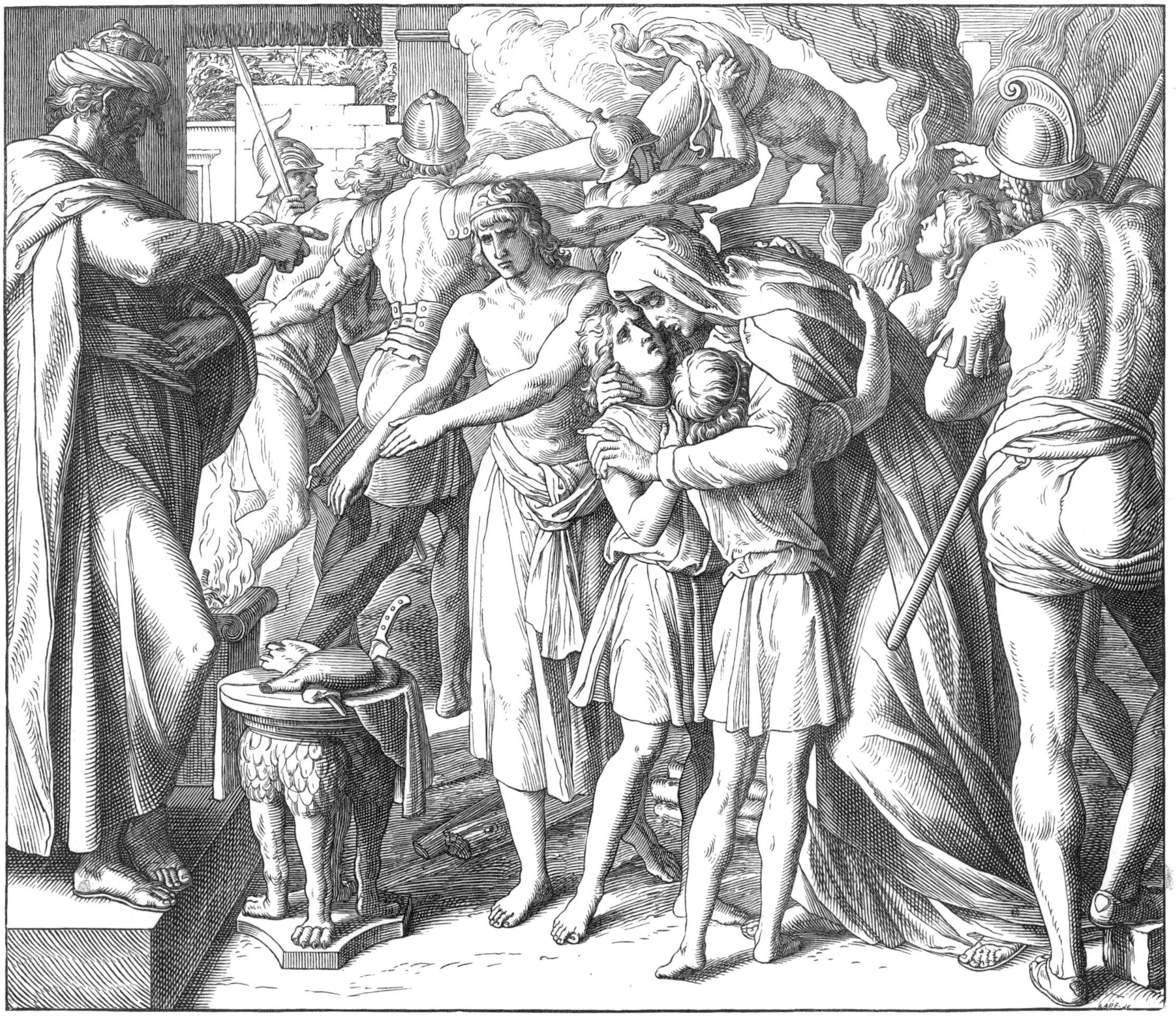

THE MARTYRDOM OF THE SEVEN BRETHREN AND THEIR MOTHER

The Second Book of the Maccabees. Chapter 7.

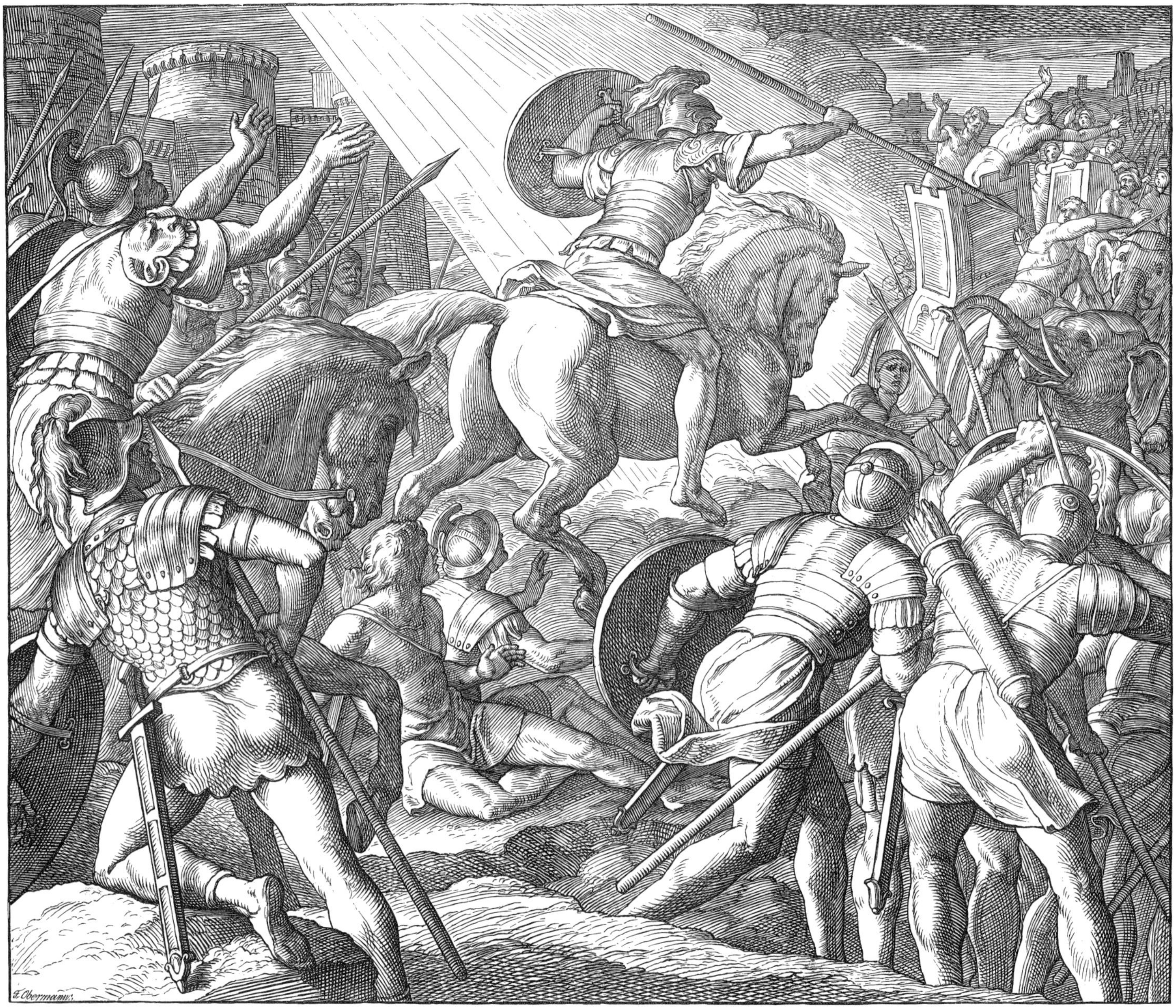

An Angel of the Lord Leads Israel Against the Enemy
The Second Book of the Maccabees. Chapter 11.

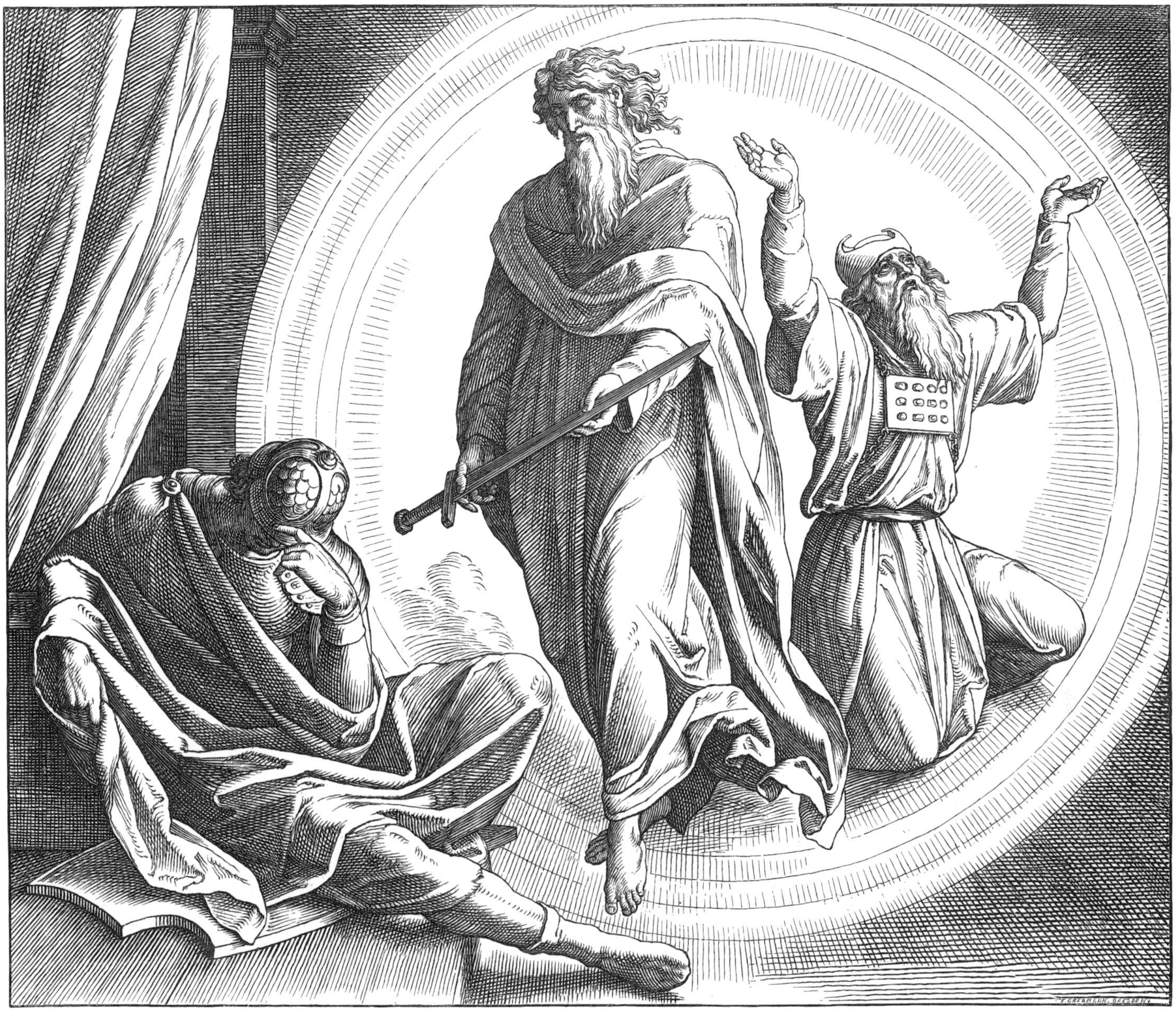

Judas Maccabeus Has a Vision

The Second Book of the Maccabees. Chapter 15.

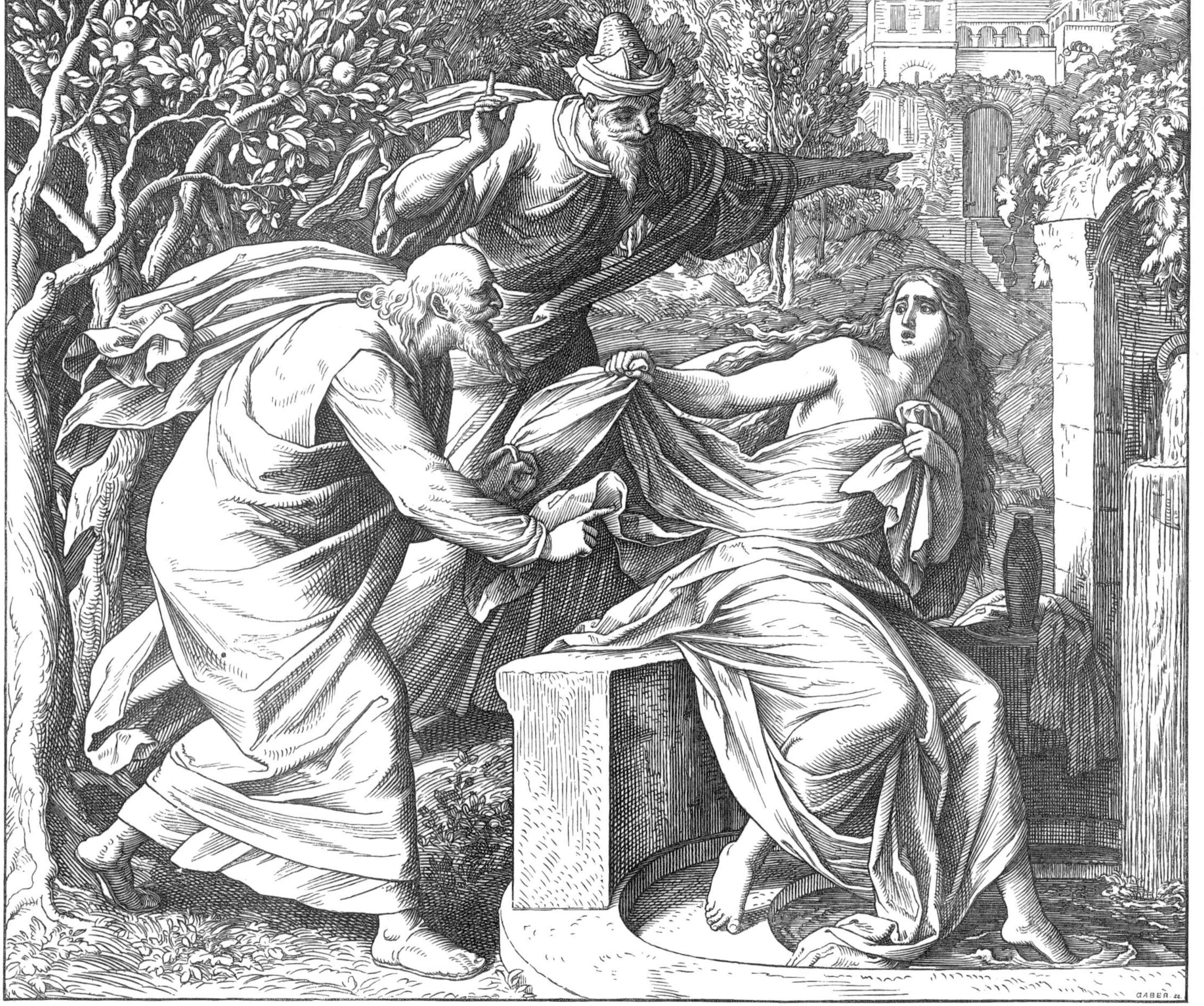

Susanna and the Two Elders
History of Susanna and Daniel.

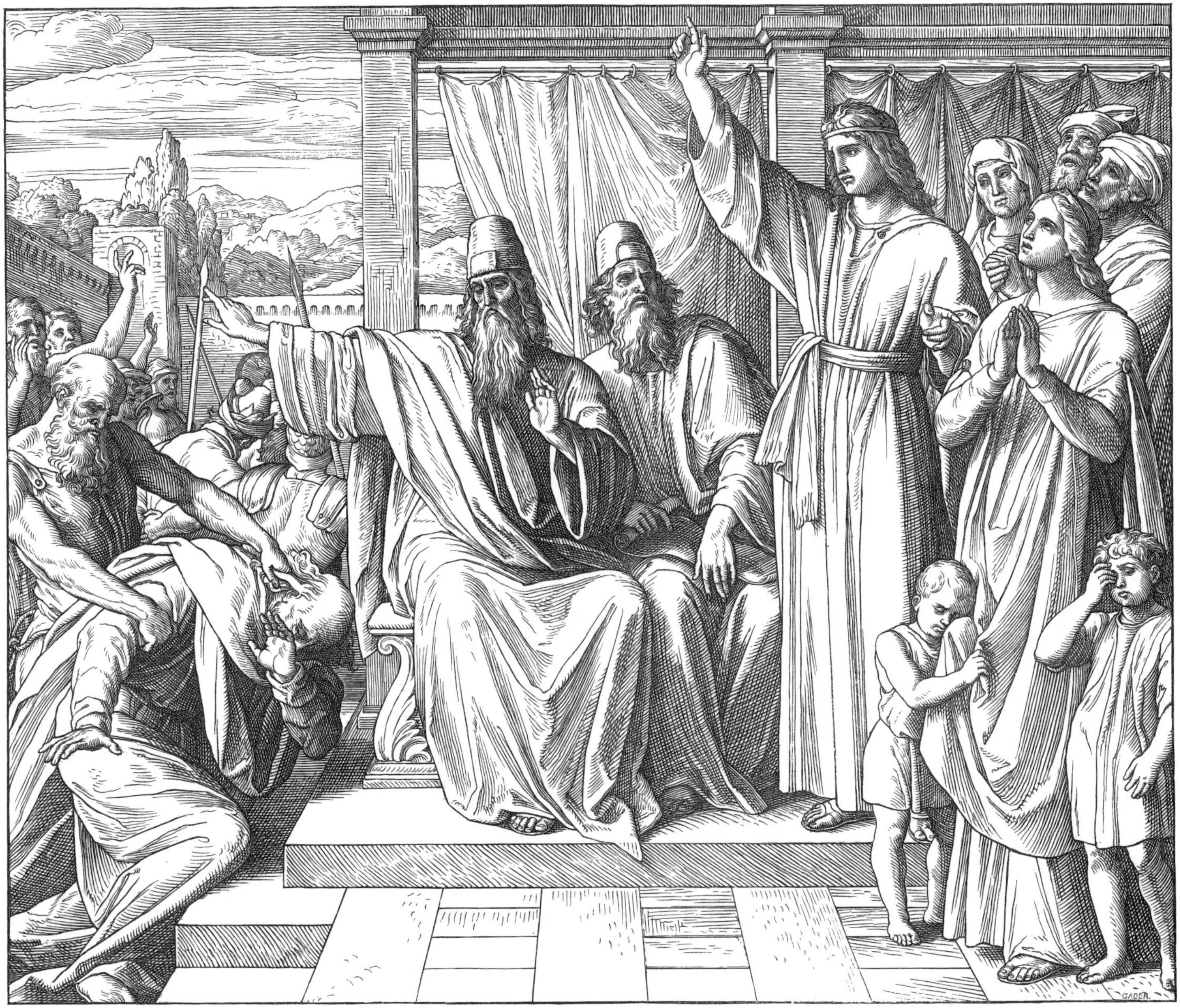

Daniel Rescues Susanna from Death
History of Susanna and Daniel.

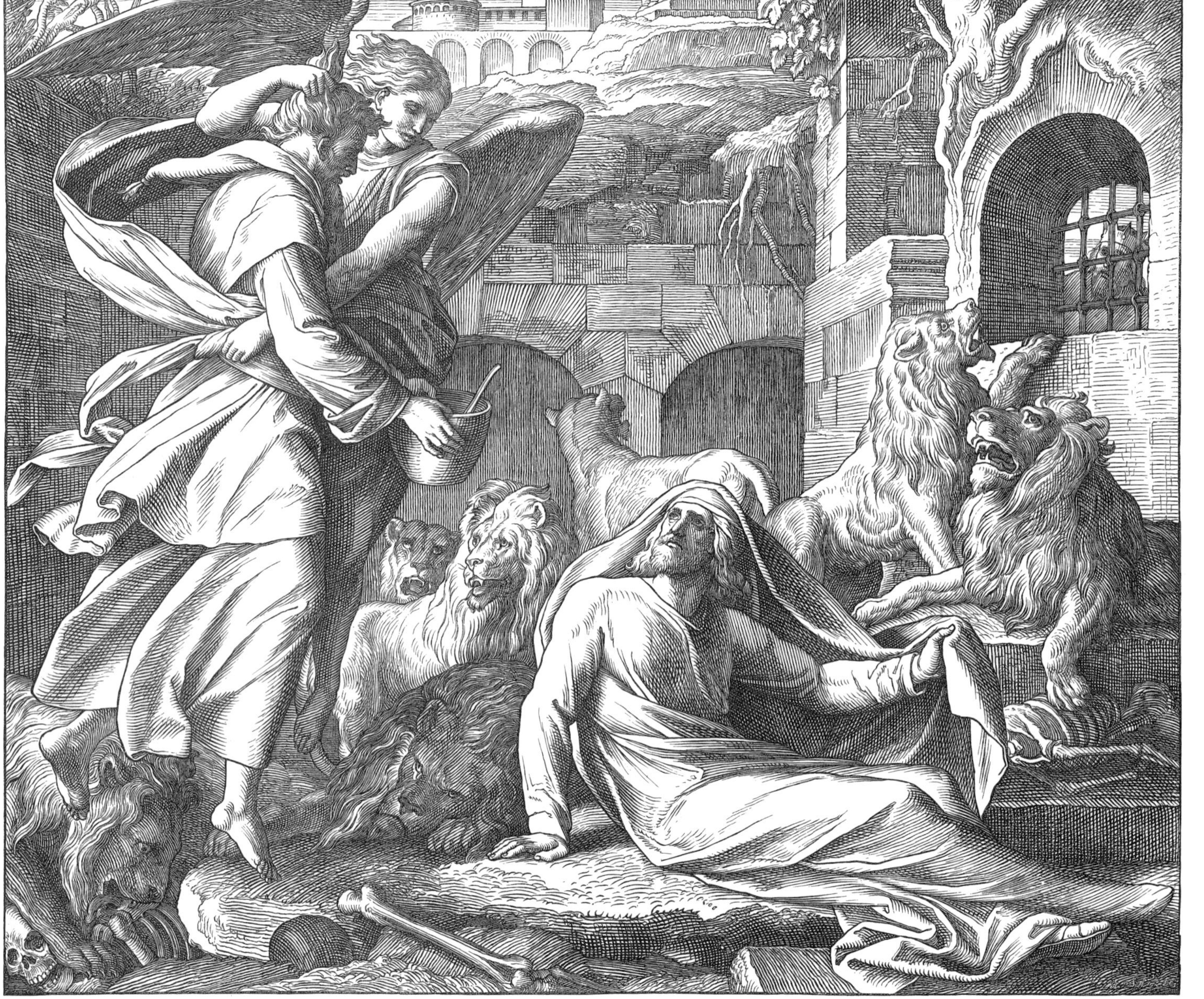

Daniel in the Lion's Den and Habakkuk

History of Bel and the Dragon.